1971

THE HARD JOURNEY
THE MYTH OF MAN'S REBIRTH

By the same Author

CHARACTER AND SYMBOL IN
SHAKESPEARE'S PLAYS
THE PRIMAL CURSE

THE
HARD JOURNEY

The Myth of Man's Rebirth

By

HONOR MATTHEWS

1968

BARNES & NOBLE Inc

NEW YORK

Publishers & Booksellers since 1873

Published by
Chatto and Windus Ltd
42 William IV Street
London W.C.2

© Honor Matthews 1968

Published in the United States, 1968
by Barnes & Noble, Inc

Printed in Great Britain

Contents

5

CONTENTS

Acknowledgements

I am grateful for permission to quote from the following copyright material: Martin d'Arcy's *The Mind and Heart of Love* (Faber & Faber Ltd. and Holt Rinehart and Winston Inc.); Erich Auerbach's *Dante: Poet of the Secular World* (University of Chicago Press) and *Mimesis: The Representation of Reality in Western Literature*, translated by W. Trask (Princeton University Press); Baudelaire's *The Voyage*, from *The Room*, translated by C. Day Lewis (Jonathan Cape Ltd.); Samuel Beckett's *All That Fall* and *Waiting for Godot* (Faber & Faber Ltd. and Grove Press Inc.) and *How It is*, *Malone Dies*, *Molloy*, *Murphy*, *The Unnamable* (Calder & Boyars Ltd. and Grove Press Inc.); Eric Bentley's *Life of Drama* (Methuen & Co. Ltd. and Atheneum Publishers); Irma Brandeis's *The Ladder of Vision* (Irma Brandeis, Chatto & Windus Ltd. and Doubleday & Co. Inc.); Bertolt Brecht's *Badener Lehrstücke*, translated by Lee Baxandall (Lee Baxandall), *Brecht on Theatre*, translated by John Willett (Methuen & Co. Ltd., Hill & Wang Inc. and Suhrkamp Verlag), *The Life of Galileo*, translated by Charles Laughton, in *From The Modern Repertoire Series*, edited by Eric Bentley (Indiana University Press), *Plays*, Volumes 1 and 2—*The Caucasian Chalk Circle*, translated by J. & T. Stern, with W. H. Auden, *The Good Person of Szechwan*, translated by John Willett, *Mother Courage and Her Children*, translated by Eric Bentley, *St Joan of the Stockyards*, translated by Frank Jones, *The Threepenny Opera*, translated by D. I. Vesey and Eric Bentley—and *Poems on the Theatre*, translated by J. Berger and A. Bostock (Methuen & Co. Ltd. and Suhrkamp Verlag), *Selected Poems*, translated by H. R. Hays (Harcourt Brace & World Inc. and Ann Elmo), and *The Threepenny Novel* (MacGibbon & Kee, Arco Publications, and Suhrkamp Verlag); Max Brod, editor, *The Diaries of Franz Kafka 1910–23* (Secker & Warburg Ltd. and Schocken Books); Joseph Campbell's *The Masks of God: Primitive Mythology* (Secker & Warburg Ltd., Russell & Volkening Inc. and the Viking Press Inc.); Albert Camus's *Caligula*, *Cross Purpose*, and *The Plague*, translated by Stuart Gilbert, *Carnets, 1942–51*, translated by P. Thody, and *The Fall*, translated by J. O'Brien (Hamish Hamilton Ltd. and Alfred A. Knopf Inc.); F. C. Copleston's *Contemporary Philosophy* (Burns & Oates Ltd. and Newman Press, Maryland); Dante's *Divine Comedy*, translated by Dorothy Sayers and Barbara Reynolds (David Higham Associates Ltd. and Ann Watkins Inc.) and translated by John Sinclair (The Bodley Head); C. Day Lewis, translator, *The Aeneid of Virgil* (The Hogarth Press and A. D. Peters & Co.); Fyodor Dostoevsky's *The Brothers Karamazov*, translated by Constance Garnett (William Heinemann Ltd. and The Macmillan Co.); T. S. Eliot's *The Cocktail Party*, *The Family Reunion*, *Collected Poems*, *Four Quartets* and *The Waste Land* (Faber & Faber Ltd. and Harcourt Brace & World Inc.); Erik Erikson's *The Young Man Luther* (Faber & Faber Ltd. and W. W. Norton Inc.); John Fletcher's *The Novels of Samuel Beckett* (Chatto & Windus Ltd. and Barnes & Noble Inc.); Angel Flores and Homer Swander, editors, *Franz Kafka Today* (the Regents of the University of Wisconsin); Frieda Fordham's *Introduction to Jung's Psychology* (Penguin Books Ltd.); Northrop Frye's *Anatomy of Criticism* (Princeton University Press and Oxford University Press); J. Gassner, editor, *Ideas in the Drama* (Columbia University Press); Maja Goth's *Kafka et les lettres françaises* (José Corti); Robert Graves and Raphael Patai's *Hebrew Myths* (Robert Graves and Raphael Patai, A. P. Watt & Son and Collins-Knowlton-Wing Inc.); Homer's *Odyssey*, translated by E. V. Rieu (Penguin Books Ltd.); Edwin Honig's *Dark Conceit: The Making of Allegory* (Oxford University Press, New York); *Poems of Gerard Manley Hopkins* (Oxford University Press); J. Huizinga's *The Waning of the Middle Ages* (Edward Arnold Ltd.); Henrik Ibsen's *Brand*, translated by Michael Meyer (David Higham Associates Ltd. and Doubleday & Co. Inc.), *The Master Builder and Other Plays* and *Three Plays*, translated by Una Ellis-Fermor (Penguin Books Ltd., Mrs Harold Weston and Mrs Elsie Brown) and *Peer Gynt*, translated by Peter Watts (Penguin Books Ltd.); Ionesco's *Plays* (Calder & Boyars Ltd. and Grove Press Inc.); C. E. M. Joad's *A Guide to Philosophy* (the author's executors); C. G. Jung's *Collected Works* (Routledge & Kegan Paul Ltd. and The Bollingen Foundation); Franz Kafka's *The Castle* and *The Trial*, both translated by Edwin and Willa Muir (Secker & Warburg Ltd. and Alfred A. Knopf Inc.); W. Kaufmann, editor, *Existentialism from Dostoevsky to Sartre* (The World

ACKNOWLEDGEMENTS

Publishing Co.); Edith Kern, editor, *Sartre: A Collection of Critical Essays* (Prentice-Hall Inc.); Sören Kierkegaard's *Concluding Unscientific Postscript*, translated by D. F. Swenson, *Fear and Trembling* and *The Sickness unto Death*, translated by Walter Lowrie (Princeton University Press); Jack Lindsay's *The Clashing Rocks* (Laurence Pollinger Ltd.); F. L. Lucas's *Literature and Psychology* (Cassell & Co. Ltd. and The University of Michigan Press); Louis Macneice's *Varieties of Parable* (Cambridge University Press); Emile Mâle's *The Gothic Image* (J. M. Dent & Sons Ltd. and Librairie Armand Colin); G. E. Mylonas's *Eleusis and the Eleusinian Mysteries* (Princeton University Press and Routledge & Kegan Paul Ltd.); Erich Neumann's *The Origins and History of Consciousness* (Routledge and Kegan Paul Ltd. and The Bollingen Foundation); R. M. Rilke's 'Baudelaire' from *Poems 1906–26* translated by J. B. Leishman (The Hogarth Press Ltd. and New Directions Inc.); Sylvia Plath's *Ariel* (Olwyn Hughes); Plato's *Phaedo*, translated by R. Livingstone, in *Portrait of Socrates* (The Clarendon Press, Oxford); Kathleen Raine's *The Hollow Hill* (Kathleen Raine and Hamish Hamilton Ltd.); Jean-Paul Sartre's *Being and Nothingness* (Methuen & Co. Ltd., Editions Gallimard and Citadel Press), *Altona*, first translated as *Loser Wins* by S. and G. Leeson, *The Flies*, translated by Stuart Gilbert, *The Age of Reason* and *The Reprieve*, translated by Eric Sutton, and *Iron in the Soul* (American title, *Troubled Sleep*), translated by Gerard Hopkins (Editions Gallimard, Hamish Hamilton Ltd. and Alfred A. Knopf Inc.); *Poem of St John of the Cross*, translated by Roy Campbell (Hughes Massie Ltd. and Pantheon Books Inc.); Dorothy Sayers's *Further Papers on Dante* (David Higham Associates Ltd.); Sophocles' *Three Theban Plays*, translated by A. E. Watling (Penguin Books Ltd.); Karl Stern's *The Flight from Woman* (Allen & Unwin Ltd.); Wallace Stevens's *Collected Poems* (Faber & Faber Ltd. and Alfred A. Knopf Inc.); August Strindberg's *Inferno* (Hutchinson Publishing Group Ltd.); A. N. Whitehead's *Religion in the Making* (Cambridge University Press); Charles Williams's *The Figure of Beatrice* (Faber & Faber Ltd., David Higham Associates Ltd. and Mrs Florence Williams); and W. B. Yeats's 'Blood and the Moon', 'The Circus Animals' Desertion', 'The Cold Heaven' in *Collected Poems*, and 'Sophocles' Oedipus at Colonus' in *Collected Plays* (Mr M. B. Yeats, Macmillan & Co. Ltd., London, and The Macmillan Co., New York).

I would also like to thank Miss Enid Crowe for her generous help in the translation of passages from *Drôle d'Amitié* and in preparing the MS of this book for publication.

There was a muddy centre before we breathed.
There was a myth before the myth began.
Venerable and articulate and complete.
From this the poem springs.
WALLACE STEVENS: *Notes towards a Supreme Fiction*

I set up a ladder to heaven among the Gods.
Book of the Dead

I must lie down where all the ladders start
In the foul rag-and-bone shop of the heart.
W. B. YEATS: *The Circus Animals' Desertion*

Prologue: In Thebes and Florence

Thebes has become a Wasteland; the priest pleads before the king:

> You too have seen our city's affliction, caught
> In a tide of death from which there is no escaping—
> Death in the fruitful flowering of her soil;
> Death in the pastures; death in the womb of woman;
> And pestilence, a fiery demon gripping the city.*   p. 26

The oracle speaks:

> There is an unclean thing . . .
> Here—the god said, Seek, and ye shall find.   p. 29

Oedipus answers the challenge:

> I will start afresh; and bring everything into the light.   p. 30

Immediately, his search for the truth becomes the search for himself:

> I ask to be no other man
> Than that I am, and *will know who I am*.   p. 59

When the shepherd recognizes, in the killer of Laius and the husband of Jocasta, their own child, whom he had saved from death as an infant on the mountain of Cithaeron, he can only look with tragic knowledge at his master and mutter:

> *If* you are the man . . .

But Oedipus has recognized himself at last:

> O Light, may I never look on you again,
> Revealed as I am, sinful in my begetting,
> Sinful in marriage, sinful in shedding of blood.   p. 63

His eyes have become clear, and as a result of what they see he darkens them himself:

> What should I do with eyes
> Where all is ugliness?
> . . . I am lost,
> Hated of gods, no man so damned   p. 67

* Sophocles: *Three Theban Plays*, tr. A. E. Watling, Penguin (1947).

11

The journey, begun so hopefully at Corinth, has led him to the bottom of the pit.

Nearly two thousand years later, another poet wrote of another traveller:

> Midway this way of life . . . .
> I woke to find myself in a dark wood . . .
>   the mere breath
> Of memory stirs the old fear in the blood.*   *Inferno*. I. 1–6

When, after his journey through Hell and Purgatory, Beatrice challenges Dante with the question:

> How hast thou deigned† to climb the hill?‡
>
> > *Purgatory*. XXX. 74

the truth about himself becomes at last visible to him:

> I dropped my eyes down to the glassy rill
> Saw myself there, and quickly to the brink
> Withdrew them, bowed with shame unspeakable.   76–8

So icy were the bonds which still compressed his heart that for a time he was even 'impotent for sighs or tears' (91) until his shame 'through eyes/And mouth burst forth in anguish' (98–9) from his breast. Between the moment in the dark wood of his hardness of heart, his pride and self-ignorance, and the moment under those other trees of the Earthly Paradise where at last he rediscovers Beatrice, Dante's pilgrim has made his journey. He has plumbed the abyss of his own being, and, after following the dark road to 'the dreadful centre', has toiled up the mount of the 'refining fire' until he reaches the stream in which the grace of God at last reveals his self to his appalled eyes.

The journey of Oedipus is concerned ostensibly with himself alone and that of Dante ostensibly with many people, but critics of the *Divine Comedy* would mostly now agree with Charles Williams when he writes: 'the whole poem is an analysis of one soul as well as the description of many'.§ The poem is indeed the supreme medieval exemplum of the search for the self, as the Oedipus plays are that of classical Greece. Both authors recognize the first state of man as

---

* Dante, *Hell*, tr. D. Sayers, Penguin (1949).

† *degnasti* (cf. John Sinclair: 'durst thou'. *The Divine Comedy* I, Bodley Head, 1939).

‡ Dante, *Purgatory*, tr. D. Sayers, Penguin (1955).

§ *The Figure of Beatrice*, Faber (1943), p. 116.

sinful, and both show also the subsequent emergence of a reborn second-self.

> I know the bottom, she says. I know it with my great tap-root:
> It's what you fear.
> I do not fear it: I have been there.*

It is because the poem is personal that it is also universal.

In spite of their different backgrounds the Greek and the medieval stories are versions of a single vision of the human condition. Separated by nearly two millennia they are based on the same imaginative concept of the nature of man. Both reflect the myth of the 'Fall' which made Man as we still know him to be. In the Judaeo-Christian version the fall was two-fold: first comes the fall of pride:

> How art thou fallen from heaven, O Lucifer, son of the morning! . . .
> For thou hast said in thine heart . . . I will exalt my throne above the stars
> of God: . . . Yet thou shalt be brought down to hell, to the sides of the pit.†

Then came Adam's fall into lust, leading quickly to the wrath and violence of the first murder. The elements of pride, lust and murder determine also the fate of the Sophoclean Oedipus.

This is the journey downward from created light and order, the world of the Sun and the heavens, into chaos and darkness, the world of the Earth, as it was without form and void, before the Spirit of the creator brooded upon it. It is unique for each individual, and yet to make it is a universal necessity, accepted even by 'a young child':

> O Margaret are you grieving
> Over Goldengrove unleafing? . . .
> Now no matter, child, the name:
> Sorrow's springs are the same . . . .
> It is the blight man was born for
> It is Margaret you mourn for.‡

But neither Sophocles nor Dante concludes here.

In Christian doctrine the descent of angel and man was followed by the descent of God himself, who was made flesh to dwell among us. Only after this could the return journey—the journey upward to worlds of experience and power and delight impossible before—begin.

* *The Elm*, From *Ariel*, Sylvia Plath, Faber (1965).
† Isaiah xiv, 12–15.
‡ G. M. Hopkins: 'Spring and Fall: to a young child', *Poems*, Oxford University Press (1950), cf. Isaiah LXIV, 6.

This spatial image is not present in the Greeks' play. For them the world of death was below the earth, although it was not intrinsically a world of sin and chaos. The good dwelt there also, in the grey Elysian fields, and Oedipus descended to his apotheosis, whereas Dante climbed to his vision of God. But though in this respect the spatial imagery is different, the concept of the journey through darkness to a second-selfhood is the same. Both poets fulfil in their manner the task Blake saw as every poet's own:

> to open the immortal Eyes
> Of Man inwards into the Worlds of Thought, into Eternity.*

In so doing they illuminate also Blake's vision of the necessity of evil:

> If I were pure I should never
> Have known thee: if I were unpolluted I should never have
> Glorified thy holiness or rejoiced in thy great salvation.

For 'the way up is the way down', 'the way forward is the way back'.† In the words of the Christian poet:

> Therefore that he may raise, the Lord throws down.

A Jewish poet offers the same consolation to the anguished spirit:

> Wherefore, O wherefore
> Is the soul
> From the highest height
> To the deepest depth fallen?
> Within itself the Fall
> Contains the Ascension.‡

---

* *Jerusalem:* Plates 5 and 61.

† T. S. Eliot, *Four Quartets*. The Dry Salvages III (London: Faber; New York: Harcourt Brace & World).

‡ Opening lines of *The Dybbuk*, Sholem Ansky, 1907. Translated from Yiddish by S. M. von Engel, Comet Press (1953).

Part I

THE JOURNEY
IN THE
ORDERED UNIVERSE

Therefore I will return from outward things to inward . . .
that I may know from whence I come and whither I go; who
I am and from whence I am: that so by the knowledge of
myselfe, I may be the better able to attaine to the knowledge of
God. For by how much I profit, and goe forward in the knowledge of myselfe, by so much the nearer I approach to the
knowledge of God.   S. BERNARD

Religion . . . translates into significant words, images and
codes the exceeding darkness which surrounds man's existence,
and the light which pervades it beyond all desert or com-
prehension.   ERIK ERIKSON. *The Young Man Luther*

CHAPTER I

The Origins of the Mythical Journey

Up above there is a certain tree where the souls of the shamans
are reared ... and on the boughs of this tree are nests in which
the souls lie and are attended ...
　　According to our belief, the soul of the shaman climbs up
this tree to God when he shamanises. For the tree grows during
the rite and invisibly reaches the summit of heaven.
Quoted by G. V. KSENFONTOV.
Schamanengeschichten aus Siberien

It cannot be stated too categorically that this chapter does not pre-
tend to recount or interpret the great myths famous in either
Western or Eastern cultures which embody the concept of man's
journeys up and down through macrocosm and microcosm. Its far
slighter purpose is to illustrate the primordial images of space which
lie behind such myths and to show them informing later literature.

For myth is the foundation of life; it is the timeless pattern, the religious
formula to which life shapes itself, in as much as its characteristics are a
reproduction of the Unconscious. There is no doubt about it, the moment
when the story-teller acquires the mythical way of looking at things, the
gift of seeing the typical features of characteristics and events—that
moment marks a beginning in his life. It means a peculiar intensification of
his artistic mood, a new serenity in his powers of perception and creation.*

Since the appearance of Sir James Frazer's *The Golden Bough* the
research of anthropologists has brought to civilized man new knowledge of the ways of thought of his ancestors. Professor Mircea Eliade,
for example, in his *Patterns in Comparative Religion†* deals in detail
with much primitive thought concerning what he names man's
'Journey to the Centre'—that is his journey from what he directly
experiences, the world of extension in space and time, to other worlds
either below or above it, and also to that 'primordial time' when, on

---

* Thomas Mann: *Freud and the Future* (1936).
† Sheed & Ward (1958).

earth itself, the limitations of such extension were unknown. The 'other' worlds may be either worlds of chaos and horror—usually but not always imagined as lower worlds—or the heaven of an imagined order of ideal beauty and security, generally conceived as above the sky. Such a journey must always start from some special and sacred spot, though such spots can be made by man as he needs and will use them. They are frequently marked by an omphalos or sacred stone, like the ka'aba of Mecca, Jacob's pillar of stone at Bethel, the stone of Abraham's sacrifice in the temple of Jerusalem and the omphalos of Delphi which has given a name to the image. The ka'aba is said to have fallen from heaven, leaving a hole in the sky immediately above its resting place on earth, and Jacob watched the angels ascending and descending above his pillow as he slept. Through such spots the Axis Mundi passes, both upwards and downwards, so that they are junctions of hell, earth and heaven. For example Golgotha, where the rock resembled a skull, was held to be the place where Adam was both created and buried. When the crucifixion opened a way up to heaven, Christ's blood was said to have reached Adam below so that by it he was baptized and saved. Any true temple was such a centre, and every ritually consecrated house could become one for the family that lived in it.* Thus the hard journey could begin as well at home as after a long pilgrimage. But men do not choose the place, it is shown to them, possibly by an animal, and one remembers that the dark portal of the Inferno was known to the leopard, the lion and the wolf, who revealed their knowledge of it by striving to keep the pilgrim away from the sacred entrance.

The stone might be developed into the temple, or associated with a cosmic mountain, reaching from earth to heaven. Where a temple was built in the form of rising terraces, or contained towers or spires, these levels were identified with the levels of the universe so that they reproduced the holy mountain up which the saint or hero could climb to heaven, as Moses, for example, climbed Mount Sinai, and the saved souls of the *Divine Comedy* climbed the Mount of Purgatory.

The image of the zones of the cosmos need not necessarily be in depth, and in point of fact it is not so in the early Hebraic-Christian myths. Although an early Jewish source, the Babylonian Talmud, says that 'Earth is to Gehenna as a small lid to an immense

---

* v. Mircea Eliade, op. cit., pp. 227 ff. and *Myth of the Eternal Return* (Routledge & Kegan Paul), pp. 12 ff.

pot',* other rabbinical works place Gehenna on the same level as Earth or may give it rising levels instead of the falling ones which we are accustomed to think significant. 'Arqua the Fifth Earth, contains Gehenna and its seven layers, each with its store-houses of darkness. The highest of these is *Sheol*, and beneath lie others named Perdition, The Lowest Pit, The Bilge, Silence, The Gates of Death and The Gates of the Shadow of Death. The fire of each layer is sixty times fiercer than that immediately below. Here the wicked are punished and angels torture them.'†

In the canonical Hebrew literature space symbols are developed with the—to us—familiar significance of evil below and good above. The psalmist sings: 'What profit is there in my blood when I go down to the pit?', and Jonah prayed from the belly of the whale:

> I went down to the bottom of the mountains, the earth covered me with her bars closed upon me for ever, yet hast thou brought up my life from the pit.

The image of Jonah, however, reminds one that the significance of the 'lower world' was not primarily concerned with morality. The future saviour drew power from his visit to the lower world; Joseph was cast into the pit before he ruled in Egypt and Jesus descended to hell before he rose again. The apocryphal gospel of Nicodemus does not recount the travelling but only the triumphant arrival in the lower world, and the spatial symbolism is as much in extension as in depth. The description of the city of darkness however remains a constant factor, and it reappears in Dante's fiery Dis. Satan, 'the prince and captain of death' is ordered to 'shut the brass gates of cruelty and make them fast by iron bars and fight courageously lest we be taken captive'. But while the devils are still talking 'on a sudden there was a voice as of thunder and the rushing of winds, saying, Lift up your gates O ye princes, and be ye lift up, O everlasting gates, and the King of Glory shall come in'. The victorious hero leads the souls of the virtuous dead upwards as all the saved souls will mount at the end of the dramatized cycles in which this episode was a prominent section.‡

For the Greeks and Romans also the descent to Avernus was at

---

* Quoted from *Hebrew Myths:* 'The Book of Genesis', Robert Graves and Raphael Patai (London: Cassell, 1964; New York: Doubleday, 1964).

† Ibid.

‡ E.g. in the Wakefield Cycle where the material is treated with conspicuous power. It also provides one of the most deeply poetic sections in Piers Ploughman.

first an image completely divorced from moral significance. Aeneas descends to Avernus seeking mantic power for his future efforts; he did not find it a place of punishment, although it was terrifying in its strange beauty:

> A deep, deep cave there was, its mouth enormously gaping,
> Shingly, protected by the dark lake and the forest gloom.
> Dimly through the shadows and dark solitudes they wended,
> Through the void domiciles of Dis, the bodiless regions:
> Just as through fitful moonbeams, under the moon's thin light,
> A path lies in a forest, when Jove has palled the sky
> With gloom, and the night's blackness has bled the world of colour.*

Virgil's imagery has been traced to the Roman mystery rites and even specifically associated with the initiation of Augustus. Miss Maud Bodkin, for example, insists on the religious and ritual nature of the experience Virgil seeks to convey.†

The same material, attributed in this case to Themistios' essay *On the Soul*, has been interpreted by P. Foucart‡ as a factual description of the ritual of the Eleusinian mysteries, but recent archaeological discoveries suggest that this is impossible, and G. E. Mylonas considers the passage to be a literary account of the imagined after-life:

> at first one wanders and wearily hurries to and fro, and journeys with suspicion through the dark . . . then come all the terrors . . . shuddering, trembling, sweating, amazement: then one is struck with a marvellous light, one is received into pure regions and meadows, with voices and dances and the majesty of holy sounds and shapes: among these he who has fulfilled initiation wanders free, and released and bearing his crown joins in the divine communion and consorts with pure and holy men, beholding those who live here un-initiated, an uncleansed horde, trodden under foot of him and huddled together in mud and fog . . .§

No definitive moral judgments can be embodied in Virgil's Other

---

* *The Aeneid*, tr. C. Day Lewis, Hogarth Press, pp. 124–5.

† v. *Archetypal Patterns in Poetry*, Oxford University Press (1934) and cf. *Pagan Background of Early Christianity*, W. R. Halliday, University Press of Liverpool (1925), pp. 242 ff.

‡ v. *Recherches sur l'origène et la nature des Mystères d'Eleusis*, Extrait des Mémoires de l'Académie des Inscriptions et Belles Lettres. Paris, 1895.

§ Stobaios IV, p. 107. Commented on and quoted in *Eleusis and the Eleusinian Mysteries*, G. E. Mylonas, Princeton (1961), p. 264.

World, since the souls are expecting re-incarnation, and for the same reason it cannot be a place for the making or re-making of the individual selves. The bridge between Homer's Tartaros and the moralized underworld of Christian legend must therefore be sought not in the Latin poet but in the Greek mystery religions—in particular Orphism —and in Plato's *Phaedo*.* Plato acknowledges his debt to his predecessors:

> The founders of the Mysteries would appear to have had a real meaning and were not talking nonsense when they intimated in a metaphor long ago that he who passes unsanctified and uninitiated into the world below will be in the Slough, but that he who arrives there after initiation and purification will dwell with the gods.

The 'Slough' subsumes the mud imagery which is persistent in Plato and later in Dante and is revived in this century by Beckett.

The Celtic 'other' world, Annwn, was also sometimes reached by a descent. A few miles from Glastonbury one may still enter a cave which we can assume with near certainty was once an acknowledged entry to the Celtic otherworld kingdom of Annwn. One enthusiast even believes it to have been the prototype of the classical Avernus itself.† Where the river Axe flows through the Mendip Hills it has created a series of caves, at least seventeen in number, of which the last two have been re-discovered by divers as recently as 1966. Three of them are accessible on foot; they are of limestone, and vividly beautiful in shape and colour. In the first of the caves is a large black stalagmite, in shape resembling a grotesquely distorted sphinx. Local tradition, going back to the Middle Ages, knows this figure only as the Witch of Wookey, but she is still strangely disturbing to the imagination, and she ante-dates by millenia any conception of a human witch. The extraordinary noises, heard within living memory but apparently more common before the river level was changed by modern drainage, must have added to the spot's awesomeness, and it is an assumption, but not an unlikely one, that the 'witch' was first thought of as a tutelary guardian of the lower world or even as its dark goddess. Mrs Anderson, to whose book the present author owes her exploration of Wookey Hole, quotes from Hesiod passages which confirm the similarity of the entries to the underworld imagined in the cultures of both Eastern and

* *Phaedo*, p. 107. Quotations from Plato are all from the translation by R. Livingstone in *Portrait of Socrates*, Oxford University Press (1938).
† v. Flavia Anderson: *The Ancient Secret*, Gollancz (1953), chapter VII.

Western Europe. He tells that the way into the dark realm is protected by a being 'half nymph, with dark eyes and fair cheeks; and half, on the other hand, a serpent huge and terrible and vast—speckled and flesh-devouring 'neath caves of Sacred Earth . . . There in front stand the resounding mansions of the infernal god . . . and a fierce dog keeps guard in front'.* From the entrance to the cave may be seen Glastonbury Tor on whose sides the ancient ridges still suggest a spiral path by which a ritual ascent to the summit might be achieved, and as late as the sixteenth century the other-worldly associations of the district were still alive.

In the year 1568, a Jesuit named William Weston visited an aged recusant in his house near Glastonbury and wrote:

> This was on a high hill . . . . He told me it was possible to hear there the groaning sighs and wailing voices of people in distress, so that he thought it must be a kind of approach or vestibule for souls passing into the pains of purgatory.†

This is clearly an old tradition re-interpreted after centuries of Christian teaching, when the natural magic of places—the sea, hills, meres, fords and misty woodlands—had been forgotten. Certainly in late Roman days Britain was apparently believed to be a land particularly concerned with the dead, indeed in the sixth century Procopius writes as though Britain itself was an 'Other World' and tells of the voyages made across the English channel by boatmen from the Netherlands who are mysteriously summoned to make the crossing by night, rowing heavy but apparently empty boats, whose invisible passengers are summoned ashore by name so that the boats return unloaded and light in the water. Procopius believed that the tale is founded on some form of dream. More often the Celtic Annwn is reached without a descent as when Arthur sails in the magical boat, Prydwen, to seek the life-giving cauldron, shining with blue enamel and guarded by nine maidens‡ or when St Brandon—that strange popular recension of Dante's pilgrim—sails to find heaven and hell across the waters of the Atlantic.§

---

* *Theogony*, Bohn's Classical Library, p. 17.

† Quoted by G. Ashe in *From Caesar to Arthur*, Collins (1960), p. 232.

‡ v. *Wales and the Arthurian Legend*, A. M. Loomis, University of Wales Press (1956), Chs. IX and V.

§ v. *South English Legendary*, E.E.T.S., O.S. No. 187 where the story of Sir Owayn's descent to St Patrick's Purgatory may also be found.

In many cults the climb upward could be achieved by means of a ladder; Osiris is called 'Lord of the Ascent and the Heavenly Ladder' and also 'the God at the top of the staircase', and the Mithraic mysteries used a ladder of seven rungs. Similar rituals are found today in Asia among the shamans of the north and also in certain Indian cults, and the stairway also remains a basic symbol in much Christian mystical writing.

The medieval image of the Ladder of Perfection which links heaven and earth and each of whose rungs is a virtue, was first developed by Horonius of Autun.* Professor Emile Mâle writes of its use by the miniaturist of the *Hortus deliciarum*:†

> He gives a faithful representation of the mystic ladder which resting upon earth loses itself in heaven, and on it he places the race of men. Clerk and layman climb painfully from rung to rung, while the vices, who remain on the ground, beckon to them from below. A bed, symbol of idleness, invites them to come and rest from their labours, and Luxuria smiles at them. The gold in the baskets, the food on the dishes, the horses and the shields, all arouse their eager desire. Some cannot resist the temptation, and from the heights to which they have attained return with a sudden drop to earth. But one woman, a religious no doubt, hearing and seeing nothing, mounts towards the crown which awaits her at the summit. Could a more dramatic rendering be given to an allegory? How it must have affected the childlike souls of the nuns for whom it was designed, and even today its evident sincerity makes an appeal.

Dante in the heaven of Saturn sees a golden ladder:

> Coloured like gold that flashes back the light
> I saw a ladder raised aloft so far
> It soared beyond the compass of my sight.
>
> Thereon I saw descend from bar to bar
> Splendours so numerous I thought the sky
> Had poured from heaven the light of every star.
>
> *Paradise*, XXI. 28–33‡

St John of the Cross symbolizes the steps of mystical perfection by the winding paths which ascend Mount Carmel, and in *En una nocte oscura* the soul reaches her lover 'on the ramparts' at mid-night.

* *Scala coeli minor*, col. 869, *Spec. Eccles*, col. 869, Patrol CLXXII.
† *The Gothic Image*, Fontana Library (1961), pp. 105–6.
‡ Tr. D. Sayers and B. Reynolds, Penguin (1962).

THE HARD JOURNEY

O venture of delight
With nobody in sight
I went abroad when all my house was hushed
In safety, in disguise
In darkness up the secret stair I crept.*

To modern man the knowledge informing such imagery may be revealed in dream. Jung reports a patient's dream in which the dreamer:

> saw on a mountain a kind of Castle of the Grail. He went along a road that seemed to lead straight to the foot of the mountain and up it. But as he drew nearer he discovered to his great disappointment that a chasm separated him from the mountain, a deep darksome gorge with underworldly water rushing along the bottom. A steep path led downwards and toilsomely climbed up again on the other side. But the prospect looked uninviting and the dreamer awoke.†

The likeness to the journey of Oedipus on the road to Thebes and that of Dante seeking the heavenly entrance in the darkness, both of them ignorant of the path which actually lay before them, is plain.

It is probable that the earliest representations of the primordial myths were not narratives but rites, and Professor Joseph Campbell claims that such rites go back to Cro-Magnon and even Neanderthal man. Writing of the painted caves of Southern France, he suggests that they were not simply sanctuaries of a hunting cult, but places for the performance of initiation rites. He believes that 'a constellation of images denoting the plunge and dissolution of consciousness in the darkness of non-being' (p. 65) was an important aspect of such ceremonies, and continues:

> A terrific sense of claustrophobia and simultaneously of release from every context of the world above, assails the mind impounded in those more than absolutely dark abysses, where darkness no longer is an absence of light but an experienced force. And when a light is flashed to reveal the beautifully painted bulls and mammoths, flocks of reindeer, trotting ponies, woolly rhinos, and dancing shamans of those caves, the images smite the mind as indelible imprints.‡

* Tr. R. Campbell, *Poems of St John of the Cross*, Penguin Classics.
† *The Archetypes and the Collective Unconscious*, C.W. IX, Part I, tr. R. F. C. Hull. Bollingen Series XX. Distributed by Princeton University Press; London: Routledge & Kegan Paul Ltd (1959), p. 19.
‡ *The Masks of God*, Secker & Warburg (1960), p. 66.

Professor Campbell also claims that evidence exists for an even earlier apprehension of a myth of the journey through darkness to life, through death to re-birth. 'Neanderthal skeletons have been found interred with supplies (suggesting the idea of another life), accompanied by animal sacrifice (wild ox, bison, and wild goat), with attention to an east-west axis (the path of the sun, which is reborn from the same earth in which the dead are placed), in flexed position (as though within the womb), or in a sleeping posture—in one case with a pillow of chips of flint. Sleep and death, awakening and resurrection, the grave as a return to the mother for re-birth.'* In this primitive material the cosmic journey is linked to that of the hero through a faith in the goodness of the beginning of things. As the gods and goddesses of Spring bring back fertility to the wasted earth so the individual, in the success of his personal quest, finds himself in a spring-time world once more.

When Dante reaches the Earthly Paradise it images man's return to the joy that without the sin of Adam he would never have lost. The wheel has come full circle to his second birth.

> And the end of all our exploring
> Will be to arrive where we started
> And know the place for the first time
> At the source of the longest river
> The voice of the hidden waterfall
> And the children in the apple tree
> Not known because not looked for
> But heard, half heard, in the stillness
> Between two waves of the sea.†

Erich Neumann has written that though the 'extrovert'‡ will accept the myths that tell of the hero entering the cave or passing the sea or the desert or reaching the underworld as images of the quest for material success or the hand of the ideal mate, yet this is not more valid than the equally primary interpretation of the introvert, which equates the sought-for treasure 'as something within—namely the soul herself'. The 'Treasure' may thus be regarded, as it is by Jung

---

* Ibid., p. 67.

† T. S. Eliot, *Four Quartets, Little Gidding.*

‡ *The Origins and History of Consciousness,* tr. R. F. C. Hull. Bollingen Series XLII. Distributed by Princeton University Press; London: Routledge & Kegan Paul Ltd (1957).

25

and Neumann, as a return to the unconscious, intuitional mode of being. Neumann insists that 'the correlation "consciousness-light-day",* and "unconsciousness-darkness-night" always holds true', and that the latter is always and necessarily concerned with the feminine power. As interpreted by this school of thought the most fundamental forms of the myth of the journey are two—one cosmic, one individual. There is the image of the 'night sea-journey' in which the sun is submerged in the western ocean and rises next morning in the East. This is a form of the myth which underlies many initiatory rites, including that of Christian baptism. There is also the conception of the *'regressus ad utero'* which is frequently associated with the image of a cavern, or the mouth of a pit, which represents the dreaded *vagina dentata* where the young male seeking to achieve virility fears he may be destroyed but where success, like the journey up the hill, may image the triumphant development of conscious 'masculine' thought. This is the substance behind the story of Jason's passage between the moving rocks on his quest of the Golden Fleece. Homer alludes to one such legend when Circe is directing Odysseus on his homeward voyage:

> Two ways will lie before you . . . One leads to those sheer cliffs which the blessed gods know as the Wandering Rocks. Here blue-eyed Amphitrite sends her great breakers thundering in, and the very birds cannot fly by in safety . . . while for such sailors as bring their ship to the spot, there is no escape whatever. . . . Of all ships that go down to the sea only one has made the passage, and that was the celebrated Argo, homeward bound from Aeetes coast. And she would soon have been dashed upon those mighty crags, if Here, for love of Jason, had not helped her past.†

Homer here describes Jason's return through what we still name the 'jaws of death', and some forms of the story recount that he successfully exorcises the evil power of the rocks, which thereafter are stationary for ever. Jack Lindsay, in his recent exhaustive study of the myth, has convincingly related it to accounts of trance journeys to another world. After comparing Jason's experience with a variety of initiation ceremonies and of Shamanistic rites from both Asia and Europe, he concludes:

---

* *The Origins and History of Consciousness*, tr. R. F. C. Hull. Bollingen Series XLII. Distributed by Princeton University Press; London: Routledge & Kegan Paul Ltd (1957).

† *The Odyssey*, tr. E. V. Rieu, Penguin (1946), pp. 1958.

The Rocks represented the decisive moment of entry into the spirit world . . .
We may reasonably hold that in the tale of the Argo . . . we touch a myth
of the spirit-journey comparable with that of Gilgamesh.*

He might well have added: 'and with that of Dante'. Jason's voyage is
constructed, of course, on a horizontal, not a vertical, space pattern,
and his search is concerned with a precious object and not directly
with the self. Nevertheless it is not unrelated to the discovery of the
true self and the terrors of rebirth.†

Wittgenstein wrote that 'we make to ourselves pictures of facts',
but today it is only when the pictures are recreated by an artist that
they are perceptible to most of us. Freud has said that: 'It is an
immutable truth that what comes from the heart, that alone goes to
the heart', and it is equally certain that only imagery which has its
source in the unconscious mind can reach the unconscious mind of its
observer. Never has the need to move in a world where our real wants
and the possibility of their satisfaction are revealed, and where the
'double think' and the pseudo-wants of a commercial society are
exposed, been more urgent than it is today. 'Without his mythologies',
writes Coleridge, 'man is only an unruly animal without a soul . . . a
congeries of possibilities without order and without aim.'‡ Only
by allowing a response to the symbols created or re-created for us by
our artists can our symbol-less minds recover something of the lost
awareness and sensibility in regard to ourselves, each other and the
cosmos of which we are a part, which are our rightful inheritance.

* *The Clashing Rocks*, Chapman & Hall (1965), p. 381.

† In a twelfth-century boss in Chichester Cathedral a figure is shown emerging
from a great toothed mouth, which is visualized as that of a dragon, but the creature
emerging is no conventional hero; it is a tiny human foetus ready to be born.

‡ v. I. A. Richards: *Coleridge on the Imagination* (Routledge), pp. 171–2.

CHAPTER 2

The Journey to the Dreadful Centre

i *Oedipus Tyrannus*

O dark dark dark. They all go into the dark,
The vacant instellar spaces, the vacant into the vacant.
. . . . I said to my soul, be still, and let the dark come upon you
Which shall be the darkness of God.

T. S. ELIOT. *Burnt Norton*

THE theme of Sophocles' *Oedipus Tyrannus* has already been out-lined, and it now remains to consider the play's substance in rather more detail. We may begin by glancing at a comparison made by Mr F. L. Lucas* who refers to the case of a patient treated by the German psychiatrist Stekel. After saying that the young man in ques-tion 'is no lord of Thebes, merely an unhappy kleptomaniac', he describes his wretched childhood in the care of a nymphomaniac mother to whom he became emotionally tied, falling in love with women of her age, or occasionally with very young girls. 'After arrest for one of his thefts, he first tried to hang himself in prison, like Sophocles' Jocasta; then like Sophocles' Oedipus, blinded himself—with glass splinters. It was, indeed, a step long meditated to end his sexual temptations. . . . It has also to be remembered that blinding can be a common symbol for castration. We may recall Cranmer thrusting first into the flames the hand that signed his recantation and realize that with Oedipus also the punishment fitted the crime.'

Such pictures of self-punishment bring into prominence the problem of the guilt of the hero. J. T. Shepherd, in his introduction to his translation of *Oedipus Tyrannus*,† writes a chapter entitled 'The Innocence of Oedipus'. On one level, perhaps at what Dante would call the 'literal' level, that is to say in the tale of the events, Oedipus

---

* *Literature and Psychology*, Cassell (1951), pp. 26–7.
† Cambridge University Press (1920).

is indeed innocent, since the narrative emphasizes that the murder of his father and the marriage with his mother were deeds committed in ignorance, and there remains a Sophoclean fragment which declares that 'no-one who sins unwittingly is evil'. Yet these deeds were actually committed. Jung writes that nature is not at all lenient with unconscious sinners and can ensure that guilt follows the unknowing acts unmodified by the apparent ignorance of the performer.*

> There exists a terrible law which stands beyond man's morality and his ideas of righteousness—a law which cannot be cheated.
>
> It is no good having sceptical ideas about this—nature does not care a pin for our ideas. If we have to deal with the human soul we can only meet it on its own ground and we are bound to do so whenever we are confronted with the real and crushing problems of life.

The appeal of the play is indeed enhanced rather than diminished by the hero's ignorance and the consequent absence of a deliberate choice on his part, for his action is given a mantic quality of inevitability.

Dr Immanuel Velikovsky believes that he has found the historical origin of the story of Oedipus.† Puzzled like many other readers by the appearance of a sphinx outside the gates of Boetian Thebes, he sought an explanation in the homeland of the first sphinx. In Egyptian Thebes is set the story of a prince who returned from exile to his home land and after killing his father, married his mother and had a daughter by her, afterwards passing again into exile, perhaps a blind man and leaving behind him two sons who slew each other and a daughter who possibly gave one brother secret burial and was immured herself to die in a rocky tomb. Only an Egyptologist is equipped to evaluate Dr Velikovsky's evidence, but he has collected enough written and visual material to merit attention at least for the first part of his thesis, which is what concerns us here.

A female sphinx first appears during the Eighteenth Egyptian dynasty and has a head which clearly bears the features of Tiy, the Queen of Amenhotep III. The figure has female breasts and in one case is shown rampant and tearing apart or strangling 'its victim'.‡

---

* *Development of Personality*, C. W. XVII, tr. R. F. C. Hull. Bollingen Series XX. Distributed by Princeton University Press; London: Routledge & Kegan Paul (1954), p. 40.

† *Oedipus and Aknaton*, Sidgwick and Jackson (1960).

‡ Op. cit., p. 42.

It is Aknaton, the son of this sphinx-queen, whom Velikovsky casts as the historical Oedipus. He shows that Aknaton, who is always pictured not with swollen ankles certainly but with abnormally thickened thighs, returned mysteriously after long absence to assume the throne after his father's death, and that he symbolically murdered him by defacing his name and sign wherever he could, thus killing his *ka* or soul in its after-life. Professor A. H. Gardiner writes: 'In Ancient Egypt to destroy a person's name was actually to destroy himself, and Aknaton certainly obliterated his father's name in many places, notably on his memorial tablet.'* After Aknaton became king the sphinx figures also were mutilated. Selun Hassan, quoted by Velikovsky writes of a stele in the Cairo museum: 'These sphinxes have been systematically erased, only their outlines remain to show what was originally there. Before each sphinx was a standing figure of the king, which has also suffered erasure . . . these are clearly the erasures made by the iconoclasts of Aknaton.'† The King is certainly shown in many pictures, notably in the murals on the tomb at Egyptian Thebes of one of his principal officials, with his mother, who wears the double crown and is seated apparently as his principal queen. The beautiful Nefertiti, mother of most of his children, appears in these pictures behind the king and is drawn quite small. In the accompanying writing Tiy is described as: 'The hereditary princess, the most praised, the lady of grace. . . . The great wife of the king who loves her, the lady of both lands, Tiy.'‡ Although the 'king who loves her' is usually held to be Amenhotep, this is not self-evidently true. The most exquisite and interesting of the tomb murals shows Aknaton leading Tiy by the hand into the temple of Aton, 'to let her see her sunshade', and the pair are followed by a child-princess, next to whom is written: 'the king's daughter of his body beloved by him, Bekatatem'.§ Egyptian scholars appear to be agreed that this princess was the daughter of Tiy, but it remained for Velikovsky to show that dates made it impossible for her to be the child of Amenhotep and to go on to identify her father, not with Tiy's first husband, but with her son, Aknaton.

* Quoted op. cit. p. 84. Cf. 'His strongest hatred was directed against his father whom he could not reach because he was no longer among the living'. Karl Abraham, Imago (1912) quoted op. cit. p. 68.
† v. S. Hassan. *Annales du Service*, XXXVIII (1957), p. 61.
‡ Translated by G. Maspero, op. cit., p. 94.
§ Op cit., p. 91

The relationship of this mother and son differed from that of Jocasta and Oedipus in that it was no secret and was not based on ignorance. By the pair themselves it must have been accepted as not only proper but especially sacred. Such a union was so held by certain Persian tribes with whom the kings of the Eighteenth Dynasty had close relations. It was however abhorred by the Egyptians, and together with Aknaton's belligerent monotheism, also presumably Persian in origin, it may well have precipitated his deposition and exile. The fate of the wife-mother remains a mystery. She apparently received no royal burial and the catafalque marked with her name was found in modern times to contain the body of a young man, not, in spite of certain identifying marks, her grandson, the pharaoh Tutankamen, but possibly that of his brother, secretly buried after his father's fall.

The important point is, of course, not that the name Oedipus may possibly be a corruption of Aknaton, or that the story of royal murder and incest with its tragic consequences reached pre-historic Greece from Egypt and was repeated by story-tellers there until Sophocles made it into the play we know: the story of Aknaton, as Velikovsky tells it, fascinates because it shows the repetition in fact of a situation apparently experienced in fantasy by every European male child for whom the sphinx to be destroyed has the face of the mother who is at once desired and feared, and it is for this reason that it wins its universal response. It is such fantasies of which Jung writes:

It is they which make kings or pawns of the insignificant figures who move about on the checker-board of life, turning some poor devil of a casual father into a ferocious tyrant, or a silly goose of an unwilling mother into a goddess of fate. For behind every individual father there stands the primordial image of the Father, and behind the fleeting personal mother the magical figure of the Magna Mater.*

In the play by Sophocles both the hero and the chorus believe that some of Oedipus' suffering is due to his daimon:

> What demon of destiny
> With swift assault outstriding
> Has ridden you down?†

To the contemporary reader it will appear that compulsions spring from within, but they are not the less mysterious, and the drives from

* *Development of Personality*, C.W. XVII, pp. 44–5.
† v. *Three Theban Plays*.

31

which Oedipus acts and suffers will seem not inappropriately imaged by the old belief of daimonic compulsion. Professor William Arrowsmith stresses the social rather than the philosophic content of the play. 'Oedipus looks into the abyss that yawns beneath him—the frightful knowledge of his nature which fifth-century man had learned from the war, the plague and the atrocities, the sophistic revolution and the collapse of the old world order—and dashes out his eyes.'[*]

When Oedipus guessed the riddle of the Sphinx, he recognized himself in her words. He knew himself as Man, the being who walks erect at the height of his powers and is doomed to creep later with the help of a stick, as certainly as he is doomed to die. But although Oedipus knew of this innate frailty, he was unable to apply his knowledge. He could boast to Tiresias:

> Where were you when the Dog-faced Witch was here?
> . . . all were silent
> Until I came—I, ignorant Oedipus came—
> And stopped the riddler's mouth.   p. 38

He forgot, in his arrogance, what the Sphinx had revealed concerning the beginning and the end of man. Even on the verge of self-discovery he claimed:

> I am the child of Fortune,
> The giver of good, and I shall not be shamed.   p. 59

He could not accept that he too would descend to walking on three legs like the rest of mankind.

It may be noted in passing that a recent school of thought has arisen in which Oedipus is again judged to be a guilty man, responsible for his own failure. Erich Neumann[†] takes Oedipus as an example of the mythical hero who fails to fulfil his heroic destiny—that is to say, fails to become a prototype of the mature man. Of the true hero he writes: 'By conquering his terror of the female, by entering into the womb, the abyss, the terror of the unconscious, he weds himself triumphantly with the Great Mother'. But, he continues: 'though Oedipus conquers the Sphinx, he commits incest with his mother and murders his father unconsciously . . . and when he finds out, he is unable to look his own deed, the deed of a hero, in the face'. For this reason, he fails to fulfil his destiny, and his suffering springs, not from

---

[*] *Ideas in the Drama*, ed. John Gassner, Columbia (1964), p. 3.
[†] *Origins and History of Consciousness.*

committing incest and murder, but from failing to accept the need to do so, since these acts are the symbols of necessary steps on the road to maturity.*

We are not here primarily concerned, however, with either the guilt or the innocence of Oedipus. The ancient judgment of guilty as much as the humanistic verdict of innocent are both of secondary importance. His deed and his own reaction to it create the central symbol of the play, and its form is exactly calculated to image—among other things —the gradual approach not to judgment but to truth. Among the glories of Sophocles' drama is its clarion statement that the man who makes this approach, for all his defects, is a heroic figure, taking the terrible but necessary journey towards his final salvation.

Although Sophocles' *Oedipus* is based on material similar at a deep level to Dante's, it is built on a completely different *maquette*. Its power stems from the events of its narrative, extended in chronological order and leading one to another in a sequence unbroken save at one point. The original breach of obedience committed by Laius when he marries and begets a son, leads to Oedipus' exposure and adoption, his fears concerning his parentage, his flight from Corinth, his meeting with Laius and with the Sphinx on his journey to Delphi, the reward of marriage with Jocasta, the plague, the second oracle, the curse on the murderer of Laius and the institution of the search. Jocasta's further blasphemy and the sending for the old slave are linked one to another with the inevitability which has always been admired. The one coincidence is the arrival of the messenger from Corinth with news of Polybus' death at the moment when Oedipus is set to discover whether or no he is the slayer not indeed of his father—that he does not yet suspect—but of Laius. After this all is causally ordered once more; the messenger has a motive for revealing his secret, and Oedipus' true parentage is confirmed by the shepherd whose presence has already been demanded. The one break in human causality—the death of Polybus at the same time as the plague of Thebes—is, however, sufficient to convey the whole other-world nature of the fable. The events in human time are part of a larger whole; they are over-ruled by supernatural powers in the interest of a numinous pattern of which the actors are unaware. At first this supernatural purpose seems one of horror and cruelty, but this is in fact not so. As in the Christian mythology, the 'Fall', tragic in its

* This interpretation equates the action of Oedipus with the *mauvaise foi* so important to Sartre. v. inf. p. 97.

immediate consequence, was at last revealed as the *felix culpa* from which mankind's true adventure and final glory sprang, so Oedipus, gaining wisdom in suffering and sight in blindness, reached at last a goal beyond the lot of ordinary men. The divine pattern matches achievement with preliminary failure, power with weakness and at last glory with shame and ignominy.

Sophocles' vision is communicated by the structure of the events of the plot, a structure as closely woven as that of Dante's scholastic philosophy. The strangeness and mystery of Dante's settings give his poem an indisputably romantic *ambiance*, but it shows none of the vagueness or shapelessness which may cloud the nostalgic beauty to which we respond as 'romance'. For all the differences in method the *Divine Comedy* is as perfectly articulated as *Oedipus Tyrannus*—the most economical and balanced of classical tragedies. Dante is the poet of what T. S. Eliot has called the 'intellectual soul', and he communicates a coherent philosophy as well as a dream adventure and the religion of a mystic poet. Religious truth is not a matter of vague feeling; if it is to be found it 'must be developed from knowledge acquired when our ordinary senses and intellectual operations are at their highest pitch of discipline'.* It is such high and disciplined intellectual operations which give its structure to the *Divine Comedy*. Sophocles and Dante would both have agreed with Rilke: 'the important thing is not to express feeling, but to shape it', for the poet's aim is 'the complete integration of the poetical image and the subjective experience'.

ii *The Divine Comedy: The Inferno*

Man is in no sense perfect but a wretched creature who can yet apprehend perfection.

T. E. HULME. *Speculations.* 1924

The night-sea journey begins with the encounter with the world and ends with the heroic birth of the self.
ERICH NEUMANN. *Origins and History of Consciousness*

IN the following analysis it is, of course, never intentionally suggested that the traveller through the three worlds of the *Divine Comedy*

* A. N. Whitehead: *Religion in the Making*, in *Anthology, A. N. Whitehead*, Cambridge University Press (1953), p. 513.

is the central figure of an autobiography in the modern sense of that word. Nevertheless Dante, although he sometimes stands apart from him, does give his pilgrim his own name, and it is convenient for us to do so here. It is also necessary to remember that it is the poet himself who explains, in his famous Epistle XIII to Can Grande della Scalle, that poetry may be interpreted at as many as four different levels of meaning. Of the subject of his own poem, Dante says that it:

> in the *literal* sense is the 'state of the soul after death straightforwardly affirmed' . . . But if, indeed, the work is taken *allegorically*, its subject is: 'Man as by good or ill deserts, in the exercise of his free choice, he becomes liable to rewarding or punishing Justice.*

We have the author's own authority therefore to consider the poem as, at one level, a description of Everyman as he lives his life in this world, and the story, or literal element, shows clearly enough that in many of Everyman's spiritual adventures Dante was remembering his own.

Like that of *Oedipus Tyrannus* Dante's story opens with its hero in mid-career; he is self-confident and apparently successful but is made suddenly aware that he has strayed from the straight way. As we have already seen, his journey only gradually reveals to him what he truly is, and when he sees the truth it is almost unbearable to him. The bony structure thus shows the essential similarity between the two great artefacts, one classical and the other gothic, but the flesh in which each structure is clothed reveals not likeness but difference. Although each poem reflects the basic human condition, each poet interprets this condition in the light of a philosophy which would be incomprehensible or repugnant to the other.

Beatrice's words of Dante's pilgrim are true also of Oedipus:

> he who yonder weeps should comprehend,
> And grief with guilt maintain the balance true.
> . . . to such a depth he fell
> That every means to save his soul came short
> Except to let him see the lost in hell.

Purgatory, xxx. 107–8, 136–8

Oedipus certainly saw himself lost in hell, but his creator's 'sense of sin' was very different from Dante's. The medieval mind was in this regard like Donne's,

---

* Quoted and translated by D. Sayers, *Divine Comedy* I: *Hell*, Introduction, p. 15.

To seize and clutch and penetrate
Expert beyond experience.*

To the classical Greeks, and so to Sophocles, the act was the sin, for whatever reason it was committed; it was sin apart from the moral responsibility of the sinner. To Dante every sin is sin because it is an act of free choice, a choice made with knowledge, for which therefore the sinner's moral responsibility is complete:

Light's given you to know right from wrong at need.

Purgatorio, XVI, 75

He shows that even those who strive to evade choice cannot succeed. Both men and angels who did not decide for good found themselves within the gates of hell, futilely pursuing their whirling ensign round the rim of the abyss. For them it proved true that 'he that saveth his life shall lose it'. Their personal responsibility remains absolute.

Nevertheless, the two journeys are in many ways similar. The immediate starting point for Oedipus was the word of the oracle, for Dante it was that of Beatrice, who descends to Limbo to beg Virgil's aid:

A friend of mine, who is not Fortune's friend,
Is hard beset . . .

Beatrice am I, who thy good speed beseech;
Love that first moved me from the blissful place
Whither I'd fain return, now moves my speech.

Inferno, II. 61–72

Both pilgrims, after the original divine intervention, pursue their course by their own intelligence and determination, for Virgil represents human wisdom and therefore, among other things, Dante's own poetic imagination and intellectual vigour.

The pilgrim's descent to the lowest circle of the pit reveals Dante's descent into himself, into his previously subconscious mind. Each sinner that he meets is a symbol of the evil, potential or actual, of his own soul, for this is the only evil he can know. As an existential psychoanalyst has written in our own day: 'The Passion is all that man can know of God; his conflicts, duly faced, are all that he can

* T. S. Eliot: *Whispers of Immortality* in *Collected Poems* (London: Faber; New York: Harcourt, Brace & World).

know of himself. The last judgment is the always present self-judgment.'*

> This dark road downward to the dreadful centre   II. 83

was indeed to prove 'a savage path and froward' (II. 142) and it led to 'hidden things' (III. 21) which he would willingly never have seen. The entrance to the City of Desolation, whose inhabitants have abandoned hope, proved to be unexpectedly close at hand, but the road on which his feet were set was unexpectedly long. The spatial imagery is used repeatedly to suggest the dangers of the hardest of journeys—that into the depths of the self.

> Hear truth: I stood on the steep brink whereunder
> Runs down the dolorous chasm of the Pit. . . .
>
> Deep, dense, and by no faintest glimmer lit
> It lay, and though I strained my sight to find
> Bottom, not one thing could I see in it.   IV. 7–12

This is that personal and spiritual guilt known only to the truly religious man of which Baudelaire wrote:

> Pascal avait son gouffre, avec lui se mouvant.
>
> J'ai peur du sommeil comme on a peur d'un grand trou
> Tout plein de vague horreur, menant on ne sait ou.†

A detailed survey of Dante's treatment of particular sins both enforces an 'autobiographical' interpretation of the poem and also establishes further links with the play of Sophocles. Oedipus, in his moment of truth, recognizes in himself the sins of lust and wrath, and behind these all the time was the shadow of the *hubris* which led to his overwhelming confidence in his 'Luck', and hence to his defiance of Creon, of Tiresias, of Jocasta, and most important of all, of the gods whose oracles he expected to circumvent by his own cunning.

These are exactly the sins which Dante attributes to his pilgrim, his 'other self', and he uses the same pattern. The pilgrim, as will be shown, is particularly concerned with lust and wrath. There is no specific punishment for pride in the circles of hell, but it is clearly a basic attitude of which the pilgrim is continually aware, and it is a sin of which he shows both his guilt and his repentance in Purgatory.

---

* E. Erikson: *The Young Man Luther* (London: Faber; New York: W. W. Norton).

† *Le Gouffre. Selected Verse*, Penguin Poets (1961), p. 245.

Aristotle divides sin into three classes: incontinency or uncontrolled appetite, bestiality or perverted appetite, and malice. The animals who pursue the pilgrim in the dark wood represent Dante's interpretation of these three classes: the leopard is incontinence, the lion the violence which is a perversion in man, and the wolf is malice, which includes fraud. This makes up the pattern of Dante's hell except that there is added an extra circle for the heretics, whose existence depends on the acceptance of an established orthodoxy of faith—a thing inconceivable to the Greeks—where intellectual pride and perverted appetite are analysed and condemned.* Within this complex of material it is possible to distinguish certain sins with which Dante is especially concerned.

Miss Dorothy Sayers in the notes to her translation of the *Purgatorio*† writes:

> Only on three of the Cornices does Dante . . . associate himself with the punishment of the spirits, viz on those of Pride, Wrath and Lust. Since these are precisely the three failings of which Dante has always been accused, one may perhaps infer that he knew his own weaknesses as well as anybody.

Using this as a clue towards uncovering the psychological thread which is woven through the fiction, we find that at least two of these sins—wrath and lust—are those associated with the beasts who originally strove to deflect the pilgrim from pursuing his course directly upward to the sunlit mountain. It is because they have already succeeded in this that Virgil, Dante's own reason as well as his mentor, priest—analyst if you will—is obliged to lead him by a longer way:

> But, as for thee, I think and deem it well
> Thou take me for thy guide, and pass with me
> Through an eternal place and terrible.   I. 112–4

This is the beginning of the journey into the mind which is a unique yet universal experience. Every man can eventually recognize himself as potentially Judas; our difference from Dante is that, having accomplished this, we are less likely than he to have faith in our capacity still to love Beatrice and attain the vision of God. At the tremendous gate the sense of whose inscription 'was dreadful' to him

---

* These types of sin are well analysed and discussed by D. Sayers in her Introduction to *Divine Comedy*. I. *Hell*, pp. 139 ff.

† *Divine Comedy*. II. *Purgatory*, Penguin Classics (1955), p. 162.

(III. 12) Virgil insists that the 'savage path' (II. 142) on which the pilgrim has set his feet, leads through it:

> We are come to the place where I told thee thou shouldst see the woeful people who have lost the good of the intellect.* III. 16–18

—that is those who have lost the knowledge of God, but it is also those who have lost even that measure of understanding which would lead them to accept the necessity to attempt the journey to the dreadful centre. Dante's pilgrim is at last saved because he accepts this necessity and welcomes it as good:

> He laid his hand on mine, and with a face
> So joyous that it comforted my quailing,
> Into the hidden things he led my ways. III. 19–21

In the *Comedia* there are certain scenes which because of their exceptional power are picked out again and again for praise. It is significant that these scenes—with perhaps two exceptions—are all concerned with the sins of lust, wrath or violence, and with the underlying disposition of pride. Immediately inside the Gateway is the circle of the Laodiceans, those who had made no positive choice of either good or evil—'This scum who never lived' (III. 64) as Dante calls them. Alas, their number is legion:

> such an endless train
> It never would have entered in my head
> There were so many men whom death had slain. 55–7

They are maybe the majority of us, identified by T. S. Eliot when he watched the workers of London drifting over the city's bridge and was amazed:

> I had not thought death had undone so many.†

The episode is, so far as we know, Dante's own invention, but though it is vivid, the pilgrim and Virgil pass through it quickly. Dante was never a man to be 'neither hot nor cold', or ever to consider making 'through cowardice the great refusal' (III. 61). It is very different when he reaches the first circle of the spirits who have deliberately chosen their sin. Gazing into the depths beneath he hears the voice of Reason speak:

* Translated by John Sinclair. *Divine Comedy* I, Bodley Head (1939).
† T. S. Eliot. *The Waste Land*.

'Down must we go, to that dark world and blind' . . .
So, entering, he made me enter.   IV. 13

Their first discovery is lust, in a place 'Where nothing shines at all'
(151). Here is Francesca drifting on the wind, and at the sight of her
and Paolo in one another's arms Dante's response is immediate: 'Pity
came upon me and I was as one bewildered' (V. 140).* Here he sees
the fate of a love the like of which his own love might so easily have
become. Paolo had distantly worshipped his lady as Dante had worshipped his, and the traveller naturally longs to know what happened
to these other lovers; even in his tact and delicacy he presses Francesca
to tell him details of the change from bliss to pain. Recognizing his
sympathy she answers willingly:

> O living creature, gracious and so kind,
> Coming through this black air to visit us, . . .
> Hear all thou wilt.   88–94

When she has told the story of their guilty but so gentle love, the poet,
'hearing those wounded souls', is silenced.

> When I could answer, I began: 'Alas!
> Sweet thoughts how many, and desire how great,
> Brought down these twain unto the dolorous pass'.   112–4

Dante knew love as a 'lord of terrible aspect', but he could also
imagine the simplicity of the first kiss exchanged between the young
lovers—the kiss which he himself had never given to Beatrice. The
whole canto has been said to be 'faint with its goal-less sweetness',†
but the pilgrim did not find it so:

> While the one spirit thus spoke, the other's crying
> Wailed on me with sound so lamentable,
> I swooned for pity like as I were dying,
> And, as a dead man falling, down I fell.   139–42

This is the Dante who loved Beatrice, who sublimated his love,
forgot it, and remembered it again in middle life. No breath of criticism
of the lovers is even implied; Francesca's egotism is unremarked. But
although *the pilgrim* recognizes as yet no evil here, *the poet* places the
lovers in hell. They had taken that first step which if not repented and

---

* Sinclair. Op. cit., p. 77.
† I. Brandeis: *The Ladder of Vision* (London: Chatto & Windus; New York:
Doubleday), p. 34.

abandoned leads to the ice in which mutual association becomes mutual hatred, and contact is contact only to destroy. This—the first of Dante's intimate encounters with the sinners in hell (for the ancient dead in Limbo stand apart from the rest—they are always and inevitably the Other, never the self)—must be compared with his meeting with his own mistress in the Earthly Paradise. Here he discovers—or possibly rediscovers—what love really is, its tension and its power. When we are made aware of this other love, Francesca and Paolo appear to have accepted damnation in exchange for a very slender 'good'. The tender but flaccid emotion of Francesca as she drifts on the dark wind is suddenly exposed as betrayal and adultery, as a 'shrinking from the adult love demanded' of her,* and for all its pathos, is remembered, if it is remembered at all, as a thing of naught, a kind of loving which Dante had left behind for ever.

It is in the fifth circle that Dante first encounters the sins of wrath and violence, and an intensely personal note is at once introduced. As the boat crosses the filthy ooze in which the wrathful are sunk: 'There started up at me a mud-soaked head,' (VIII. 32) that, when asked his name, replied that the voyagers may see that he is 'one who weeps' (36). This has something of the same pathos as Francesca's words about the bitterest woe of woes being to 'remember in our wretchedness/Old happy times' (III. 121–3) but Dante's response is very different. To Filippo Argenti's apparently harmless question: 'Who art thou, come here before thy time?' his answer comes like a whip-lash:

> Though I come I stay not; thou that art made
> So rank and beastly, who art thou?   33–5

The scene marks his first recognition of himself in the person of another, and he is both horrified and angry:

> Amid the weeping and the woe,
> Accursed spirit, do thou remain and rot!
> I know thee, filthy as thou art—I know.   37–9

That is to say, he knows himself, and he acts accordingly. When the sinner stretches out his hands to clutch the boat, Virgil, i.e. the pilgrim's own rational mind,

---

* Charles Williams: *The Figure of Beatrice*, p. 118.

> thrust him back,
> Crying, 'Hence to the other dogs! Trouble him not!'
> And after laid his arms about my neck
> And kissed my face and said: 'Indignant soul,
> Blessed is the womb that bare thee'.   41–5

Dante actually begs to see the spirit's further punishment, and this is granted him:

> And soon I saw him set upon so sore
> By the muddy gang, with such a pulling and hauling,
> That I still praise and thank my God therefor.   58–60

The sin once admitted can be forgotten:

> There we left him, as doth this tale of mine; . . .
> And I craned forward.   64–6

At the level of narrative Dante abjures Filippo Argenti; at the level of allegory he abjures an aspect of himself, and Virgil therefore approves his action.

After this the pilgrim passes the glowing walls of the fiery city of Dis and begins to discover the sins not of the body but of the mind, those not so much of weakness as of will, which culminate in the sin of Lucifer, that of direct rebellion against God. The battle for self-knowledge is intensified.

> Dante underlines . . . the significance of the Furies and the Gorgon, their traditional character as the spirits of remorse and despair. Against the forces of denial and refusal with these dreadful allies, the conscience is all but paralysed and the reason itself for the time baffled.*

The image of Medusa's head, used by the devils to deflect or destroy the pilgrims, has been variously interpreted, but it seems to be a metaphor for some sort of irrational impulse strong enough to paralyse the will and destroy the personality. It is therefore of interest that although it is at first Dante's reason that protects him—Virgil turns him round and, not content with bidding him close his eyes, lays his hands across them—yet the defeat of the irrational is not finally by reason but by another irrational, the angel who 'came to us . . . sent from Heaven' (IX. 80–6).

In the sixth circle the heretics are buried, each in a separate grave, so that when he sat bolt upright in his, the great Ghibbeline rebel,

* John Sinclair: op. cit.

Farinata, was visible to the waist. The meeting with Farinata, justly
one of the famous episodes of the first canticle, is vivid but at first
sight objective. It is certainly impossible to believe that Dante felt
himself personally involved in the sin of heresy. He is certainly however involved with the sin of pride, and his retorts to Farinata are in
the latter's own language and fully as arrogant. When Farinata, learn-
ing who Dante's kindred were, boasts that he had routed them from
Florence, Dante's answer comes pat:

> 'Quite true; and by that same arithmetic',
> Said I, 'they rallied all round and came back twice;
> Your side, it seems, have not yet learned the trick'.   X. 48–51

Yet the poet's sympathy with this great rebel soon becomes obvious,
and in human terms it is well merited:

> Already my eyes were fixed on his; upright
> He had lifted him, strong-breasted, stony-fronted,
> Seeming to hold all Hell in deep despite.   X. 34–6

When Dante accuses him of rebellion against Florence, Farinata
admits the charge but claims that he had also defied his closest friends
in her support. Dante's obvious concern (so different from his clear-
sighted repudiation of Filippo Argenti) causes Virgil to refer him to
the higher wisdom which alone can illuminate him on the essential
arrogance of such self-sufficiency:

> When thou shalt stand bathed in the glorious ray
> Of her whose blest eyes see all things complete,
> Thou'lt learn the meaning of thy life's whole way.   130–2

In the first round of the seventh circle are found the violent against
others, and here for one stanza the voice of the poet himself takes the
words over from his *alter ego*.

> O blind covetousness and foolish anger, which in this brief life so goad us
> on and then, in the eternal so steep us in misery.*   XII. 49–51

Dante here directly identifies himself with the sins he contemplates.
He is recognizing himself in their horror and ugliness with increasing
clearness.

In the next circle he meets the suicides, and here is one of the
exceptional cases where intense personal feeling exists without apparent

* Sinclair: op. cit.

43

involvement in the sin. Dante is dumb with pity before the protest of the bleeding tree that was once Pier della Vigne and that he has unwittingly wounded:

> So from that broken splint came words and blood
> At once: I dropped the twig, and like to one
> Rooted to the ground with terror, there I stood.

XIII. 42–5

It may not be too fanciful to believe that in the bitterness of exile 'on another's stair' Dante had once contemplated the escape of suicide, although he could not then have been one who made his 'own roof-tree his scaffold' (151) as Pier had done. For some reason he was able to conceive the horrifying image of the risen bodies, desired at last, but never to be worn:

> Here shall we drag them, to this gloomy glade;
> Here shall they hang, each body ever more
> Born on the thorn of its own self-slaughtering shade.

106–8

Irma Brandeis points out that all suicides are not in this circle — Cato and Cleopatra for example are elsewhere — but here Dante places the soul who *chose* 'to be out of reach of what distresses it'. It was Pier's conceit which had made his disgrace unbearable to him.* In some measure this experience is not uncommon, and Dante may well have known it.

In the third round of the circle Dante places the famous meeting of the pilgrim with his old teacher, Brunetto Latini. In this touching conversation between tutor and student, no mention whatever is made of the former's sin. If we had not learned earlier from Virgil that the men walking in the burning sand were Sodomites, we should not know it. The pilgrim voices only his joy at seeing his master and at being able to tell him of his own predicament and to receive his encouragement:

> And he made answer: 'Follow but thy star;
> Thou canst not fail to win the glorious heaven,
> If in glad life my judgment did not err.
> Had I not died so soon, I would have given
> Counsel and aid to cheer thee in thy work.'

* Op. cit., p. 50 ff.

This, with its delicate psychological truth to a relationship as old as the earliest academies, presents not a sin condemned, but a nostalgic memory relived. The pupil replies just as his old teacher could wish:

> I keep with me still
> Stamped on my mind, and now stabbing my heart,
> The dear, benign, paternal image of you,
> You living, you hourly teaching me the art,
> By which men grow immortal; know this too:
> I am so grateful, that while I breathe air
> My tongue shall speak the thanks that are your due.
>
> XV. 81–7

The Dante that, fainting for pity, can yet consign Francesca to the first circle, can also consign Brunetto Latini to the seventh, but his love for him is such that he knows and speaks the words that every teacher would choose to hear from his pupil:

> This much I'd have you know: I can stand steady,
> So conscience chide not, facing unafraid
> Whatever Fortune brings, for I am ready.   91–3

Canto XVI marks the descent to the third principal division of hell, that wherein the specifically intellectual sins—the sins demanding the prostitution of man's unique perquisite—his reason—are housed. First comes the eighth circle, Malbolge, divided into its ten terrible ditches or bowges, linked for the most part by tenuous bridges from which the horrors below can be observed. In this great circle of the Fraudulent there are many brilliantly drawn figures, but for the most part they are viewed externally, and often Dante's only contact with them is through Virgil. For example, Virgil summarizes Jason's epic tale, telling of the capture of the golden fleece and the betrayal of the women who had helped him, and then simply adds:

> Suffice thee so much knowledge of this ditch.   XVIII. 98

'This is not a canto of passion . . . He (Dante) feels . . . an olympic contempt . . . (which) allows him to abandon himself to the pleasure of creation . . . from the satiric comedy of Venedice to the majesty of Jason.'* Recognizing the flatterers and the simoniacs, Dante condemns the sin but does not identify himself with the sinners. He weeps for the sorcerers who are so twisted that their tears water their buttocks,

---

* Rossi. Quoted Sinclair: op. cit., p. 253.

but he does not speak to them and relies on Virgil to tell him who they are. There is a particularly vivid image of his escape from the bowge of the barrators,* and there is a personal reference here, for Dante had been accused of barratry by the Florentines. Since it is a sin of which he was innocent however, he could feel secure in the rational judgment of men:

> my master went at a run
> Carrying me off, hugged closely to his breast,
> Truly not like a comrade but a son.   XXIII. 49–51

In the seventh bowge, that of the thieves, is found the horrific image of the loss of identity through the mutual interaction of man and serpent. The visual material probably owes much to Ovid's metamorphoses, but these shifting shapes are true sub-conscious images of a universal fear, familiar today and obviously greatly distressing to Dante—the fear of the disintegration of the self:

> Lo! while I gazed, there darted up a great
>   Six-legged worm, and leapt with all its claws
>   On one of them from in front, and seized him straight,
> Clasping his middle with its middle paws,
>   Along his arms it made its forepaws reach,
>   And clenched its teeth tightly in both his jaws;
> Hindlegs to thighs it fastened, each to each,
>   And after thrust its tail between the two,
>   Up-bent upon his loins behind the breech. . . .
> Two heads already had become one head,
>   We saw two faces fuse themselves to weld
>   One countenance whence both the first had fled; . .
> All former forms wholly extinct in it,
>   The perverse image—both at once and neither—
>   Reeled slowly out of sight on languid feet.   XXV. 49–78

This terrible punishment is, surprisingly to the men of an affluent society in which property is no longer sacred, allotted to the thieves. We are asked by scholars to remember that to the medieval mind property was considered—as it was by Roman law—an extension of a man's personality, but to the present author the episode appears to draw its shuddering power from dread rather than from guilt. It is

---

* i.e. men who sell justice.

an image of Dante's personal fear and of his very real danger. After the daring of a full analysis will the personality again be integrated, will the fragments fit into place, and the subject once more know himself, or will the so dearly loved identity vanish or be changed beyond recognition for the rest of the patient's life? The doubt is real, and Dante in his creative activity was forcing himself through a similar experience.

Among the false councillors in the eighth bowge Dante meets Ulysses twinned with Diomede in one sheath of flame. The story is an epitome of the excellences of objective narration, and yet there is also strong emotional involvement. It is once again a sinner's pride and daring with which Dante identifies himself, and as before he is not afraid to condemn his own most dearly loved faults. In the Christian world-order in which man's place and function are allotted to him by his Creator, the unbounded self-assertion of Ulysses is what the Elizabethans would have called the 'Luciferian sin', and the Greeks *hubris*. Here the pride of Oedipus, who thought he could save Thebes from the wrath of the gods single-handed, finds a supreme statement. Dante could admire it, even envy it, but he could also condemn it, and he did so. 'Here if anywhere Dante's imagination beats at the bars of his day and creed.'* Maybe so, but that this imagination was firmly disciplined by the intellect the very structure of the poem bears witness.

There is a Marlovian ring about Ulysses' appeal to his men to make their last effort westward:

> Think of your breed; for brutish ignorance,
> Your mettle was not made; you were made men,
> To follow after knowledge and excellence.
>
> XXVI. 118–20

The fate of this daring was inevitable, and although he saw it Ulysses could not set foot on the Mountain of Purgatory, up which a Christian might have climbed to his redemption:

> . . . a whirlwind struck the forepart of the ship;
> And three times round she went in a roaring smother
> With all the waters; at the fourth, the poop
> Rose, and the prow went down, as pleased Another,
> And over our heads the hollow seas closed up.   133–42

* Sinclair: op. cit., p. 131.

There is a ballad which tells of a voyage made by a faithless wife with her lover in which the coasts of the Other World are sighted, and the story tells quite plainly what they were and who the captain of that ship was:

> 'What hills are yon, yon pleasant hills,
> The sun shines sweetly on?' —
> 'O yon are the hills o' Heaven', he said
> 'Where you will never won'. —
>
> 'O whaten-a mountain is yon', she said,
> 'So dreary wi' frost and snae?'
> 'O yon is the mountain o' Hell', he said
> 'Where you and I will gae'.
>
> 'But haud your tongue, my dearest dear,
> Let a' your follies a bee,
> I'll show you where the white lilies grow
> In the bottom o' the sea'.
>
> He strack the top-mast wi' his hand
> The foremast wi' his knee,
> And he brake that gallant ship in twain,
> And sank her in the sea.*

As the two voyagers traverse the bridge over the ninth bowge and look down on those who create discord, Virgil with something of the objectivity of the analyst, gives to Mahomet this explanation of their presence:

> To give him full experience, I, who am dead, must bring him here through
> Hell from circle to circle.   XXVIII. 49–51†

Dante watches them all fascinated, but he is very much a detached spectator, so much so that he is even upbraided by Virgil for his improper enjoyment of their obscene arguments.

Now comes the final descent. Ulysses showed the wrong use of intellectual daring; in Cocytus is shown the wrong use of passion. Passion, which alone can unite men, may also and finally separate them. If all 'real living is meeting'‡ then the betrayal of meeting is death. The reverse face of the fire of love is the ice of hate. This is a universal dilemma. No one is immune from the terrible law that what

---

* *The Demon Lover*, Oxford Book of Ballads, pp. 125–6.
† Sinclair: op. cit.
‡ M. Buber: *I and Thou*, T. &. T. Clark (1958), p. 11.

can be used to cherish can equally well be used to destroy, that what is the source of life is inescapably, if it is perverted, the source of death. Here is the basic evil, and its part in each of us must be seen and accepted if we are ever to know ourselves. Here indeed is 'I', and we might well adapt Donne's words and say: every man's sin diminishes me for I am a part of mankind. Still there are, it appears, zones and degrees even in treachery. The first realm, Cain's, is for traitors to their kin, the second, Antenor's, for traitors to their country, Ptolemy's is for traitors to guests and that of Judas for those who betray lords and benefactors. The cold silence of Cocytus seems at first unbroken. Even Virgil's voice sounds strangely unreal and impersonal:

> I heard it said: 'Take heed how thou dost go,
> For fear thy feet should trample as they pass
> On the heads of the weary brotherhood of woe.   19–21

It is a curious monastery indeed—its cells holes in the ice, its vowed silence broken only by a sound like the chattering of teeth. Dante sees 'thousand faces, and thousands yet/Made doggish with the cold'. (70–1). Threading their way among these silent brothers, he and Virgil come at last to two, frozen together in the same cell. They are Ugolino and his murderer, archbishop Rogiero, locked in their last and eternal embrace:

> So that one head capped the other head;
> And as starved men tear bread, this tore the poll
> Of the one beneath, chewing with ravenous jaw,
> Where brain meets marrow, just below the skull.

> 126–132

Here is the last of the famous dual episodes alluded to earlier, and it glows with its own putrescent light. Ugolino's sin is never mentioned. He was in fact a political turncoat, who built his own career out of the fratricidal strife of Guelf and Ghibbeline. What we are shown instead is hatred. Pure, unforgiving ferocity in revenge for wrong suffered is sufficient to destroy humanity, and by indulging it Ugolino destroys himself. In this deathly cold men can no longer even grieve, for their tears freeze and 'the mere weeping will not let them weep' (XXXIII. 94). This treachery to himself is a more potent cause of the ice in which he is immured even than his treachery to Pisa. It is in fact the latter's final result.

Three double figures in hell show, as has often been remarked, the mutuality which should have been meeting and living, abused and turned to the uses of destruction. The corruption of the love which began so tenderly with Francesca's kiss ends at last here. Three silent figures, mere ghosts of what they were born to be, accompany each of the protagonists, their partners in sin: Paolo, whose kiss should never have been given and whose love should have been refused, Diomede, whose friendship was exploited to make him a traitor and Rogiero whose unscrupulous ambition led him into the ice with the man he betrayed. The pairs show a declining scale of that mutuality in living which is necessary for man's salvation—even for his mere survival. What is potentially the relationship of a Dante to a Beatrice can slide through the triviality of Francesca's love to the cleverness of Ulysses' intrigue and on to the pure horror of two bodies locked together for eternity in the stasis of the ice.

And at last Dante reaches Satan himself, the final externalization of his own hates and fears.

> How cold I grew, how faint with fearfulness,
> Ask me not, Reader; I shall not waste breath
> Telling what words are powerless to express;
> This was not life, and yet it was not death.

At the nadir of earth he sees the creature that was once so fair in his 'shimmering and shining'.*

> If he was once as fair as he is now foul, and lifted up his brows against
> his maker, well may all sorrow come from him.†   XXXIV. 34–6

He still has the six wings of the cherubim, changed now to bats' wings, and he has six eyes with which to weep both tears and blood. When Dante has also seen Judas in Satan's mouth he knows that within man is what makes it possible for him to betray the source of his own creation and the maintainer of his own existence: to betray Love itself, Love unflawed by any individual blemish or eccentricity that might in the slightest degree motivate such treachery. Now in Virgil's words 'we must depart', for indeed Dante 'has seen all' (69).

> This is the end of the Way that began with the girl in Florence or
> London or anywhere, the end of the young people and poets in the City,
> the end of the leopard at daybreak and of Francesca's kiss when she lifted

* *York Cycle of Mystery Plays*, S.P.C.K. (1957).
† Sinclair: op. cit.

her eyes from the book, of Brunetto's teaching and of the Pontiffs of the Holy See.... Dante has become Judas, and the power that champs him was once Beatrice and Florence. The City is every way betrayed.*

Dante is here using what Professor Northrop Frye calls a 'demonic imagery' which presents

> the world as it is before the human imagination begins to work on it and before any image of human desire, such as the city or the garden, has been solidly established.

Frye sees the demonic presented as a parody of the divine world and appears to suggest that it draws its power over men's imagination from their fear of 'the vast, menacing, stupid powers of nature as they appear to a technologically undeveloped society' (p. 147).

> Dante's last vision of human hell is of Ugolino gnawing his tormentor's skull:... the demonic erotic relation becomes a fierce, destructive passion ....The demonic parody of marriage, or the union of two souls in one flesh, may take the form of hermaphroditism, incest or homosexuality.

Here again we may remember Thaïs and, alas, Brunetto Latini, while the 'parody' of incest relates directly to Oedipus. The vegetable demonic world is very familiar; the sinister forest, in which Dante finds the terrifying gateway, is also Lear's heath, Timon's desert and the waste of Egdon. The burning city of Dis is a parody of the heavenly Jerusalem, and the involved pathway through hell is Dante's labyrinth with Satan at its core.

At last however, the direction of the journey changes and the downward exploration of the self is succeeded by the long climb to the final vision of God. When Dante and Virgil accomplish the last desperate stage down and up the narrow opening at the fundament of hell, they

Come forth to look once more upon the stars. 139

Now the journey upward can begin. Ascending the circles of the mountain of Purgatory, the pilgrim is, by his own will as well as by grace, cleansed of the sins which would blind him to the beatific vision he seeks. It is only after this purgation, when the final barrier of searing flame is passed, that the sinner can realize the quality of the corruption from which he is at last to be redeemed. Dante has been drawing steadily nearer to this moment, when he will have no option

* Northrop Frye: *The Anatomy of Criticism*, Princeton University Press (1957).

but to see himself as he really is. He has gathered the necessary information, as it were, by which he can assess himself, but he is only now about to do so. Without the presence of Beatrice we may well believe that had he achieved self-knowledge it would have been mortal to him. For most of us it is only love which makes it possible to endure a clear vision of ourselves. At another level of interpretation we may say that the true nature of evil is known only to God and is revealed to us in such measure as we can receive it only by His grace.

Chapter 3

The Rebirth

i *Oedipus at Colonus*

Out of the eater came forth meat, and out of the strong came forth sweetness.

Judges. XIV. 14.

WE can know little of Oedipus' journey after the revelation of his identity; there are only a few references made by himself. He says that:

Time passed and the pain abated,*

admitting that there was some small measure of comfort to be found in the privacy of home and family. We know this did not last but was followed by exile, and that 'the suffering stranger', however meekly he adapted himself to the country where he was, looked for refuge and help without much hope of success. Like Dante he had learned:

How salt the bread of strangers is, how hard
The up and down of someone else's stair. *Par.* XVII. 59–60

He speaks of the principal lesson he has learnt:

Three masters—pain, time, and the royalty in the blood—
Have taught me patience. p. 77

Although this is not a lesson that events demonstrate he has learnt well, yet before his apotheosis Oedipus does arrive at an Earthly Paradise—wood and garden in one.

Antigone: Here, where we are,
There is a kind of sacred precinct, overgrown
With laurel bushes, olive, and wild vine;
And it is full of the voices of many nightingales:
There is a seat of natural rock. Sit down and rest.
You have come a long way, father. p. 78

* *Oedipus at Colonus, Three Theban Plays,* p. 92.

But the garden is—as it must be—a sacred precinct:

Countryman: Come from that seat. That place is holy ground . . .
Dread goddesses own it, daughters of Earth and Darkness . . .
We call them here the All-Seeing Kindly Ones.

Oedipus: Then may they be gracious to their suppliant;
For this is the place where I must stay for ever.   p. 79

To these goddesses Oedipus makes his plea for final peace and gives thanks for the guidance already vouchsafed him:

O Holy Ones of awful aspect,
Whose throne, this seat, was my first resting-place
In these lands; be gracious to me . . .
And now I know it is by your certain guidance
That I have travelled the road to this sacred place.
No other hand could have led me, at my first coming,
The sober penitent, to you. . . .   pp. 80–1

The guidance is thus admitted to have been feminine; the dread goddesses have played the role of Beatrice, and from this place, when the events of the last tumultuous day of his earthly life are over, he will 'no leading need'.

Follow, my children.
It is my turn now to be your path finder. . . .
This way . . . This way . . . Hermes is leading me,
And the Queen of the Nether World.   p. 129

Before he takes this last stage of his journey, however, Oedipus has proclaimed his own innocence. He is prevailed upon to reveal his story to the old men of Colonus and tells them first of the marriage with Jocasta.

Chorus: What you did—
Oedipus: No doing of mine.
Chorus: How so?
Oedipus: A gift—it was my city's gift,
A prize for what I did for her!   p. 95

He continues by telling of the death of Laius:

Chorus: You killed him?
Oedipus: *Yes,* with justice.
Chorus: Justice?

Oedipus: Yes. You shall hear.
He whom I killed
Had sought to kill me first. The law
Acquits me, innocent, as ignorant
Of what I did.   p. 96

That is to say Oedipus has transcended blind horror at his deed, at the facts of his own nature. He has looked beyond them to the spiritual reality of *motive*. He has achieved the near-miraculous; he has forgiven himself. The answer to his own earlier question—'Am I made man in the hour when I cease to be? (p. 90)—is thus in the affirmative: he is indeed made man at last.

The chorus' farewell, by a direct inversion of the Christian symbolism, sends him to peace and to triumph *below* the earth among the images of Dante's *Inferno:*

> I call upon Persephone, queen of the dead,
> And upon Hades, king of night, I call;
> Chain all the Furies up that he may tread
> The perilous pathway to the Stygian hall
> And rest among his mighty peers at last,
> For the entanglements of God are past.
>
> Nor may the hundred-headed dog give tongue
> Until the daughter of Earth and Tartarus
> That even bloodless shades call Death has sung
> The travel-broken shade of Oedipus
> Through triumph of completed destiny
> Into eternal sleep, if such there be.*

For Sophocles the purpose of redemption was peace while for Dante it was ecstasy, but Oedipus, like the Christian pilgrim, has been redeemed by suffering, and the gods put their seal on his own claim to innocence. The messenger describes the scene:

> He went as far as the brink of the Chasm, where the Brazen Staircase plunges into the roots of the earth . . . There he stood, among those hallowed objects—the Basin, the Rock of Thoricus, the Hollow Pear-tree, the Stone Tomb. He sat down . . . . until suddenly a Voice called him, a terrifying voice at which all trembled and hair stood on end. . . . 'Oedipus!

* W. B. Yeats: 'Sophocles' *Oedipus at Colonus*' in *Collected Plays* (Macmillan, London and New York, 1934).

Oedipus!' it cried again, again and again . . . He heard the summons, and knew that it was from God.

All, obeying his instructions, leave him, and when the children and the servants dare to look once more behind them:

> Oedipus was nowhere to be seen; but the King was standing alone holding his hand before his eyes . . . Certain it is he was taken without a pang, without grief or agony—a passing more wonderful than that of any other man.   pp. 130–2

At the beginning of the journey of his life Oedipus appeared as the young saviour bringing succour by the slaying of the Sphinx; as an old man his body retained, or rather retrieved, its power to protect his people from beneath their soil. Between these two points had been the descent into hell and the anguish and mutilation which made the final triumph possible. Sophocles was probably familiar with the mystery religion of Egypt, and he may or may not have realized that he was re-telling in human terms a version of the great Osiris myth. Of this god, Erich Neumann writes:*

> On the one hand, as the dismembered god, he is the bringer of fertility, the young king who passes away and returns; on the other hand, as the procreative mummy 'with the long member', he is everlasting and imperishable. . . . In this mysterious symbol of the fertile dead, mankind has unconsciously stumbled on a vital factor . . . the everlastingness and fruitfulness of the living spirit as opposed to the everlastingness and fruitfulness of nature.

The plays of Oedipus tell the same tale.

ii On the Mountain of Purgatory

> Thine own consciousness, shining, void, and inseparable from the Great Body of Radiance, hath no birth nor death and is the Immutable Light—Buddha Amitabha.
> EVAN WENTZ. *Tibetan Book of the Dead*

THE journey of Dante's pilgrim up the Mount of Purgatory is recounted in much detail. After the terrible 'rite of passage' from the

* Op. cit., p. 227.

womb of Earth, after the completion of the analytic experience, comes a reaction into a relief which reaches us through the poetry like the fulfilment of all desire:

> Colour unclouded, orient-sapphirine,
>> Softly suffusing from meridian height
>> Down the still sky to the horizon-line,
>
> Brought to mine eyes renewal of delight
>> So soon as I came forth from that dead air
>> Which had oppressed my bosom and my sight.
>
> The lovely planet, love's own quickener,
>> Now lit to laughter all the eastern sky,
>> Veiling the Fishes that attended her. I. 13–21
>
> Gently upon the turf my master spread
>> Both hands; and I, not taken unawares,
>> But understanding what this purported,
>
> Held up to him my face begrimed with tears;
>> And so he brought my native hue once more
>> To light, washed clean of hell's disfiguring smears.
>
>> 124–9

Into the peace comes the promise of new life. The pilgrim sees 'a light come speeding o'er the sea' and two strange 'whitenesses' beside it, which he at last recognizes as wings. Virgil interprets:

> Behold the angel of the Lord ...
> And near and nearer as he came full sail
>> The bird of God shone momently more bright.
>
>> II. 37–8

The boat wafted by the angel towards the base of Mount Purgatory carries many souls, among them Dante's friend, the musician Casella. The Mount of Purgatory is full of singing; on every cornice an angel's voice greets or comforts the aspiring spirits with song. Dante, like Shakespeare, knew much of the curative value of music. Here, for once only, the music is secular, for Casella sings a setting of one of his friend's own love poems:

> '*Love in my mind his conversation making*',
>> Thus he began, so sweetly that I find
>> Within me still the dulcet echoes waking.

My master and I and all that spirit-kind
   That came to him, hung on those notes of his
   Entranced, as bearing nothing else in mind.

II. 112–17

But they are interrupted by the firm command 'Run to the mountain' (122). The music has done its therapeutic work; the time for effort and action has arrived. The obedience is willing, for here:

heavenly justice keeps desire
Set towards the pain as once 'twas towards the sin.

XXI. 65–6

It is unnecessary here to follow and interpret Dante's climb in detail; we shall consider only the cornices of the three sins we have already noted: pride, wrath and lust. First Pride: to this cornice the way leads 'Bare as a desert track and lonelier' (X. 21). First the pilgrim broods on the *contrary* of the sin, 'The image of the great humilities' (X. 97). These are figures carved on the rock face, notable among them Mary at the time of the annunciation, accepting meekly her mission from:

The angel that to earth came down and bore
   The edict of the age-long wept-for peace
   Which broke the long ban and unbarred Heaven's door.

34–6

The penitent Proud, bowed to enforced humility by the great burdens they carry on their heads, move forward praying:

Let come to us, let come Thy Kingdom's peace;
   If it come not, we've no power of our own
   To come to it, for all our subtleties.   XI. 7–9

Among them are many artists and if it is true, as must surely be the case, that Dante had the self-confidence to mean himself when he wrote of the coming poet, 'born, belike, already' (98–9) who would succeed Guido Cavalcanti as the glory of Italian letters, it is the more noticeable that the particular warning he is given concerns the professional pride of any great craftsman:

Once, Cimabue thought to hold the field
   In painting; Giotto's all the rage to-day;
   The other's fame lies in the dust concealed.   94–6

Dante accepts the implied rebuke:

> 'True words', said I, 'that rightly teach my heart
> Meekness, and prick my blown-up self-esteem'.   118–19

Beside these men Dante walks, bowed like them that he may speak with them, until Virgil urges him to renewed effort, and he leaves them behind him as he climbs. Soon he notices a difference in his power of movement:

> Wherefore I said: 'Master, what heavy load
> Has slipped from me, so that I walk with ease,
> And scarcely feel fatigue upon the road?'   XII. 118–20

and Virgil assures him that he moves now with the burden of Pride purged away.

On the cornice of the Envious, Dante gives the pilgrim words which justify the personal interpretation of the poem which is followed in this study:

> 'Mine eyes have yet to be deprived of light
> Up here, though not for long; their sin,' I said,
> 'In casting looks of envy has been slight'.   XIII. 133–5

On the cornice of Wrath, Dante is first wrapt, as he was on that of the Proud, by images of its opposite. Charles Williams has written of the 'ecstasy of tenderness' shown in the vision of Mary seeking her son in the temple. His translation of her words runs: Little Son, why have you done this thing to us? See, your father and I have been looking for you with tears.* The Wrathful, whose song is always of the meek *Agnus Dei*, go their way in a blanket of smoke:

> So gross in grain and gritty to the touch   XVI. 5

that Dante is blinded by it. They are concerned, as Virgil explains, with 'loosening the knot of wrath' (p. 24), and this purgation is bitter for the poet also. By clutching Virgil's shoulder, however, he is able to keep on his course through 'that foul and acrid air' (p. 13), for although anger is of its nature irrational, yet reason can assist in mastering it. The tension of the struggle is revealed by the relief which follows its cessation when at last the travellers see:

> faintly winking
> Through thin-drawn veils, the pale disc of the sun.
>   XVII. 5–6

* *Figure of Beatrice*, p. 161.

The passage of the last cornice, that of Lust, is especially protracted, and a still more personal note is sounded:

> Here the bank belches forth great sheets of flame,
>   While upward from the cornice edge doth blow
>   A blast that shields it, backward bending them,
> So that in single file we had to go,
>   Where space allowed; and I was sore afraid,
>   On this side, fire—on that, the depths below.
>
> XXV. 112–17

Through this fire all spirits, whatever their particular sins on earth, are obliged to pass. The reason is explained to the pilgrim in Canto XVII: love, since it is the root of all goodness, is also, in perversion, the root of all evil. Men act—for good or ill—through desire:

> Bethink thee then how love must be the seed
>   In you, not only of each virtuous action,
>   But also of each punishable deed.   XVII. 103–5

Dante knows well why he is on his journey: it is, as he has told a spirit before approaching this very cornice, 'to have my sight made clear'. (XXVI. 58) Nevertheless when he sees the fire he is afraid, and not even the sounds of music can assuage his fear. This is the ordeal by fire, which Mozart dramatised in The Magic Flute, and which Dorothy Sayers calls:

> that 'Pass of Peril', which in so many folk tales of other-world journeys, the hero has to leap through in order to attain the lady, or other object of his search.*

At first Dante hesitates: his flesh recoils from the agony it foresees:

> I leaned across my clasped hands, staring hard
>   Into the fire, picturing vividly
>   Sights I had seen, of bodies burned and charred.
>
> XXVII. 16–18

But Virgil is able to tell—which means of course that Dante himself knows intellectually in spite of his intuitive fear—that the passage through the fire is essential:

> 'Look, my son', he said,
>   'Twixt Beatrice and thee there is this wall'.   35–6

* Divine Comedy I. Hell, p. 285.

The motive is sufficient and the barrier is passed.

> *'Venite benedicti patris'* welled
> In song there from a core of blinding light.   58–9

That night the pilgrims rest on the topmost stair before their entry to the Earthly Paradise, where Virgil will cede to Beatrice, and reason will be superseded by spiritual wisdom. His farewell words mark the distance achieved:

> 'I've brought thee here by wit and by address;
>   Make pleasure now thy guide. . . .
> No word from me, no further sign expect;
>   Free, upright, whole, thy will henceforth lays down
>   Guidance that it were error to neglect,
> Whence o'er thyself I mitre thee and crown'.   XXVII. 124–42

Dante's Earthly Paradise is, like Milton's Garden of Eden, a poet's vision of the state of innocence from which Man should have started his life's journey; it is the paradisal bliss described in all the mythical cosmogonies which tell of the original world as created by God. Here the sounds of water and the murmur of leaves fall on the ear as sweetly as the colours of the flowers, red and yellow, fall upon the eye, and Mathilda, wandering by the brook, reminds the pilgrims, as Eve reminded Milton, of the spring goddess of the Greeks:

> O thou dost put me to remembering
> Of who and what were lost, that day her mother
> Lost Proserpine, and she the flowers of spring.
>
> XXVIII. 49–51

The journey up to now, therefore, has been one of return to a lost innocence:

> We shall not cease from exploration
> And the end of all our exploring
> Shall be to arrive where we started
> And to know the place for the first time.*

Here at last Dante re-discovers Beatrice, the human love through whom was revealed, long before, the grace of God, and who is indeed now for him the perfect symbol of that grace. She calls him by his name — the only time in the poem in which it is used — 'Dante weep

---

* T. S. Eliot: *Four Quartets:* Little Gidding.

not'. (XXX. 55) In all the flaming wonder of the Masque of the Sacrament, by which Dante believed that divine grace was mediated to man, and of which she is the central figure, she can still say to him, even through the cloud on cloud of flowers, flung by angelic hands: 'we are indeed, we are Beatrice' (XXX. 73–4). It is at this moment that Dante sees his own face mirrored in the stream that still separates him from Beatrice and shrinks in anguish from the sight, recognizing himself, also, 'for the first time'. The lines have already been quoted, but they must be repeated here:

> I dropped my eyes down to the glassy rill,
>   Saw myself there, and quickly to the brink
>   Withdrew them, bowed with shame unspeakable.

XXX. 76–8

'We are indeed, we are Beatrice', and at this climactic moment the image of the beloved is also the image of the mother:

> even as a little boy may think
>   His mother formidable, I thought her so.   79–80

At the corresponding moment of crisis Oedipus cannot accept the loved woman as both mother and wife, but Dante does so and goes on to learn the lesson of love's complexity and essential ambiguity. For a time his agony of self-abasement continues, but it loses the deathly coldness which reminds us of the death of love in Cocytus:

> The icy bonds which held my heart compressed
>   Melted to breath and water, and through eyes
>   And mouth burst forth in anguish from my breast.   97–9

Beatrice's aim, 'that he who yonder weeps should comprehend' (107) is at last achieved.

It is probably easier for us in the second half of the twentieth century to respond to Dante's presentation of Beatrice as did her creator and his contemporaries, than it was for intermediate readers. It is not a strange idea for us that we see in each other both a distinct object and the projection on to it of our own needs, hopes and fears, and a modern poet can use such imagery without self-consciousness.

> Dante knew love as immeasurable absence
> And turned from the world to find elsewhere a presence
> Where after long-time Purgatory dawns the eternal light.
> He in that soul who gazed upon his soul

Beheld the aspect and the vehicle of wisdom
Which lay beyond, further than he had come.*

Dante himself writes that 'the literal truth should always come
first',† and in this sense Beatrice remains to the end of the story the
woman whom he knew in Florence:

It was not Theology with which Dante fell in love at the age of nine,
nor Revelation which descended into hell to send Virgil to the rescue.‡

T. S. Eliot lends his authority to the view that there is nothing un-
natural in the fixing of a child's emotion on a glimpsed figure when he
was nine years old. He merely comments that such an occurrence is
more common at a still earlier age. This is, however, only one half of
the truth; for years Dante had recognized, in the seldom seen but
constantly worshipped face, an image of all that was desirable at every
level of living. When he could no longer see it he lost touch also with
what he had identified with it, and it was this that led to his straying
in the dark wood. We must believe Beatrice's own words:

> I with my countenance some time indeed
>   Upheld him; my young eyes his beacons were
>   To turn him right and in my steps to lead;
> But when . . .
>   risen from flesh to spirit, free I ranged,
>   In beauty greater and in virtue more,
>   His mind was turned from me, his heart estranged;
> And by wild ways he wandered, seeking for
>   False phantoms of the good. . . .   XXX. 121–31

The phantom images, like the siren of his dream,§ were no less and no
more real than the other phantoms born of the beauty he had earlier
loved. Losing his love of Beatrice, he actually, though not necessarily,
lost Grace, although Grace persistently sought him out:

> Vainly in dreams and other ways as well
>   I called him home.   134–5

Irma Brandeis has seen that it is 'not his sins of commission but his

---

* Kathleen Raine: 'Soliloquies upon Love' from *The Hollow Hill*, Hamish
Hamilton (1965).
† *Epistle to Can Grande*. v. sup. p. 35.
‡ Brandeis: op cit., pp. 103–4.
§ v. *Dante*, Faber (1930).

insufficiently tenacious love of the good' that brought him low. Dorothy Sayers offers a more subtle interpretation.

> It seems to me useless to ask what sin 'exactly' it was which led to those sharp reproaches and those miserable tears—whether it was a *pargoletta* or a theological error or a loss of faith. One has only to compare the Dante of the *Convivio* with the Dante of the *Vita* and the *Commedia* to see what it was that had happened to him and then unhappened. The Dante of the *Convivio* has everything that the other Dante has—the great intellect, the great curiosity, the great poetry, the great piety, even—but without humility, and without charity. The sin is . . . simply the thing known as hardness of heart . . . not 'a' sin, but simply sin.*

When Beatrice demands if he admits her charges:

> Terror and shame inextricably knit
> Forced from my miserable lips a 'Yes'
> Such that the sight must needs interpret it.   XXXI. 13–15

Beatrice continues in her maternal rôle and he accepts this:

> As children when they are rebuked, stand dumb, . . .
> Just so stood I.   64–7

He is not let off lightly. Beatrice reminds him that he is not a child, for whom such rebukes as she gives him are fitting, but a grown man:

> hold up thy beard
> And thou by looking shalt have greater grief.   68–9

So son and lover are conflated once again as they were centuries earlier in Oedipus and centuries later in Hamlet.

The 'nettles of remorse' (85) are at last so bitter to the poet that Beatrice knows the time has come for him to find relief and instructs Mathilda to draw him through the waters of Lethe. There the disabling vision of guilt and self-loathing was obliterated, so that after the cleansing he can protest:

> I can't recall
> That ever I estranged myself from you;   XXXIII. 91–2

and Beatrice answers:

> 'And if thou hast forgotten it—go to,
> Remember'—she was smiling as she spoke—
> 'Thou'st drunk today of Lethe'.   94–6

---

* Sayers: *Further Papers on Dante*, Methuen (1957), p. 3.

After this 'his fainting powers' vitality' is recovered by him in the healing streams of Eunoe:

> From those most holy waters, born anew
>   I came, like trees by change of calendars
>   Renewed with new-sprung foliage through and through,
> Pure and prepared to leap up to the stars.   142–5

iii THE ARRIVAL IN PARADISE

There the eye goes not, speech goes not, nor the mind.
Kena Upanishad

WHEN the pilgrim enters Paradise the nature of the pilgrimage changes. There is no longer a road to follow; the passages from sphere to sphere are made smoothly and supernaturally. Moreover the pilgrim is no longer concerned to find himself; he is concerned to find God. His eyes are open, and as more light is given to see by he sees more and more. The balance is delicately held: the charisma is a gift, but the soul is responsible for its acceptance.

> Grace is conferred freely and outweighs all merit, but to receive it is meritorious, for it can be received only by the help of good will. Grace engenders the vision; the vision determines the degree of celestial love, the *caritas patriae*, which in turn is manifested in the degree of light that the soul radiates.*

Moreover the power to receive the grace must be developed by effort and by suffering. In the eighth heaven Beatrice can challenge him to look at her more clearly than before:

> Lift up thine eyes and look on me awhile;
>   See what I am; thou hast beheld such things
>   As make thee mighty to endure my smile.
>   *Paradise* XXIII. 46–8

And still the progress in vision continues, as the poet's 'sight by seeing learned to see' (XXXIII. 112).

---

* Auerbach: *Dante: Poet of the Secular World* (University of Chicago Press, 1961), p. 118.

The light, brought to the pilgrim by Beatrice, reveals the central and characteristic matter of Dante's revelation. Beatrice says:

> The bliss of all—set this among thy knowns—
> Abounds in measure as, with sight, they plumb
> The depths of Truth where all disquiet drowns.
> Their blessedness, therefore, is shown to come
> From seeing, if thou reasonest aright,
> Not loving, which is subsequent.　　XXVIII. 106–11

This is Dante's most distinctive attribute—that he brings the imaginative intensity of a great poet to glorify intellectual not emotional passion. Man must *know* before he can truly *love*. His prayer to the Virgin, presented by St Bernard, runs:

> This man, who witnessed from the deepest pit
> Of all the universe, up to this height,
> The souls' lives one by one, doth now entreat
> That thou, by grace, may grant to him such might
> That higher yet *in vision* he may rise
> Towards the final source of bliss and light.　　XXXIII. 22–7

Mary answers by removing all remaining 'mortal clouding' from the pilgrim's eyes. While Dante does not, like Sophocles or Milton, use the symbol of physical blindness, he shares their passionate concern with the significance of eyesight, so that the climax of his experience is, as Beatrice foretold it would be, not that he loves but that he *knows*. In blindness to empirical knowledge he discovers transcendent truth at last:

> O grace abounding, whereby I presumed
> So deep the eternal light to search and sound
> That my whole vision was therein consumed!
> In that abyss I saw how love held bound
> Into one volume all the leaves whose flight
> Is scattered through the universe around;
> How substance, accident, and mode unite
> Fused, so to speak, together in such wise
> That this I tell of is one simple light.　　82–90

The vision was of the unity with diversity which must for ever remain invisible to mortal eyes, unless they can trust the rare illumination of grace. And the widest diversity which Dante perceived recon-

ciled in the primal unity, was the diversity of God and Man. Within
the light that was the godhead, he glimpsed the form of God made
man and of man made in the image of God:

> Eternal light, that in Thyself alone
> Dwelling, alone dost know thyself. . . .
> The sphering thus begot,* perceptible
> In Thee like mirrored light, now to my view—
> When I had looked on it a little while—
> Seemed in itself, and in its own self-hue,
> Limned with our image. 124–31

Amazed, like a geometer who has suddenly squared a circle
(XXXIII. 133) or the physicist who has reconciled the movement
of the sphere with the point of rest which is its centre, Dante feels the
wings of his imagination fail, but this is not before he has glimpsed
one last paradox—the unity of love and law:

> High phantasy lost power and here broke off;
> Yet as a wheel moves smoothly, free from jars,
> My will and my desire were turned by love,
> The love that moves the sun and the other stars. 142–5

Professor Auerbach has written in words of great distinction about
the philosophical basis of the *Comedy*:

> Ordered and transfigured by the divine vision, earthly appearance
> becomes the true, definitive reality which, by its essence and the place in
> which it is manifested, discloses the plenitude of the divine order, so pre-
> supposing and encompassing everything else contained in it. The *Comedy*
> is an eminently philosophical work, not so much because of the actual
> philosophical doctrines set forth in it as because the spirit of those doctrines
> compels Dante to write philosophically. . . . Very much in the spirit of
> philosophy which abstracts pure ideas from phenomena, this poetic work
> draws from earthly appearances the true personality which is body and
> spirit in one.† p. 157

In this study we have been particularly concerned with the process
by which one human person has reached his potential stature. His
philosophy gave Dante the framework within which he could conceive
of this process of integration into true individuality, and that framework, accepted in his day, is no longer widely accepted in ours. The

---

* i.e. Christ. † *Mimesis*, tr. W. Frask, Princeton University Press (1953).

growth of the individual, however, we can understand very well, for the process of such integration is basically unchanged. Its reality in Dante's poem is clear once the span of human experience between the opening and ending of the poem is grasped. The man who, in the first canto of the Inferno, wanders helpless 'through the long horror of that piteous night' (I. 21) in such terror that 'the mere breath/Of memory stirs the old fear in the blood,' (I. 5–6) pursued by beasts in 'that place wherein the sun is mute' (40), who calls to the form he can hardly see: 'Have pity on me', is the same who after a childlike dependence first on Virgil and then on Beatrice can at last accept her words: 'Not in mine eyes alone is Paradise', (*Par.* XVIII. 21) and is content to view her image as a part of the single celestial rose. His words to her then are a triumph song:

> O thou in whom my hopes securely dwell,
> And who to bring my soul to Paradise,
> Didst leave the imprint of thy steps in Hell,
> Of all that I have looked on with these eyes
> Thy goodness and thy power have fitted me
> The holiness and grace to recognise.
> Thou hast led me, a slave, to liberty.   XXXI. 79–85

When we remember the genuine but too easy sympathy for Francesca, the uncontrolled anger at Filippo Argenti, the arrogance with Farinata, the shame in front of Beatrice in the Earthly Paradise, of which he admits that 'gnawing self-reproach my heart so clove/I swooned' (*Purg.* XXXI. 88–9), we can realize in the same measure the distance that was covered before St Bernard can say:

> That thou mayst draw
> Thy journey to a perfect close . . .
> Over this garden with thy vision fly
> For looking on it will prepare thy gaze
> To rise towards God's luminance on high.
>   *Par.* XXXI. 94–9

At last, a personality torn into shreds and tatters has been knit up into a unity able to face reality without disintegration: 'Will and desire' have been 'Turned by love' (XXXIII. 144) so that they are subdued at last to the creator's purpose for his creature, and in a service which is perfect freedom a man is born.

At the end of the *Paradise* Dante, using all the conceptions and imagery of his Christian belief, has imagined and projected the final union of man and the universe with their creator at a level of intensity untouched in any other work of literary art. Only in Shakespeare can an adequate comparison be found.

When Lear asks the question: 'Who is it that can tell me who I am?' and receives the fool's dusty answer: 'Lear's shadow', he sets out on a road towards self-discovery in a society that is ordered indeed, but in which true values are reversed. He hears its door slam behind him and descends into a wilderness where neither order nor value appears to exist. From the nihilism of his madness he is carried at last to the Earthly Paradise. For Lear does not climb Mount Purgatory; he is carried up it in sleep, as mysteriously as Dante moves from sphere to sphere in Paradise. Nor does he recover his Beatrice among the trees and flowers although 'All the unpublished virtues of the earth' have sprung with her tears to 'be aidant and remediate' to his distress; instead he meets her to the strains of music. At first he does not recognize either himself or her, but he finds both in the moment when he kneels, as Dante knelt beside the stream, and speaks not as king or beggar but as what he had long longed to be. At last after eighty years of journeying he can say:

> *As I am a man*, I think this lady
> To be my child, Cordelia.   IV. 7

This is a story told in the form of secular drama, but in Christian terms such as Dante might have used, Cordelia is the god-bearer, the bringer of grace, for love is a given 'good'; it can be neither earned nor deserved, only accepted in humility. For Shakespeare the first possibility of man's reconciliation with God is expressed as the possibility of his reconciliation with himself through love of another, and his plays affirm that for him the uniting of male and female is both the primary image and also the source of personal redemption.* It can be seen in the dance and the feast celebrating the marriage of true lovers, and it may be imaged in the mysterious identification of twin brother with twin sister or of lover with his beloved:

> a fair divided excellence
> Whose fullness of perfection lies in him.†

* For the alchemists' use of the hermaphrodite as a symbol of human perfection v. Jung, *Psychology and Alchemy*, C.W. XII, 'The self is a union of opposites . . . it represents in every respect thesis and antithesis, and at the same time synthesis', p. 19.
† *King John*, II. 1.

In the last plays the reunion may be between a father and his daughter as it is also achieved at last by Lear and Cordelia. But although Cordelia is indeed the Beatrice who seeks Lear from without, she is also the tenderness that is a part of Lear himself, and which he had to rediscover beneath the aggression, pride and fake logic of the *persona* he had built.

> It is impossible to find the treasure unless the hero has first found and redeemed his own soul, his own feminine counterpart ... who is at once man's inspiration his beloved and his mother, the enchantress and the prophetess.*

Thus in the meeting which is living is found the love that is man's peace. Dante would have accepted this in his own terms, but writing with the whole Christian cosmogony available as a source for his imagery he transcends even Shakespeare in his power to draw the universal from the particular. The circumstances in which his vision took on shape thus ensures that it remains unique in the world of poetry.

* Neumann: op. cit., p. 212.

Part II

THE JOURNEY IN CONTEMPORARY SOCIETY

Professor Eucalyptus said, 'The search
For reality is as momentous as
The search for God'. It is the philosopher's search

For an interior made exterior
And the poet's search for the same exterior made
Interior. . . .

WALLACE STEVENS.
An ordinary evening in New Haven

CHAPTER 4

The Existentialist Journey

Acid the knowledge travellers draw. The world
Little and dull, today, tomorrow and
Tomorrow makes you see yourself—an appalled
Oasis in a tedium of sand.
Should we then go or stay? If you can, stay:
Go, if you must
> BAUDELAIRE. *Le Voyage*. Translated by
> C. Day Lewis. *The Room and Other Poems.*

i INTRODUCTION

THE impulse to undertake the hard journey has never been a rational one. Commonsense has always inclined to the preservation of the *status quo*:

Let us alone. What is it that will last?
All things are taken from us, and become
Portions and parcels of the dreadful Past.
Let us alone.*

If the earliest drives to exploration came perhaps from the need not for knowledge but for food, yet what a modern dramatist has called 'exploration into God'† appears to have had its beginnings almost as early; its primitive form can still be seen in Shamanistic dance and tribal ritual, and a seventeenth century allegory shows for how long the journey remained an effective symbol in popular European art:

So I saw in my dream that the Man began to run: Now he had not run far from his own door, but his Wife and Children perceiving it began to cry after him to return; but the Man put his fingers in his ears and ran on crying *Life! Life! Eternal Life!* So he looked not behind him, but fled towards the middle of the Plain.‡

* Alfred Tennyson: *The Lotus Eaters.*
† Christopher Fry in *A Sleep of Prisoners*, O.U.P. (1951).
‡ John Bunyan: *The Pilgrim's Progress.*

73

With the Romantics comes the glorification of the journey for its own sake:

> Once more upon the waters! yet once more!
> And the waves bound beneath me as a steed
> That knows his rider. Welcome to their roar!
> Swift be their guidance, whereso'er it lead!
> Though the strained mast should quiver as a reed,
> And the rent canvas fluttering strew the gale,
> Still must I on.*

In later Romanticism the image is associated not with positive achievement but with the fulfilling of the death-wish:

> O Mort, vieux capitaine, il est temps! levons l'ancre.
> Ce pays nous ennuie, O Mort! Appareillons!
> Si le ciel et la mer sont noirs comme de l'encre
> Nos coeurs que tu connais sont remplis de rayons!
> Verse-nous ton poison pour qu'il nous réconforte!
> Nous voulons, tant ce feu nous brûle le cerveau,
> Plonger au fond du gouffre, Enfer ou Ciel qu'importe?
> Au fond de l'Inconnu pour trouver du *nouveau*.†

Until the nineteenth century metaphysicians and philosophers gave rational justifications for man's journey towards himself, towards 'progress', towards 'truth' or towards God, but with the late acceptance of the doctrines of Sören Kierkegaard this was changed. A 'leap' forward was now demanded of men, without rational justification, yet even in the teaching of proclaimed atheists, this 'leap', like Christian's flight across the Plain, was religious in its nature. It was essential to man's well-being, yet to make it was now admittedly an utterly irrational act.

In *Notes from the Underground*, published in 1864, Dostoevsky's hero may be said to open the existentialist ball in literary form:

> You see, gentlemen, reason is an excellent thing, there's no disputing that, but reason is nothing but reason and satisfies only the rational side of man's nature, while will is a manifestation of the whole life ... and although our life, in this manifestation of it, is often worthless, yet it is life and not simply extracting square roots.‡

* Lord Byron: *Childe Harold's Pilgrimage*. Canto III.
† Baudelaire: *Le Voyage*. v. Selected Verse. pp. 189–90.
‡ v. *Existentialism from Dostoevsky to Sartre*, ed. W. Kaufmann. Meridan Books (1956), p. 73.

Dostoevsky is also the first great artist to use the word 'absurd' to express the irrationality man sees both in himself and in the universe which he inhabits. In the famous conversation between the brothers Ivan and Alyosha Karamazov, Alyosha admits his inability to defend his position rationally and Ivan accepts his admission with delight:

> 'What I said was absurd, but—'
> 'That's just the point, that "but" ', cried Ivan. 'Let me tell you, novice, that the absurd is only too necessary on earth. The world stands on absurdities, and perhaps nothing would have come to pass on it without them.'*

The need to accept 'absurdity' was developed by Kierkegaard in the second quarter of the nineteenth century in reaction against the dominant philosophic thought of the times. Two statements from his *Concluding Unscientific Postscript*† will make his belief in the insufficiency of reason clear:

> It is professed that thought is higher than feeling and imagination, and this is professed by a thinker who lacks pathos and passion. Thought is higher than irony and humour—this is professed by a thinker who is wholly lacking in a sense for the comical. How comical! . . . The facile deification of this pure thought as the highest stage in life shows that the thinker who does it has never existed *qua* human being. p. 269

In the place of the exaltation of reason Kierkegaard demands that man accept the duality of his own nature and of the universe:

> It is impossible to exist without passion, unless we understand the word 'exist' in the loose sense of a so-called existence. . . . I have often reflected how one might bring a man into a state of passion. I have thought in this connection that if I could get him seated on a horse and the horse made to take fright and gallop wildly . . . Or if a driver were otherwise not especially inclined towards passion, if someone hitched a team of horses to a waggon for him, one of them a Pegasus and the other a worn-out jade, and told him to drive—I think one might succeed. And it is just this that it means to exist, if one is to become conscious of it. p. 276

Such a fully existent 'self' is the principal quest of the existentialist philosopher. André Gide has said that: 'That which is opposed to love is not primarily hatred but the rumination of the brain',‡ but he, like

---

* *The Brothers Karamazov.* I. p. 248. Dent, Everyman Edition.
† Princeton University Press (1941); London: Oxford University Press, (1941).
‡ *Dostoevsky.* Paris, 1923.

Kierkegaard before him, was still writing within the Christian tradition which bases both the reality and the importance of the self on its creation by God and its mysterious value to Him. When this tradition is abandoned, it is possible that the discovery of the self may become even more important to a human being than before. After describing a dream of one of his patients and commenting on the occurrences of the circle or mandola image in dreams and paintings, Jung goes on to voice in terms of his own profession the same conception of selfhood as that expressed by those who think in existentialist terms. The older mandolas of both East and West contain the emblem of the worshipped deity, and Jung comments:

> If we allow ourselves to draw conclusions from modern mandolas we should ask people first whether they worship stars, suns, flowers and snakes. They will deny this and at the same time they will assert that the globes, stars, crosses and the like are symbols for a *centre in themselves*. . . .

> A modern mandola is an involuntary confession of a peculiar mental condition. There is no deity in the mandola, nor is there any submission or reconciliation to a deity. The place of the deity seems to have been taken by the wholeness of man.*

To all Existentialists the search for the self remains of central importance, not simply for its own sake but because only through knowledge of the self can a wider reality also be apprehended. Thus Heidegger believes that the philosopher should: 'lead our thinking on the way on which it may find the involvement of the truth of Being in human nature', and claims that 'the involvement of Being in human nature is an essential feature of Being'.† A mode of being which involves an awareness of the immediacy of Being is a mode of being available to man if he will accept it—as burden and privilege. It makes up his unique capacity for 'existence'.

> The being that exists is man. Man alone exists. Rocks are, but they do not exist. Trees are, but they do not exist. Angels are, but they do not exist. God is, but he does not exist. . . . To be a self is admittedly one feature of the nature of that being which exists . . . the ecstatic existential nature of man must lead through the metaphysical conception of human selfhood.‡

---

* *Psychology and Religion*, C.W. XI, pp. 81–2, tr. R. F. C. Hull. Bollingen Series XX. (Princeton University Press (1959); London: Routledge and Kegan Paul.)

† *The Way Back into the Ground of Metaphysics*, tr. W. Kaufmann in *Existentialism from Dostoevsky to Sartre*, p. 212.

‡ Ibid., pp. 214–5.

In her introduction to an American symposium on J.-P. Sartre,* Mrs Edith Kern after speaking of Heidegger's 'hauntingly poetic' use of language, goes on to paraphrase his conception of the relationship between the self and the universe:

> In human existence Being is as it were localised and temporalised. Man is the 'here and now' of Being, for through Man alone does Being disclose itself. Man or *Dasein* is, in Heideggerian terms, the 'openness' of Being. It is its *lumen naturale* through which Being comes to light in its manifold-ness and acquires meaning—within man's horizons of place and time. To live *authentically* man must let Being come to light through him—let it speak through him. The essence of humanity is that a man, and only a man may say: 'I am the being by which there is being'.

With minor reservations, all existentialists would agree with their master, Kierkegaard, that man's knowledge of himself is an irrational knowledge, and that the price to be paid for it is suffering. It is in *Fear and Trembling*† that Kierkegaard proclaims most simply the impossibility of obtaining the knowledge of truth by reason, and he illustrates this by his analysis of the story of Abraham:

> By faith Abraham went out from the land of his fathers and became a sojourner in the land of promise. He left one thing behind, took one thing with him: he left his earthly understanding behind and took faith with him—otherwise he would not have wandered forth but would have thought this unreasonable. p. 31

The crisis of Abraham's life is, of course, the command to sacrifice Isaac; Kierkegaard finds here the crux of his thesis, and his account of Abraham's journey to Mt Moriah contains some of his finest writing:

> He mounted the ass, he rode slowly along the way. All that time he be-lieved...He believed by virtue of the absurd; for there could be no question of human calculation, and it was indeed the absurd that God who required it of him should the next instant recall the requirement. He climbed the mountain, even at the instant that the knife glittered he believed. p. 46

It is the only way by which man, the Word made flesh, can transcend his flesh and gain knowledge of that other aspect of Reality which

---

* *A Collection of Critical Essays*, ed. E. Kern, Prentice Hall (1962).

† *Fear and Trembling* and *The Sickness unto Death*, tr. W. Lowrie, Doubleday Anchor Books (1954).

is the Word. The acceptance of obedience to God as a higher imperative than the ethical duty owed to man, is the *leap of faith*—'the great
leap whereby I pass into infinity' (p. 47)—which Kierkegaard
demands of every man who would become a genuinely human being.
This irrational 'leap', which man's nature enables him to make, is
the hallmark of Kierkegaard's complete man, his *knight of faith*. The
cost of living in 'infinity' rather than in the commonsense world of
measured time is the suffering which Kierkegaard calls 'despair', and
of which he urges all men to be proud:

> Is despair an advantage or a drawback? . . . The possibility of this sick-
> ness is man's advantage over the beast, and this advantage distinguishes him
> far more essentially than the erect posture, for it implies the infinite erect-
> ness or loftiness of being spirit. The possibility of this sickness is man's
> advantage over the beast.*   pp. 147–8

The catholic and protestant successors to Kierkegaard agree that
the experience and the transcendence of anguish are possible for
men:

> The soul is in sound health and free from despair only when, precisely
> by having been in despair, it is grounded transparently in God.   p. 163

The atheistic existential writers, however, must show their heroes
carrying the burden of their anguish till death. The single source of
genuine despair is thus man's responsibility for a lonely and unguided
choice without the support of reason, and for the implementation of
that choice in action.

The experience which Kierkegaard calls 'despair' is the same sensation which Sartre names 'anguish' when he writes that man's 'freedom
will become conscious of itself and will reveal itself in anguish'.† Thus
while one aspect of genuine 'existence' is despair, the other aspect is
freedom. The 'existent individual' is the man who, having accepted the
burdens of despair and of freedom, goes forward to the making of
himself.

Of this search, and of its complexities, Jaspers writes:

> Becoming aware of a man's being means becoming aware of Being in
> time as a whole. Man is the Encompassing that we are; yet even in the
> Encompassing man is split. . . . How man achieves unity is a problem,
> infinite in time and insoluble; but it is nevertheless the path to his search.

* *The Sickness Unto Death*, pp. 147–8.
† *Being and Nothingness* (Methuen), p. 627.

After this he adds wryly: 'Man is less certain of himself than ever'.*

In a chapter on 'The Human Person in Contemporary Philosophy' Dr Frederick Copleston writes:

> Human freedom is regarded as the efficient cause of personality, or at least as its necessary condition, for personality is looked on as something to be won, something to be created and maintained with effort. In the eyes of certain thinkers one can become a person, and one can cease to be a person; one can descend, for example, into being a mere 'individual' or a mere 'self'... The word 'person'... is not equivalent to human being; it frequently has a moral conontation and denotes what a medieval philosopher might have thought of as a person who... lives and acts and chooses as a person, that is, in a way befitting a person.†

Sartre in *Being and Nothingness* writes of man's making of himself, and not himself only but, as part of this task, the making any system by which he can live, for man is the source of his own values and is free to make them what he will.

The belief in man's freedom unites all types of existentialist thought, though belief in the purpose of his freedom naturally divides the Christian from the atheistic existentialist. It is clear therefore that the refusal of choice, the refusal of the anguish of responsibility, is the one absolute evil on which all existentialists could agree. This refusal, called by Sartre *la mauvaise foi*, can only be made by those whose gifts or circumstances bring them within sight of the choice or of the leap by which they could if they would, attain existence as distinct from simple biological life. Such figures form the dark shadows which throw into relief the others who, accepting freedom with anguish, attempt the upward journey to the light.

The most famous of all the 'existentialist' heroes is perhaps a character created nearly 300 years before Kierkegaard wrote of the leap of faith or Sartre of the freedom that is man's unique and terrifying attribute.

Hamlet resembles Oedipus in that he pursued the trail of his self for the downward journey and viewed there with horror his own potential of lust and violence, discovering that, like other men, he had 'more offences at my beck than I have thoughts to put them on,

* *On My Philosophy*, tr. F. Kaufmann, in *Existentialism from Dostoevsky to Sartre*, p. 151.

† *Contemporary Philosophy*, F. C. Copleston (London: Burns and Oates; Newman Press, Maryland).

imagination to give them shape, or time to act them in'. *Hamlet* opens with a question of identity: Who's there? and its hero finds himself only a few minutes before the end of the play. Hamlet answers his own cry: 'What a piece of work is a man?' with the muttered 'a handful of dust', and he tells Ophelia not to believe more complacent replies. 'What should such fellows as I do, crawling between earth and heaven? We are arrant knaves, all; believe none of us.' He has also a horror, unknown to the Greek, of the physical basis of his own identity. Gertrude was wrong when she accused Hamlet of seeking 'his noble father in the dust', but Hamlet, picturing the body of Polonius at its last and grimmest supper, told Rosencrantz and Guildenstern that he had 'compounded it with dust whereto it is kin', (IV. 2) and holding Yorick's skull in his hand he sees in it all mankind, and his 'gorge rises at it'.

But the prince, although a late-starter, yet covers his road and finds at its end the integrated self which is not merely a handful of dust:

> What is a man
> If the chief good and market of his time
> Is but to sleep and feed? A beast, no more.

Challenged by the appearance of Fortinbras' army, he faces and accepts the dichotomy of the self:

> Sure he that made us with such large discourse
> Looking before and after, gave us not
> That capability and god-like reason
> To fust in us unused.   IV. 4. (quarto II)

But reason is not enough; what Shakespeare would have called 'will', and Freud the libido, must also be engaged. Hamlet's bodily leap into the pirate ship is no bad symbol of Kierkegaard's 'leap' required for the acceptance of the values which transcend reason and can only be accepted by faith.

> Rashly
> And praised be rashness for it, let us know
> Our indiscretions sometimes serve us well
> When our deep plots do pall.

He starts his counterplot against his enemies and discovers that 'heaven was ordinant' in his support, but he also accepts his responsibility for his own deed. He still uses the language of the old order:

> is't not perfect conscience
> To quit him with this arm? . . .
> and is't not to be damned
> To let this canker of our nature come
> In further evil? V. 2

His words and his attitudes are thus an early and not unsuccessful attempt to set the fortuitous, the irrational and the 'absurd' within the pattern of an ordered universe.

It is after this triumph that he can at last assert his own function and identity as both King and man:

> it is I
> Hamlet, the Dane. V.1

Meeting Laertes he makes a supreme effort to separate the grain from the chaff in his newly discovered self:

> Was't Hamlet wronged Laertes? Never Hamlet:
> If Hamlet from himself be ta'en away
> And when he's not himself doth wrong Laertes,
> Then Hamlet does it not . . . V. 2

The ground has been prepared, and with the revelation of Claudius as the murderer not only of his father but also of his mother and himself, Hamlet could have said, with Sartre's Orestes, that he felt his freedom crash down on him 'like a thunderbolt'. He was utterly free at last and he found his freedom in his action.

> Here thou incestuous, murd'rous damned Dane,
> Drink off thy potion: Is thy union here?
> Follow my mother.

When Laertes begs:

> Exchange forgiveness with me noble Hamlet:
> Mine and my father's death come not on thee
> Nor thine on me,

Hamlet can reply as one whose 'withers are unwrung' by calamity and, as a 'free soul', can offer the boon of freedom to another:

> Heaven make thee free of it.

In such a moment the burden of the weariness, the heart-ache and the fret are truly lightened, but Hamlet, like so many of his 'existentialist' successors, achieves it only at the point of death:*

'The readiness is all'.

Shakespeare is writing not as an atheistic existentialist, but in the tradition of medieval Christianity. If his hero is to find redemption it will not be only in the power to act, to judge and to forgive. Hamlet, like Lear, finds his redeemed self when he rediscovers the truth of love. After his 'leap' he admits his love of the previously despised woman, the girl whom, because of his mother's frailty, he had rejected in despair:

> I loved Ophelia; forty thousand brothers
> Could not with all their quantity of love
> Make up my sum.

Hamlet had indeed been worthy of the rebuke given by his creator to another 'beauteous niggard':

> Profitless usurer, why dost thou use
> So great a sum of sums yet cannot live?

It is too late now to repair the loss, for Ophelia has been dragged to muddy death, and her fate has sealed her lover's. It is Hamlet's 'other love' who is to prove 'of comfort not despair'. His 'better angel is a man right fair' (Sonnet 144), and his love for Horatio whom his soul's election had sealed for herself was his 'ever fixed mark' in the Valley of the Shadow of Evil.

> Give me that man,
> That is not passion's slave, and I will wear him
> In my heart's core, ay, in my heart of heart,
> As I do thee.   III. 2

Horatio, like Cordelia, cannot easily heave his heart into his mouth; his reply is delayed until his friend is dying in his arms. At first it is the offer of death:

> I am more an antique Roman than a Dane:
> Here's yet some liquor left.   V. 2

But Hamlet's final plea invoked by its echo an earlier and mutual commitment:

* Cf. In particular the deaths of Brunet and Vicarios in Sartre' *Drôle d'Amitie.* v. inf., p. 113.

If thou didst ever hold me *in thine heart*
Absent thee from felicity a while,

he can only assent to live that he may:

speak to the yet unknowing world,
How these things came about.

So we find here not only the irrational decision, the forging of an identity and the discovery of the freedom in action—all hall-marks of the existentialist creed—but also the pair of friends so important later to Sartre and Beckett.

The lunatic, the lover and the poet
Are of imagination all compact,

and the 'shapes' they body forth do not greatly change over the centuries.

ii Ibsen's Brand: an Existentialist Hero?

There are elements in the drama of Henrik Ibsen which justify his inclusion both as the forerunner of modern existentialist literature and also as, like Shakespeare, a link between contemporary writing and the products of the Middle Ages. Ibsen is much concerned with man's creation of himself—with what might be called today, the making of the fully existent individual—and with the anguish which follows the moment of self-recognition and the consequent knowledge of failure or inadequacy. He dramatizes also the self-destruction which, he believes, is almost certain to follow this moment. Moreover in *Brand* there is such an obvious relationship to Kierkegaard's *Fear and Trembling* that this alone would make the play a prototype of existentialist drama.

Brand's story is that of a man's self-conscious and highly disciplined effort to find his full stature by consistently willing and performing what he believes to be his creator's purpose. We watch the hero develop from the raw, enthusiastic young priest to the harrowed man, aware of the dichotomy of his divided nature, deserted by his flock and facing his God in the 'ice-church' of the mountains. In the course of this desperate adventure Brand repeatedly enforces his decisions on others, and he takes responsibility for allowing his own infant son to die. Much that Kierkegaard says of the patriarch Abraham in *Fear*

and Trembling is true also of Brand, and the Hebrew myth is referred to by Ibsen more than once. Kierkegaard writes: 'Before the result (i.e. the saving of Isaac) Abraham was every minute a murderer, or we are confronted by a paradox which is higher than all mediation. The story of Abraham contains therefore a teleological suspension of the ethical. As an individual he became higher than the universal. . . .*
If such is not the position of Abraham then he is not even a tragic hero but a murderer. . . .'† The acceptance by Abraham that the religious duty of obedience to God is a higher imperative than the ethical duty he owes to man is the *leap of faith*. This leap Brand has apparently taken. He dedicates himself absolutely to the task which he believes is appointed him by God, and in order to accomplish it he is prepared to forgo all prospects of worldly prosperity and personal ease.

On his first fear of his son's illness Brand refers directly to the parallel with Abraham:

> *Agnes:* There is one sacrifice which God dare not demand.
> *Brand:* But if he should dare? If he should test me
> As he tested Abraham.‡   p. 57

Agnes also accepts the analogy implicitly. She lifts the child high in her arms with the words:

> O God! This sacrifice you dare demand
> I dare to raise towards your heaven.   p. 65

Ibsen implies the possibility of the existential, integrated self when Brand says:

> Be wholly what you are,   p. 26

and makes his hero seek his own true existence in commitment to society:

> *Brand:* I know that I
> Was born into this world to heal its sickness.   p. 27

Brand also experiences the genuine existential loneliness and *angst*:

> It is terrible to stand alone.
> Wherever I look I see death.

* Cf. 'the ethical as such is the universal', p. 64.

† *Fear and Trembling*, p. 77.

‡ All quotations from *Brand* are from the translation by M. Meyer (London: Rupert Hart Davis; New York: Doubleday and Co), 1960.

> It is terrible to hunger for bread
> When every hand offers me a stone.   p. 88

But Ibsen never shows Brand facing the depths of his own nature. Such an experience is left to the father who in the famine slew his own child and whose subsequent suffering is described by his wife:

> His grief burst forth like a river and he turned
> His hand on himself . . .
> . . . He cannot live and dare not die.
> He lies clasping the child's body shrieking
> The Devil's name.   p. 36

This nameless man is the true representative of Oedipus in the play; Brand never sees so deeply into himself; it is from another's sins that he learns that:

> Men do not understand what a mountain of guilt
> Rises from that small word: Life.   p. 40

He demands:

> A place on earth where one can be wholly oneself;
> That is Man's right; and I ask no more.   p. 42

Yet his most vivid picture of himself is based on an obviously false sense of human values, and he identifies the whole of his selfhood with a part of it. To Agnes, after the loss of their child, he callously describes his physical, fighting self as his true self. Telling of his adventure in the storm, he boasts:

> Out on the fiord
> An hour ago I was a man. The water
> Seethed around us, the mast shook,
> Our sail was slit. . . .
> But I exulted in it. I grew stronger
> I took command.   p. 67

Agnes, in her deeper grief, saw the limitation of his vision:

> It is easy to be strong in the storm
> Easy to live the warrior's life.
> But to sit alone in silence . . . is harder.   pp. 67–8

The word 'leap' is actually used in the nightmare visions which precede his death, and Brand is accused of never having taken it:

Figure of Agnes: Remember, an Angel with a flaming rod
Drove Man from Paradise.
He set a gulf before the gate.
Over that gulf you cannot leap.   p. 102

If we accept that the source of the voice is his own subconscious mind, it indicates that he was at last aware of his own failure.

In another respect also, Ibsen makes Brand the contrary of Kierkegaard's ideal. In *Fear and Trembling* we read: 'The knight of faith is obliged to rely upon himself alone, he feels the pain of not being able to make himself intelligible to others, but he feels no vain desire to guide others . . . The true knight of faith is a witness, never a teacher, and therein lies his deep humanity.' (p. 90) Brand behaves in the directly opposite way, imposing his standard of 'all or nothing' on his mother, his parishioners, his child and finally on his wife. He shows no signs of that belief in the value of the individual existence which respects individual responsibility in another as much as in oneself.

In spite therefore of Brand's likenesses to the consistent *knight of faith* who 'to the utmost limit wills' his chosen course, his acceptance by the God who calls from the thunder of the avalanche is doubtful. The ending of the play is ambiguous; Brand's success in achieving his own identity cannot be taken for granted. Ibsen's own acceptance or rejection of his hero's course may however become clearer in the light of some of his later creations. In *Peer Gynt*, the play that immediately followed *Brand*, the central character is Brand's opposite — the other half of an imaginary divided self. He has all the gaiety, charm and love of adventure which Brand lacks. He can make living relationships with other people, but he does just as much harm as his predecessor. He betrays all the women to whom he makes love: Ingrid and his green mistress; Solveig, and, though he does not desert her, his mother, whose trust he repeatedly betrays, and whom he finally deludes on her deathbed. At last Anitra betrays *him*, and he returns home alone to face the Button-Moulder and his own failure. He now learns that he has no self because he has never divined 'the master's intention'. Nor indeed had he attempted to do so. Peer lives always *à l'improviste*. When, for example, he has lost all after Anitra's departure, his reaction is an engaging but quite unscrupulous identification of his immediate needs with the highest imperative. He gives up his Eastern clothes as easily as he had done his troll's tail, and continues:

> A heathen existence is no good to me,
> I'm glad it was only put on with the clothes.*   p. 144

In breaking all bonds that held him to others—family, friends or lovers—Peer believes he has earned the right to be proud:

> It's understandable if I swagger
> And fancy myself: the man Peer Gynt
> Also called Emperor of Humanity!   p. 147

After this outburst Ibsen places one nine-line scene showing Solveig waiting in Peer's hut hundreds of miles away. Here might have been hope, but no-one, even through perfect love, can create the self of another, and Ibsen would be the last to think it. Peer goes on to find his only empire in the lunatic asylum.

From the Button-Moulder Peer learns too late that he has no self because he has not created a self. At first he is incredulous of such an accusation but he is finally driven to ask:

	What after all is this 'being oneself'?
Button-Moulder:	Being oneself means slaying oneself But that answer's presumably wasted on you, and therefore let's say: 'Above everything else it's observing the Master's intention in all things'.
Peer:	But what can one do if one's never found out what the Master intended?
Button-Moulder:	One just has to guess. pp. 209–10

Here the 'Master's surrogate is voicing just such a demand for blind committal to the irrational as Kierkegaard makes of his 'knights of faith'. Without it Peer's self-knowledge could never transcend the limited information provided by sense-perception and rational calculation. It is this 'commonsense' philosophy of life which has been his undoing. The character appears therefore to be a direct antithesis of Brand and a first impression may be that his failure demonstrates the other's success. There is however a later play which includes another pair of characters resembling Peer Gynt and Brand. In *The Wild Duck*† Hjalmar Ekdal is a close cousin of Peer Gynt, and

---

* Quotations from *Peer Gynt* are from the translation by Peter Watts, Penguin (1966).

† Quotations from the translation by U. Ellis Fermor: *Three Plays*, Penguin Classics (1950).

Gregers Werle is a reflection of Brand so malicious yet perspicacious in its distortions that it is hard to believe that its creator could ever have held his Brand to be a genuine 'knight of faith'. Hjalmar Ekdal, like Peer, plays a series of *rôles*. He poses as a photographer, but his wife does the work, and as both husband and father he receives care and affection which he enjoys, without any acceptance of the responsibility of returning them. He is more genuinely himself when he gives up all effort at living in the real world and retreats into the fantasy of the attic-forest. When his child tries to enter his fantasy, bringing with her genuine concern and involvement and without understanding the unreality into which she is thrust, the actual lovelessness of her father's world destroys her. She, Hedwig, has a real self, which she proves by surrendering it to save the father whom she truly loves, while Hjalmar's essential unreality is exposed at the end of the play:

> *Rilling:* Before the year is out little Hedwig will be nothing more to him than a fine subject to declaim on. . . . Then you'll hear him delivering himself of fine phrases about 'the child torn untimely from her father's heart', and see him wallowing in emotion and self-pity. p. 259

Gregers Werle consciously strives for complete consistency and believes that every man can discover his true self by the exercise of intellectual honesty. Once the eyes of the mind are opened men will see the truth, and will accept it. This experience will transcend any rational assessment of what is revealed, and the new life will therefore be achieved by what can properly be compared to the leap of faith. Again, however, the application of Kierkegaard's maxim, that this leap must always be an individual experience and that no knight of faith will attempt to communicate, much less impose, his unique vision on others, exposes Gregers, as it did Brand, as fraudulent. The would-be saviour is shown to be a man as blind to the truth of his own being as was Oedipus before he lost his eyes. Indeed Gregers' relationship to his parents is that of Oedipus himself. He hates his father and is obsessively devoted to his mother's memory, but he does not recognize this and never makes Oedipus' double journey, first to the original truth and then to its transcendence. He achieves no spiritual vision, and is left as centreless and unorganized a neurotic at the end of the play as he was at the beginning. His despair is absolute:

> *Gregers:* I am glad my destiny is what it is.
> *Rilling:* May I ask—what *is* your destiny?
> *Gregers:* To be thirteenth at table. p. 260

Ibsen does of course use an image from the early mythic journeys which might appear to contract this reading of the plays. Brand ends his life on a mountain top amid the shining arches of the 'ice church'. Does this convey a final apotheosis? Along Brand's straight path lie the bodies of his victims just as along his circular track lie those of Peer Gynt. The words that reach Brand as he dies: 'He is the God of Love', could indicate either condemnation or forgiveness, but what they cannot indicate is approval, for Brand has consistently opposed self-assertion to love. The intellectual passion of the play draws its strength, not from the conception of a steady progress on the road to self-knowledge and thence to redemption of the self, but from the contrary conception of the continuous dialectical conflict between half-rights and half-wrongs—ultimately, we might say, between half-selves—about which Ibsen learnt not from Kierkegaard but from Hegel.

Once again a consideration of later plays is relevant, for Ibsen creates other characters who finish their lives on a height—notably Solness, Borkman and Rubek. The futility of the hero's attempted ascent is clearest in *John Gabriel Borkman*,* for Borkman is plainly labouring under a paranoic delusion when he attempts the final ascent which destroys him:

Ella: But where will you go to?

Borkman: Just go on and on and on. . . . Do you see the mountain ranges *there*, far away? One behind another. They rise up. They tower *That* is my deep, unending, inexhaustible kingdom!

Ella: Yes, John, but there's a freezing breath coming from that kingdom!

Borkman: . . . that breath comes to me like a greeting from imprisoned spirits. . . . I feel the veins of metal that stretch out their curved, branching, luring arms to me . . . I love you, you treasures that crave for life—with all the shining gifts of power and glory that you bring. I love, love, love you!   pp. 365 and 367–8

This is madness, and Borkman dies in the snow before setting out on his last ascent.

In *The Master Builder*† Solness' situation is similar. He climbs his tower in the blind belief that he can 'bring back yesterday' and be the

---

* Translated by U. Ellis Fermor: *The Master Builder and Other Plays*, Penguin Classics (1958).

† Ibid.

successful lover of a young girl. His motive is clear: 'hereafter I will build only the most beautiful thing in the world—build it together with the princess whom I love'. But he recognizes that the most beautiful thing is only a 'castle in the air'. In spite of his promises he can give it no foundation. After he has hung the wreath on the tower he makes his last descent headlong:

> *Voices:* He's falling! He's falling! ...
> *A Voice:* His whole head is crushed—He fell straight into the quarry.
> *Hilde:* I can't see him up there now ... But he got right to the top. And I heard harps in the air.   pp. 210–11

The music of their fantasy was all they either of them ever heard. The reality was the quarry.

Brand never sees himself, but Peer Gynt does, clearly enough, in the mirror of the onion that he peels, although he neglects its warning.

> There's quite a multitude of layers.
> When am I going to get to the heart?
> God, it hasn't got one! Right to the middle,
> It's layers and layers, each getting smaller.
> Nature is witty! To hell with thought.   pp. 145–6

Gregers Werle discovers himself as he looks at the child whom he betrayed to her death and can find no words for what he sees. Solness sees himself in Hilde's eyes and realizes he must climb the tower or lose her. Rosmer learns to know himself when he finds he cannot live without Rebecca and goes with her to face the dark waters of the mill-stream.

> *Rebecca:* Is it you that go with me, or is it I that go with you?
> *Rosmer:* We shall never search that to the bottom.
> *Rebecca:* I should like to know, though.
> *Rosmer:* We two go with each other, Rebecca. I with you and you with me. . . . For now are we two *one*.*   p. 118

Ibsen is here approaching Shakespeare's images of the two divided excellencies who find themselves in union with their opposite. In his last play, Rubek responds in the same way to Irene† and it is after such self-recognition that the two pairs of lovers move upward or downward to their salvation, while the men like Brand, Solness and Borkman, whose eyes continue blind or whose vision remains distorted, move forward only to death.

---

* *Rosmersholm*, trs. by U. Ellis Fermor: *The Master Builder and Other Plays*, Penguin Classics (1958).   † *When the Dead Awaken.*

THE EXISTENTIALIST JOURNEY

iii THE HARD JOURNEY IN THE PLAYS OF ELIOT AND SARTRE

THE myth of the journey is a useful tool for the existentialist dramatist; it is a central image in *The Family Reunion** and *The Flies*† and is
repeated rather more heavily disguised in *The Cocktail Party*‡ and *Les
Séquestrés d'Altona*.§ Since *The Family Reunion* and *The Flies* are both
based on the Greek myth of the son who returns to avenge his murdered father on his mother and her lover, the likenesses and differences
of the two plays illustrate in particularly vivid form the contrast between Christian and atheistic existentialism.

In *The Family Reunion* Harry-Orestes returns home from exile and
goes on to make the backward journey into his childhood. He rediscovers places and people but knows there is more to be found:

> At the same time, other memories,
> Earlier, forgotten, begin to return.
> Out of my childhood. p. 52

> Here I have been finding
> A misery long forgotten, and a new torture,
> The shadow of something behind our meagre childhood,
> Some origin of wretchedness. p. 100

As he learns more of his parents' loveless marriage he discovers something of the cause of his present anguish and self-loathing in a childhood:

> Where the dead stone is seen to be batrachian,
> The aphyllous branch ophidian. p. 56

In the unloved child who became incapable of love and who, when
married, could only desire his wife's death, he recognizes himself and
with this knowledge comes at last a faint hope.

Sartre's Orestes also attempts a journey back to childhood when he
revisits the Argos which, for him, had no memories because he had

---

* T S. Eliot (London: Faber, 1939; New York: Harcourt Brace).

† J.-P. Sartre, *The Flies*, translated by Stuart Gilbert (London: Hamish Hamilton, 1946, and Penguin, 1962; New York: Alfred A. Knopf).

‡ T. S. Eliot (London: Faber, 1939; New York: Harcourt Brace)

§ J.-P. Sartre, tr. as *Loser Wins* (Hamish Hamilton, 1960), and as *Altona*
(London: Penguin Books, 1962; New York: Alfrd A. Knopf).

been rejected and exiled by his mother. Touching the great door of the palace of Argos he attempts to deny his unhappy past:

> I might have lived there . . . I'd have come in and gone out by that door
> ten thousand times. . . .*
> And now I'm going to say . . . This is not *my* palace, nor *my* door. And
> there is nothing to detain us here.   p. 21

But such a course is not possible for a human being; like Oedipus Harry and Orestes can only find the way forward, can only find what they have to do in the future, when they have recognized and admitted their past. Orestes discovers that the door of the palace *is* his door and that Argos is his city as irrevocably as Clytemnestra is his mother and Electra his sister. Only through them can he find the deed he has to do and the path he has to take, although when it is found he has to follow it in solitude.

The Family Reunion is more complex than *The Flies*, for although both plays develop the statement 'In my beginning is my end', Eliot gives us the psychological matrix from which the hero's dilemma has grown, and his play reflects an individual's recovery from an infantile trauma as vividly as it does a universal human dilemma. After their discovery of the past the fate of the two heroes diverges. To the Christian the 'leap' forward in blind faith means the discovery of God and of the self in relation to God; to the atheist it means the discovery of the self in its relation to other people. Both authors use the Greek image of the Furies who follow the man who has killed; to Orestes they are the Flies of an unnecessary and wrongful remorse, who can plague, but never destroy, the man who is prepared to carry consciously the burden of his own freedom and the responsibility of his own deed. To Harry they are the enigmatic but benevolent emissaries of a divine power, and he trusts them to save him from the 'sickness unto Death':

> . . . . Strength demanded
> That seems too much, is just strength enough given.
> I must follow the bright angels.   pp. 114–15

Guidance was given to him as surely as it was given to Dante and, in another form, to Oedipus in the divinely ordered societies in which each lived. Harry does not know the future, but he knows he has at last escaped from 'the fearful privacy of the insane mind'.

* Page references to translation by S. Gilbert, Hamish Hamilton.

Where does one go from a world of insanity?
Somewhere on the other side of despair.
... It is love and terror
Of what waits and wants me, and will not let me fall

pp. 114–15

Unlike his prototypes Sartre's Orestes goes forward alone and his journey may lead him to the 'nothingness' in which he will find himself. Without faith the loneliness of the journey means anguish, for it 'means isolation, and there is no more comforting word for it'.*
At first he hopes Electra will accompany him:

Orestes: You will give me your hand and we shall leave.
Electra: Where to?
Orestes: I do not know; towards ourselves. Beyond the rivers and the mountains there are an Orestes and an Electra waiting for us. We shall have to search for them patiently.

It is misleading, however, to say that their selves are waiting for them, for their selves, their essences, are what they have still to create. 'You are no more than the sum of your acts', says Inez to Garcin in *Huis Clos*. Earlier Jung had written:

Our personality develops in the course of our life from germs that are hard or impossible to discern, and it is only our deeds that reveal who we are.†

The traditional idea that man commits such or such act because he is thus and so, is replaced by its opposite; by committing such or such act, man makes himself thus or so.‡

Orestes admits this to Zeus when he says that there is:

Nothing left in heaven, no Right or Wrong, nor anyone to give me orders. . . . For I, Zeus, am a man, and every man must find his own way.

p. 97

God's orders, the true Right and Wrong, are, on the other hand, what Harry believes exist, and what he goes to seek. It is significant that neither play concerns itself with crime. Either directly or indirectly each man causes death, but the significant facts do not lie there; these are Harry's loveless heart and Orestes' assumption of responsibility. As Agatha says to Harry:

* Jung: *The Development of Personality* p. 172.
† Ibid., p. 173.
‡ J. Guicharnaud: *Man and his Acts.* In *Sartre*, ed. Kern, p. 85.

What we have written is not a story of detection.

Her continuation however is true for the Christian only, not for the atheist, for she says that the story is:

> Not of crime and punishment but of sin and expiation.
> It is possible that you have not known what sin
> You shall expiate, or whose, or why. It is certain
> That the knowledge of it must precede the expiation
>   . . . . You may learn hereafter,
> Moving alone through flames of ice.   pp. 104–5

Both dramatists are concerned with anguish. But for Sartre there can be no question of atonement, only acceptance of and pride in the deed, done by the free choice of the doer; his S. Christopher carries no Christ-child:

> *Orestes:* I have done *my* deed, Electra, and that deed was good. I shall bear it on my shoulders as a carrier at a ferry carries the traveller to the farther bank. . . . The heavier it is to carry, the better pleased I shall be; for that burden is my freedom.   p. 79

Father Martin d'Arcy, who does not, of course, agree with Sartre, writes that in the existentionist view:

> there is nothing beyond the self which exists. . . . Man's existence is the only primary and plenary datum, and all other reality is relevant to it and subject to it. Such a view puts man in the first place and God and all else in the secondary place; in other words, necessary existence or the identity of essence and existence, which belongs to God alone, is displaced and given to the ego.*

That final comment is the inevitable response of the committed Christian, and it may be complemented by another:

> In the end, the hero, the leader, the saviour, is one who discovers a new way to a greater certainty. Everything could be left undisturbed did not the new way demand to be discovered . . . classical Chinese philosophy names this interior way 'Tao', and likens it to a flow of water that moves irresistibly towards its goal. To rest in Tao means fulfilment, wholeness, one's destination reached, one's mission done; the beginning, end, and perfect realization of the meaning of existence innate in all things. Personality is Tao.†

* *The Mind and Heart of Love* (London: Faber; New York: Holt, Rinehart and Winston).

† Jung, *The Development of Personality*, p. 186.

THE EXISTENTIALIST JOURNEY

In *The Cocktail Party* the central characters all attempt the journey into the self. Edward and Lavinia do not get very far. In the psychologist's consulting room they discover some of their deficiencies, admitting that one is unloving and the other perhaps unloveable, and from there a correspondingly short ascent takes them to the point at which they can mutually support each other through the ordeal of a cocktail party.

Celia, however, makes a spiritual journey deep into herself, and it shows her, to her own amazement, sin. To the psychologist, who is to her rather the confessor, she says:

> It's not the feeling of anything I've ever *done*,
> Which I might get away from, or of anything in me
> I could get rid of—but of emptiness, of failure
> Towards someone, or something, outside of myself;
> And I feel I must . . . *atone*—is that the word?   p. 121

Celia is the Orestes figure in this play, and again the story is not one of 'crime and punishment'. Celia has committed no legal offence. She is horrified simply at what she sees as her own nature; she does not blind herself to it but accepts guidance, and this in the end leads her—by what steps we are not told—to martydom in Kinkanja.

> . . . from what we know of local practices
> It would seem she must have been crucified
> Very near an ant-hill.   p. 155

One of the 'guardians' explains:

> Every one makes a choice, of one kind or another,
> And then must take the consequences. Celia chose
> A way of which the consequence was crucifixion;   p. 165

This marks Celia's as the existentialist act of commitment, the creation of the self by action, but she, like Harry, can follow bright angels and does not face isolation, like Sartre's Orestes, who after his 'deed' discovered he 'was like a man who's lost his shadow. And there was nothing left in heaven, no Right or Wrong, nor anyone to give me orders' (p. 96).

In *Les Séquestrés d'Altona** the journey symbol is almost lost in naturalistic psychology, but the skeleton is clear beneath the flesh. From the moment when Franz, held down by four storm-troopers,

---

* Page references are to *Loser Wins*, tr. S. and G. Leeson (Hamish Hamilton).

95

watches them beat a Polish rabbi to death, he moves step by step, as
inevitably as did Oedipus, to the moment where he sees what he has
become and is revolted by his own image. On the last day of his life
he makes his confession to his father:

> *Franz:* I was clean when I left you. I was pure.
> (*crying out*) I wanted to save the Pole.   p. 143

But this is not the whole truth:

> The rabbi was bleeding, and I discovered at the heart of my power-
> lessness, some strange kind of approval.   p. 139

That is the beginning of the journey. The end is reached, hundreds of
miles and eons of life-years away, on the Russian front, where, cut off
from their regiment, a small group of Germans hold two Russian
partisans, who possess information which may mean the life or death of
them all.

> *Father:* Did they talk?
> *Franz:* What's that? No. They died without talking . . . I hadn't the
> knack—then.   p. 140

For Franz there is no ascent. He finds a momentary peace in reconciliation with the father he has always loved but knows he is incapable of
allowing it to last. 'In an hour I should hate you' he says (p. 148), and
the two men seek death together. Like Rosmer and Rebecca they fall
from a bridge into the river below them. The time that has elapsed
since the writing of the earlier play is marked only in the device by
which the Sartre pair drive to the waters of death in a fast sports car:

> *Leni:* What time is it?
> *Joanna:* Six thirty-two.
> *Leni:* At six thirty-nine my Porsche will be in the water. . . .
> *Joanna:* Why?
> *Leni:* Because the Teufelbrücke is seven minutes from here. . . . What
> does it matter? He didn't want to live.   p. 150

Both Eliot and Sartre show, behind their protagonists, lesser figures
who will not undertake the journey and refuse to endure the existential
anguish. In *The Cocktail Party* even the least perceptive characters
are allowed their little vision of truth and live by it as best they may,
but in *The Family Reunion*, the aunts and uncles are mercifully permitted to remain blind to the revelation which they would certainly

betray. In this they resemble the people of Argos, and are distinct from those who have faced the moment when the leap forward is necessary but have refused to make it. Electra is the clearest example of this *mauvaise foi*, but Sartre portrays it also in the von Gerlach brothers and in the three characters of *Huis Clos*. They are all confined either liter-ally or figuratively in hell because they will not accept as theirs their own 'essences', the selves they have made during their earthly lives, even though they are clearly mirrored for them in the eyes of their companions.

Both Eliot and Sartre set their plays in a naturalistic medium which is deceptively banal. In *The Family Reunion* people change for dinner, arrange flowers, refer to early editions of the evening paper, draw the window curtains and have a birthday cake with candles. Yet through this lacquered surface erupt — even in visible form — the furies of divine love, and the poetry expresses the anguish of human beings at the very end of their capacity for endurance. Although sometimes, as in *The Flies* and *Lucifer and the Lord*, Sartre uses situations far re-moved in time and place, yet most of his plays are set in contemporary surroundings. Even hell appears as a Louis Quinze hotel sitting-room where the electric bell does not ring, and a cellar, a prostitute's room or the stuffy opulence of a rich man's home are the places where love, violence and treachery explode. Each dramatist is prepared to trust his philosophy to interpret the experiences of the 'everyday life' in which reality must ultimately cohere, and where it must be sought if it is ever to be found.

iv Sartre: *Roads to Freedom*

Only three novels of the tetralogy *Roads to Freedom* are complete: *The Age of Reason,** *The Reprieve*† and *Iron in the Soul*.‡ Of the fourth Sartre has published two fragments only, entitled *Drôle d'Amitié*, which appeared in *Les Temps Modernes* (Nos. 49 and 50), for July and December 1949. The work is constructed round the development of three men, all friends, who at the time of the story, 1938–40, are in early middle life. Each seeks to discover himself or to

* *The Age of Reason*, tr. Eric Sutton (*L'Age de la Raison*, 1945), Penguin (1961).
† *The Reprieve*, tr. Eric Sutton (*Le Sursis*, 1945). Penguin (1963).
‡ *Iron in the Soul*, tr. Gerard Hopkins. (*La Mort dans l'âme*, 1949). Penguin (1963).

create his own 'essence'; each does at last find himself in answering the challenge of unforeseeable and surprising circumstances, and each is destroyed by his discovery. For two the destruction is triumphant, for the third calamitous. The trio are a pattern of two bright figures and a shadow. The bright ones are each other's antitheses, for whereas one refuses all commitment to person or cause other than himself, the other offers his total being—love, energy and judgment—to the group with which he is identified. Yet each seeks both to know and be himself, either by saving himself, or losing himself. Their 'shadow' is the man who believes he is already and irremediably the self he will for ever be, and whose aim is to destroy that self. Yet, as has been said, the positive figures too find themselves only in death; human society, it would seem, offers its more sensitive children no place in which to live; its growing shoots are nipped off in the bud. The man who believes he was born to kill and be killed, like the man whose last words are a promise to start again and live better, find death with equal inevitability at the moment when they also find themselves.

All three men are drawn with insight and with compassion, and two of them suggest a large measure of self-identification on the part of their creator. Mathieu de la Rue, the intellectual, the successful teacher of philosophy, adored by his pupils, intent always to hold himself uncommitted so that he may be free to espouse the cause which shall finally demand his allegiance, clearly suggests the young Sartre; Brunet, the communist, forced to choose between party solidarity and personal responsibility and at last deciding to trust his own judgment about basic values, mirrors with equal clarity the older Sartre who finally separated himself from his communist allies in post-war France. These are the two positive figures; their black shadow is Daniel Sereno, the self-destroying homosexual. In *The Age of Reason* Mathieu figures as a self-contained intellectual, whose commitments, apart from his teaching, are to his not greatly-loved mistress, Marcelle, and to two of the pupils of his lycee, the Russian brother and sister, Boris and Ivich. He cares dutifully for Marcelle and enjoys forming the boy's mind and watching—sometimes caressing—the girl's body. His real concern, however, is solely with himself. Marcelle says to him:

'You've acquired the taste for self-analysis. . . . It helps you to get rid of yourself; . . . you want to be nothing.'
'To be nothing?' repeated Mathieu slowly. 'No, ... Listen. I—I recognize no allegiance except to myself.'   p. 13

These are the words of a man who cannot act because he has refused to commit himself to others, in co-operation with whom action is alone possible. As an intellectual of the '30's, his political allegiance, could he give it, would inevitably be to the Left. He knows with one part of himself that he ought to be fighting in Spain. Indeed the novel actually begins with his meeting with a vagrant who gives him his most cherished possession—a Spanish stamp on a card written to a Paris group of the Communist Party. Mathieu fully understands the symbolic importance of the stamp both to the tramp and to himself, but he cannot act on his understanding, for one choice, one decision, would take from him for ever the freedom to make other decisions at the behest of that self to which alone he owes ultimate loyalty. Yet that self perpetually evades his search. Since Marcelle is pregnant by him he has, in fact, done a deed which should commit him to at least one other person. This responsibility, however, although he acknowledges it, he is determined to side-step at any cost, short of deserting her. Indeed he actually steals the money necessary to pay for an abortion.

Mathieu's true position at this time is pin-pointed in a talk with his old friend, Brunet, who has solved his own problem and decided his own fate by joining the Communist Party:

'You have gone your own way', said Brunet. 'You are the son of a bourgeois, you couldn't come to us straight away, you had to free yourself first. And now it's done, you are free. But what's the use of that same freedom if not to join us?'

Mathieu realizes that Brunet has gained what he himself knows nothing of. 'He is freer than I, he is in harmony with himself and the Party.'

'Well', said Mathieu, 'you're lucky.'
'Lucky to be a Communist?'
'Yes.'
'What a thing to say. It's a matter of choice, old boy.'
'I know. You're lucky to have been able to choose.'   p. 121

Mathieu is not able to choose, although, as he admits, he has nothing to defend, and his 'freedom' is merely a burden to him. He can make no use of it for, as yet, there is no cause for which he is prepared to die. When his friend has left him, he bitterly sums up his opinion of himself: 'I am an utter wash-out' (p. 125).

The elements of unreality and of frivolity which vitiate so much of Mathieu's relationship with the young Russian girl, Ivich, are shown by events in a night-club, when Ivich, in a desire to distract herself and horrify her neighbours, jabs her hand with her brother's knife:

> Mathieu felt himself growing pale with rage, . . . He jabbed the knife into *his* palm, and felt almost nothing. When he took his hand away, the knife remained embedded in his flesh, straight up, with its haft in the air . . . p. 195

> Ivich was looking at him with an affectionately fierce expression; she hesitated for a moment, and then suddenly applied the palm of her left hand to Mathieu's wounded palm, with a sticky, smacking sound. p. 197

Ivich calls this the mingling of the blood, but although Mathieu experiences sudden flashes of desire for her, there is no genuine threat from Ivich to his non-commitment. The desperate seriousness of Daniel's desire for self-mutilation shows this episode up for what it is —a childish search for sensation. As Mathieu himself comments:

> I'm a ghastly kind of fool . . . Brunet was right in saying that I'm a grown-up child. p. 195

Such things were the merest gestures, superficial, without meaning, unreal.

While Mathieu vacillates between the desire for self-discovery and the fear of losing the self in commitment Daniel Sereno is hell-bent for destruction—the destruction of others, but, more importantly, the destruction of himself. He is shown first at the moment when he is preparing to drown his cats, the only living beings—not excluding himself—whom he is able sincerely to love.

Sartre here introduces an element of the Oedipus myth on which he barely touches in the drama, although some use is made of it in *Le Diable et le bon Dieu*. The desire of the guilty for self-punishment and for self-mutilation, which underlies the blinding of Oedipus, is present in the minds of both Mathieu and Daniel, and with Daniel it becomes an obsession from which, in his self-loathing, he cannot escape. Daniel has a powerful and beautiful body; his manner to others is meticulously courteous, and he wins easily both admiration and even devotion. Since, however, no one who meets him sees what he really is, or rather what he appears to himself to be, he is merely horrified at their approaches. When the caretaker's little daughter leaves flowers outside his door he kicks them downstairs. Any tribute to the hated self must be refused and the hatred of the self projected on to the bringer of the tribute.

When he has decided to sacrifice his cats Daniel dresses with peculiar care, as for the celebration of a private Black Mass, and finding a pimple on his chin he at first shaves carefully round it. Then appears the first sign of the obsession with mutilation, which at this time he is still able to resist:

> It wouldn't be a bad joke to deface the head they all admired—Pah, a scarred face is still a face, . . . I should get tired of it all the sooner, . . . Besides, I like to be good-looking. p. 82

Such ambivalence in his relationship to himself is further developed as he carries the cats in a basket to the river:

> Suddenly, he saw his shadow, a grotesque and stocky figure, with the shadow of the wicker basket dangling from the end of his arm. Daniel smiled: he was very tall. He drew himself up to his full height, but the shadow remained squat and misshapen, like that of a chimpanzee. p. 85

The cats in their panic maul one another, and blood begins to drip through the basket; Daniel ignores it, yet the sacrifice he is attempting to make is in fact of a part of himself. As he waited on the river bank to gain courage sufficient for his deed:

> Daniel heard himself say in mournful tones: 'When a man hasn't the courage to kill himself wholesale, he must do so retail.' He would walk down to the water and say: 'Farewell to what I love most in the world.'
> p. 90

But Daniel cannot as yet mutilate himself to this extent. He does not kill his cats; instead he turns away from the river and carries them home with 'an odd little smile on his face' because he had reprieved both them and himself.

On his return to his flat Daniel meets Mathieu and is suddenly filled with anger at what he considers the man's normality; what would his friend think if he knew what Daniel has just been doing—if he knew what Daniel *was*?

> He doesn't know me in the least, but he likes to label me, as if I were an object. p. 93

He deliberately feeds this hatred, and when Mathieu asks for the loan of 4,000 francs to cover the cost of Marcelle's abortion, Daniel pretends he has not got the money. He tries to goad Mathieu into returning his hatred. He longs to be punished, to be made to suffer, perhaps, indeed, to be killed, but Mathieu is too absorbed in his own

difficulties to notice, and Daniel is further exasperated by his inability
to reach him, to make him suffer as he himself suffers:

> 'Not for a moment', he said to himself, 'did Mathieu cease to be *balanced*,
> composed, and in perfect accord with himself. . . . All the same, it would
> be worth a packet if he were forced to marry Marcelle.'   p. 97

Before this revenge on 'normality' is achieved, however, Daniel
makes another attempt at his own destruction. After an experience of
degrading frustration with a casual pick-up in a squalid room he returns to his flat bent on achieving the direct self-mutilation of castration:

> Nothing impels him to decide, nothing stops him from doing so: . . .
> I shall be lying on the floor *inert, my clothes torn and sticky: the razor*
> *will be on the floor, red, jagged, inert.*   p. 267

But once again he fails.

Daniel's sickness had been analysed by Kierkegaard nearly a century
before it was described by Sartre:

> Despair is the sickness unto death . . . it is precisely self-consuming, but
> it is an impotent self-consumption, which is not able to do what it wills. . . .
> The fact that despair does not consume him is far from being any comfort
> to the despairing man. . . . This precisely is the reason why he despairs . . .
> because he cannot consume himself, cannot get rid of himself, cannot
> become nothing. This is the potentiated formula for despair, the rising of
> the fever in the sickness of the self.*

So it was with Daniel. His fever was not yet high enough for him to
become nothing.

The deed he does finally achieve however is more horrible even than
physical castration: he combines vengeance and self-punishment by
himself marrying Marcelle. He relishes demolishing Mathieu's
picture of himself as a man and a lover, but he is himself the victim
of his triumph.

After he has told Mathieu what he is about to do he cannot resist
turning the knife in the wounds he has given them both:

> Daniel took a few steps towards the door, and came brusquely back to
> Mathieu: he had shed his ironic expression, but he looked no more amiable.
> 'Mathieu, I'm a homosexual,' he said. . . .

* *The Sickness unto Death*, pp. 150-1.

Daniel stood motionless, his arms stiff against his sides, he seemed to have dwindled. . . .

He had turned a little green and spoke with difficulty, but he was still smiling. Mathieu . . . turned away his head. . . .

'Does she . . . Does she know?'

'No.'

'But . . .' Mathieu blushed violently. 'Do you like women too?'

Daniel emitted an odd sniff, and said, 'Not much'. . . .

'Do you hate her?'

'No.'

And Mathieu reflected sadly: 'No, it's me he hates.'   pp. 294–7

Daniel finds his punishment. The honeymoon, described in *The Reprieve*, is as was to be expected, but Daniel is a good actor; he is full of consideration for Marcelle, and she notices nothing amiss, relishing his protective kindness.

'Just imagine—I'm afraid of cows!' she said, in a low tone.

Daniel squeezed her arm affectionately: 'Go to hell!' was what he thought. . . . He wanted to laugh: . . . 'It's your own fault. You wanted a quick, high-powered catastrophe; and you've got it.'   p. 41

Mathieu, having attempted the positive commitment which Daniel has refused us is in a troop-train on his way to the front when he reads, though with scant attention, a letter sent by his friend after his marriage.

I was my own burden: but never burdensome enough, Mathieu. For one instance, on that June evening when I elected to confess to you, I thought I had encountered myself in your bewildered eyes. You *saw* me . . . you knew that entity . . . and yet you saw it. I merely saw you seeing it. p. 343

For Sartre the direct reflection of the self by the self, as in a mirror, is never an adequate source of self-knowledge: the self must be seen reflected in the eyes of others before it can be known.* It is this need which drives Daniel to his last attempt to lose himself and at the same time find his full identity in the mind of another. After the priest has assured him that God sees him as he is, he is received into the Catholic Church. As he writes to Mathieu:

I adapt for my own use, your prophet's foolish wicked words . . . I am seen, therefore I am.   p. 345

* v. *Huis Clos*, and cf. sup. p. 97.

The form in which Daniel believes God sees him has been described in a reverie during a walk to the village church while he is still on his honeymoon:

> A day of shame, a day of rest, a day of fear, the day of God, the sun rose upon a Sunday. . . . God looked at Daniel. . . .
>
> Here am I, as thou hast made me, cowardly, futile and a paederast . . . But I know that, beneath thy eye, I *can* no longer escape myself. I shall enter, I shall stand among those kneeling women, like a monument of iniquity. I shall say: 'I *am* Cain. Well? Thou hast made me, now sustain me.'   pp. 166–9

But this immolation on the altar of a faith which he does not in fact share is not the end of Daniel's story. In *Iron in the Soul* he returns alone to Paris and awaits there the entry of the German forces of occupation. In the almost deserted city he rejoices at the downfall of the society by whose values he had been condemned and destroyed. He walks the streets like a dark god and welcomes the barbarian invaders who will accomplish his own nihilistic will. At last he sees them coming:

> A tank moved past him, slow, majestical, covered with branches and scarcely so much as purring. At the back of it, his tunic thrown loosely about his shoulders, his shirt-sleeves rolled above his elbows, was a very young man with folded arms. Daniel smiled at him. . . . Other faces passed before his dimmed vision, more and more of them, each as beautiful as the last. They have come here with intent to do evil: today the Reign of Evil begins. What joy! He longed to be a woman so that he might load them with flowers.   pp. 94–5

Daniel is indeed in hell, in the realm of the evil angels whose smiles he would buy if he could with the gift of his own soul.

That same evening he meets the most beautiful and sensitive of all his 'victims':

> All life seemed concentrated in his eyes, and, with his eyes, he devoured the slim young man who, in all innocence, had his back towards him and was leaning over the river.   p. 134

Later that night, with the boy asleep in the next room Daniel began to undress:

> 'This time', he thought, 'it'll be the end of me', and in his mouth he could taste the bitterness of all the agonies still to come.   p. 167

As the fourth and concluding volume of *Roads to Freedom* has never been published, save for a fragment, Sartre leaves Daniel without hope of expiation or release. His fate is that of the damned in the Inferno: to persist endlessly as the self they chose to be, tortured by what they had imagined was pleasure, tormented by what they had conceived as bliss:

> I see
> The lost are like this, and their scourge to be
> As I am mine, their sweating selves: but worse.*

Unlike Daniel, Mathieu pursues the tortuous search of his self to a final apotheosis in a maelstrom of destruction. Strangely enough, considering his left-wing loyalties, it is in the peril of his own country that Mathieu at last sees the cause for which he is prepared to die and hence finds the self which had so long eluded his search. *The Reprieve* brings the story to the moment of the Munich capitulation. Mathieu, on holiday in the South of France, finds himself one morning reading a government poster announcing the call-up of men holding 'A white mobilization order or form numbered "2"' (p. 73). He has read it twice before he realizes that he carries this form 2 in his own pocketbook. At first he cannot act. Two days later, his call-up still unanswered, he is standing on the Pont Neuf watching the dark, viscous waters of the Seine, as Daniel had done a few months earlier. Daniel, though he may well have been making preparations for his own death, was immediately concerned with inaugurating a prolonged period of self-torment, and Mathieu, on the edge of the bridge, is contemplating the possibility of suicide:

> He need only lean a little further over, and he would have made his choice for all eternity. . . . Suddenly he *decided* not to do it.   p. 309

Instead he answers his summons and joins his regiment. This marks the first step of his upward journey. A year later, when war actually comes, he is serving as a conscript among second-line troops, and his next advance towards finding himself is made when he is able to identify himself with these men—men lacking all glamour, personal pride or sense of purpose. On the night before the signing of the armistice, the waiting troops discover that their officers are abandoning them. Hidden in the shadows they watch their leaders move secretly away:

* *Poems of Gerard Manley Hopkins*, No. 45, p. 65.

The night was cold and clear. The moon was shining. . . .

'Whoever would have believed it!' muttered Pinette. . . . Masses of shadow were moving away from the walls. Soldiers were silently creeping from alleyways, wagon entrances, and barns, real soldiers of a second line formation, ill-kempt, ill-fed, slipping past the shadowed whiteness of the house-fronts. All of a sudden, the street was full of them. So sad were their faces that Mathieu felt a lump in his throat. . . .

Suddenly a voice was heard, a voice edged with bitterness:

'They never liked us!' . . .

Mathieu dared not find expression for all this, but Latex, behind him, spoke it calmly and unemotionally:

'We're pariahs.'

There was a sputter of voices. Everywhere the word was repeated, harshly, pitilessly:

'Pariahs!'

Silence fell. . . . All present stared at one another: all present seemed to be waiting, as though something still remained to be said. Then, suddenly, Latex smiled at Mathieu, and Mathieu returned his smile. Charlot smiled. Latex smiled. On every face the moon brought pallid flowers to birth.* pp. 109–12

The necessity of such participation in a group as the pre-amble to salvation is a common, almost an obsessive, theme in Sartre's work and thought. So does Orestes strive to identify himself with the citizens of Argos and Goetz with the peasants of Germany. The only practical alternative to identification with the oppressor is identification with the oppressed: with the proletariat, with the negro, and, for Sartre, above all with the inmates of the concentration camps. After such a descent, such a plunge to the bottom of the pit, the ascent can begin. The descent into a social group which leads, or may lead, to action is thus distinguished from the descent into the abysses of the mind which stultifies and destroys, as in the case of Daniel Sereno. In affairs of self-knowledge it is true that 'Humankind cannot bear very much reality'.†

The turning-point for Mathieu comes when he finds that a companion whom he particularly prizes has decided to join a little group of francs-tireurs, who have entered the village with their lieutenant, determined on a final, useless stand against the enemy. The novel must once more be allowed to speak for itself. Mathieu realizes that his friend has found himself at last:

* *Iron in the Soul.* † T. S. Eliot: *Four Quartets. Burnt Norton.*

Over and done with was Pinette's pursuit of Pinette, for now he was wholly himself, a Pinette entire, close-packed in the final reckoning. Mathieu sighed, and in silence took his arm, the arm of a young employee of the Métro, noble, gentle, brave, and tender, who had been killed on 18 June 1940. Pinette smiled at him: from the depth of his past he smiled. Mathieu saw the smile and felt utterly alone.   pp. 177–8

They reach the first houses of the village:

Suddenly Mathieu began to shout. . . .
'I'm fed up!' he cried; 'fed up! fed up!'
Pinette stopped and stared at him.
'What's biting you?'
'Nothing', said Mathieu, dumbfounded at his own behaviour.
'I think I must be going mad.'   p. 179

In that moment of unreason, however, he takes the decision that will prove his salvation. The two men walk to the rifle store, and Pinette, with infinite care, proceeds to choose a weapon:

'Give me your torch', said Mathieu. He shone the beam over the rifles. . . . He bent down and took one at random.
'What are you doing?' asked Pinette with a look of surprise.
'Can't you see?' answered Mathieu: 'I'm choosing a rifle'.   p. 180

So Mathieu and Pinette settle down for the night on the belfry platform of the village church. The three professional soldiers with them hold themselves aloof at first, half-consciously resentful of the others' intrusion on the intimacy of their battle-comradeship, but as they start their evening meal they offer the almost starving newcomers tins of bully beef and invite them to cross the platform.

They sat down. Mathieu could feel Clapot's warmth against his leg. This was their last meal, and it was sacred.   p. 201

But Mathieu is clumsy and gashes his hand on the tin-opener. He remembers the evening, not so long ago in time, when he had struck his hand on Boris' knife and sealed blood brotherhood with Ivich. But such doings become meaningless gestures remembered from a life without meaning as Pinette notices the wound and Clapot dresses it from his first-aid kit. Mathieu, reminded of the earlier episode, begins to speak of it, but its irrelevance to the genuine comradeship, to the genuine *existence* which he is now experiencing, makes it a waste of breath to continue. The fleeting memory serves merely to enhance the preciousness of that last supper, the final communion of men faithful to their common purpose to the death.

Yet, when he is mounting guard that night, a question keeps nagging at Mathieu's newly-won peace:

Had I any right to abandon my pals? Have I any right to die for nothing?

But he reasserts his freedom—the freedom which is genuine at last because it issues in a deed:

the world can think what it likes. I'm through with remorse, with hesitations, with mental reservations. No one has a right to judge me; no one is thinking about me; no one will remember me; no one can make up my mind for me. . . . Here and now I have decided that death has all along been the secret of my life, that I have lived for the sole purpose of dying. I die in order to demonstrate the impossibility of living. My eyes will put an extinguisher upon the earth and shut it down for ever. The earth raised its topsy-turvy face to the dying man: the foundering sky swept across him with all its stars. But Mathieu kept watch without so much as deigning to pick up these useless gifts.   p. 203

Mathieu has paid the price for his freedom—loneliness—and he has chosen for himself the meaning of his own life—death. Just as Orestes is obliged in his freedom to choose to kill, Mathieu is obliged to choose to die. Yet both are free since their choices—irrational and contrary to both Christian and social morality—reveal, or rather create, in action, the essence of their real selves. Mathieu, drawn as the sceptic and rationalist, is here playing the part of one of Baudelaire's romantic voyagers, but his creator is no romantic. The experiences of Mathieu's last night are simple. The comradeship of men on the eve of battle has become proverbial, even a commonplace, but the meal before Gethsemane and Golgotha remains significant. Sartre's intellectual analysis is unsparing, and the destruction of each of his three principal characters is presented 'without mitigation or remorse of voice', but this resolute, metaphysical ruthlessness leaves still ultimately significant the simple human satisfactions found only after personal commitment to a group of persons. Positive values are found:

Not in Utopia. . . .
But in the very world, which is the world
Of all of us—the place where in the end
We find our happiness, or not at all.*

* Wordsworth. *The Prelude:* XI. 146 ff.

The third of the three friends, whose frenetic searches for the self form the core of *Roads to Freedom*, is Brunet, whose attempt to win Mathieu to membership of the Communist Party we have already noted. Their argument may perhaps be read as Sartre's apologia for his own refusal to commit himself to the communist party line. Brunet's character is very sympathetically drawn; he has most of the bourgeois or Christian virtues—which you will—denied to Daniel, the failure and to Mathieu, the ultimate existentialist success. Curiously, his story, except for the two short episodes with Mathieu, is not integrated into the finely woven tissue Sartre has made from the lives of his other characters, but is told in a solid block of narrative at the end of *Iron in the Soul* and in the two fragments, printed in *Le Temps Modernes* under the title: *Drôle d'Amitié*, which are all that Sartre has published of the fourth volume of his tetralogy.

Unlike Mathieu who, at the moment of the capitulation, decides for death, Brunet accepts it as his duty to preserve his life for the service of his fellows through the Party to which he is committed. On the day when Mathieu fires his defiance from the belfry, Brunet is rounded up with thousands of other Frenchmen and begins the slow and painful journey to a German prisoner-of-war camp. His single aim is to continue his Party work, and he begins at once. En route and on arrival at the camp he establishes contact with Party members and trade-unionists and slowly introduces some measure of discipline and self-respect. He is obliged to work on his own initiative and by his own judgment, for he has lost all contact with the Party leaders. Aided by a man named Schneider, whom he considers a fellow-traveller, he successfully combats the despair that the hardship and horrors of living as prisoners-of-war inevitably provoke, organizes an enthusiastic Party cell and keeps fervour and hope for the future alive.

Drôle d'Amitié introduces a new character into the situation, a Party activist from Paris Headquarters named Chalais. He soon reveals that the Party line has changed, and that Brunet's work has to be denied and undone. With the future still unknown Brunet introduces Chalais to the Group and hands over his own leadership:

> For a moment, he felt as though he were saying goodbye to them; then putting his hand on Chalais' shoulder, he pushed him forward and in a firm, serious voice said: 'Treat him as you would me'.*

The fleeting impression was correct, but before Chalais assumed

* The translations from *Drôle d'Amitié* are my own. (H.M.)

control, he did something else; he recognized in Schneider, a man, Vicarios, who had left the Party after writing articles critical of the German-Soviet treaty and publishing them in his newspaper at Oran. Later, this man had been circularized as a traitor who had betrayed men and secrets to the government.

Although Brunet never believes the second of these accusations, he agrees that Schneider should be exiled to another part of the camp, insisting however that he will tell him this decision himself and will tell him alone.

Facing his friend, he makes his accusation:

'You never told me you came from Oran.' . . .

'No, I didn't.'

'You are Vicarios?'

'Yes.'

Vicarios was sitting opposite Brunet as he spoke, but Brunet saw only Schneider.

Involuntarily, his mouth opened and a voice he did not recognize burst out:

'Why did you lie to me?' Then harshly, he amended:

'Why did you lie to us?'

'Because I know you,' said Schneider. 'Good-bye, Brunet, we did some good work together.'

In talking to Chalais the comrades assert their faith in the speedy intervention of the Soviet Union and seek news of resistance to the Germans by the workers of Paris. Brunet is thereupon ordered to give an account of his activities:

'I've given them an ideological foundation', he said. . . . 'Every prisoner should still think of himself as a combatant.' He spoke sternly. 'Tell me frankly, where have I gone wrong?' he asked.

The Party answered, even more sternly:

'You've got to begin all over again; you're absolutely out of touch.'

PP. 796-7

Since Germany and the Soviet Union are now allied, the imperialist war must be sabotaged in every possible way. Brunet accepts the directive and resigns the leadership in the camp to Chalais. Unable to understand the change of front demanded of them, the Group loses unity and enthusiasm. Two of them appeal to Brunet:

'We want to understand.'

'To understand,' jeered Brunet, 'to understand! What do you think of that! Go and ask Chalais.'

p. 1013

Chalais, knowing that he is failing to hold the men again challenges the former leader. At first Brunet offers to recant in public, and his tormentor agrees:

> 'Let's have no formal verdict,' said Chalais with a laugh. '. . . nothing dramatic or solemn, just a discussion among friends, and when it's over, you'll get up. . . .'

These words are the catalyst which at last precipitates revolt and lead to the formation of an independent judgment. Brunet refuses the confession:

> Chalais smiled; Brunet watched him curiously.
>
> 'How will he set about destroying me?'

p. 1020

Chalais works quickly. He first tells the men of the contents of the Party's warning against Vicarios. Again Brunet is appealed to secretly:

> 'Schneider, is it true his name is Vicarios?'
>
> 'Yes.'
>
> 'Is it true that he was in league with the Governor of Algeria?'
>
> 'No.'
>
> 'Chalais is wrong then?'
>
> 'He's wrong.'
>
> 'I thought he was never wrong.'
>
> 'He's wrong about that.'
>
> 'He says that the Party sent out a warning. Is that true?'
>
> 'Yes.'
>
> 'The Party's wrong as well, then?'
>
> 'The comrades were misinformed,' said Brunet. 'There's nothing so serious about that.'
>
> 'It's serious for Vicarios.'
>
> Brunet made no reply.
>
> Toussus observed casually: 'You liked him a lot, this Vicarios, didn't you? He was your buddy, in the early days.'
>
> 'Yes', said Brunet. 'He was in the early days.'
>
> 'But now you wouldn't give a damn if they beat him up?'

pp. 1025–26

Realizing what Chalais has already set in motion, Brunet turns:

113

Toussus checked him: 'You wouldn't like me to come with you?'
'Certainly not. It's a trap, and it has been set only for me'.

p. 1026

Brunet must at last make his personal choice. In fact, he has chosen already; he has refused to accept the judgment of others both on the political situation and on the conduct and character of his friend. Now he interrupts the beating-up by at last asserting his personal authority against that of the Party's representative:

> He thought: 'This is the crunch'. One movement and the spider's web that held him powerless would be ripped from top to bottom.
>
> 'No, Brunet,' said Rasque, with calm assurance; 'You can't give us orders any more; that's all over.'
>
> 'That may be so,' Brunet replied, 'but I can send you to hospital for a fortnight. That I *can* still do.'
>
> They hesitated. Brunet looked at them, laughing impatiently. . . . The trap was working well. Brunet struck out with his fist, and exultingly, brought it down on Souac's right eye.   pp. 1027–8

Brunet's rebellion is now public, but he has not yet achieved a fully conscious choice. He still hesitates.

> 'Friendship,' said Vicarios, 'should be possible, all the same.'
>
> 'It is possible,' answered Brunet, 'between two Party comrades.'

p. 1028

Events soon make any such mid-way stance impossible. Vicarios knowing that he has no longer any function to fulfil in the camp has decided to attempt an almost impossible escape. He had already, in fact, asked Brunet to secure for him civilian clothes. When Pinette chose the rifle for his final defiance Mathieu found that he must choose one too. Now Brunet is faced with the same situation, and he sends a message to the prisoner in charge of the secret store:

> 'I've been looking for you,' said Manoël. . . . 'Did you want to ask me something?'
>
> 'Yes; I need two sets of civilian clothing.'   p. 1031

Machine-gun fire breaks out as the pair struggle through the barbed wire. The scene for Mathieu's triumphant obsequies was blanched by moonlight, that for Brunet's by the snow against which the two fugitives were starkly visible. Vicarios is hit, and Brunet drags him down through the snow towards the temporary shelter of the nearby trees. But Vicarios is already in his death agony, and he feels only despair:

> 'Get out,' said Vicarios. 'It's your fault, all this.' . . .
>
> 'God, we'll begin again,' said Brunet. 'I'll speak to the Party comrades. I'll. . . .'
>
> 'Begin again,' yapped Vicarios, 'can't you see I'm finished?' Making a great effort, he added with difficulty: 'It's the Party that's finished me.'

The choice has come too late; the friend for whom it was made is dying:

> Brunet bent down and thrusting his hands into Vicarios' matted hair, he called out, as though still able to save him from the horror, as if two doomed men, at the final moment, could triumph over solitude:
>
> 'The Party! To hell with the Party; you are my only friend'. . . .
>
> The Germans rushed down the slope, holding on to the trees; he got up and walked to meet them.
>
> His death was only just beginning.

Brunet, unlike Mathieu, was a maker, a builder; he could not deliberately choose death, but death came as a result of his earlier false choice, and he finds himself only as he loses his life.

Sartre's concern with death as the climactic point of his novels might appear as a regression to the romanticism of earlier poets, but in fact it lacks their over-tones of sweetness and escapism, and a closer parallel exists. In *The Waning of the Middle Ages* Huizinga writes: 'No other epoch has laid so much stress as the expiring Middle Ages on the thought of death. . . . The popular preaching of the mendicant orders had made the eternal admonition to remember death into a solemn chorus ringing through the world.'* The parallel is not a coincidence, for men at that time were facing with a new sense of its urgency, the dichotomy—already elaborated by Occam in the fourteenth century —between the effectiveness of rational understanding in the sphere of material things and the apparent necessity of blind faith in all that concerned man's ultimate fate and his relationship with his God. In *The Summoning of Everyman*† the essential elements of the journey in quest of the self are vestigially present. When Everyman has faced failure with the words, 'Then of myself I was ashamed', and has found no single credit item in his 'book of count', his Good Deeds, who will at

---

* Pelican (1955), p. 140.
† *Three Medieval Plays*, Heinemann (1953).

last lead him through darkness into light uses the old familiar metaphor: Here is a *blind* reckoning in time of need.   p. 23

In this version of the myth the moment of self-recognition precedes the downward as well as the upward journey. After it Everyman must creep into the tomb, the underworld where Beauty would smother and where all his faculties desert him. Even Knowledge—his Virgil—cannot accompany him here; only Good Deeds supports him until he can make his final ascent when the angel's voice calls him to climb 'into the heavenly sphere'. The play is not simply a story of individual salvation: Everyman is committed to a society, and his lessons have been largely concerned with his use of the worldly goods which were only lent him. So although Sartre has nothing to say of a heavenly sphere and but little of a terrestrial paradise, yet perhaps it is here rather than in the nostalgia of the nineteenth century romantics that the prototype of his vision of Thanatos might well be sought.

v Albert Camus

Camus has denied that he is an existentialist, but his position is sufficiently close to that of Sartre for it to be convenient to consider his work here. In both his plays and novels he writes repeatedly of the man who discovers and repudiates his own nature, and in so doing he uses elements of the myths of the hard journey. Although the journey itself is never the maquette on which his story depends for its form, in his earliest play, *Caligula,** the hero gradually plumbs his own inadequacy, and Camus endows him with the true existential anguish.

The young emperor cannot ignore the limitations put on his freedom by the facts of the physical universe, but he does deny all the restraints on human action which inform social morality and which are expressed in the disciplines of religion and art. He is, in fact, Camus' *anti-hero*. He contradicts the thesis of the *Myth of Sisyphus* that, although in an absurd universe suicide is the rational act, yet man does and must go on living. He denies Camus' own delight in the sensuous experience of nature's beauty, which transcends the need

* *Caligula* and *Cross Purpose*. Tr. S. Gilbert (London: Hamish Hamilton; New York: Alfred A. Knopf).

of rational justification. He denies also the duty of *engagement*. He stands free and in his isolation because he sees no reason for commitment, and, since man can create only in co-operation with his fellows, the only use he can make of his freedom is destruction. Although he deliberately chooses this course, he is fully aware of its horror. Beating wildly on a great gong, he calls the world to judgment, and to condemnation. As soldiers and patricians surge into the hall in response to his clamour, Caligula takes his mistress Caesonia up to a great mirror and 'with a wild sweep of his mallet' smashes their reflection. Then by a twist of the old symbol, he plants himself in the frame 'in a grotesque attitude'. As he sees himself, he shows himself to others. Gazing at him in horror Caesonia murmurs his name, and the figure in the mirror answers, assuming 'a new, proud ardour':

Yes . . . Caligula.   p. 26

Now Caligula's downward journey to self-knowledge begins, and it leads only to self-destruction. In his freedom he violates all taboos, all the loyalties of kindred, sex and friendship, all social responsibility until it becomes impossible to recover what he has lost through violence and deliberate isolation. The consummation comes when he strangles Caesonia, the one human being who still loves him, as she lies on his breast:

Caesonia: Tell me you mean to keep me with you.
Caligula: I don't know. All I know—and it's the most terrible thing of all—is that this shameful tenderness is the one sincere emotion that my life has given up to now.   p. 91

With this last tie severed, Caligula faces himself once more in the mirror. Kneeling in tears before his reflection he voices mankind's despair:

I've stretched out my hands; see, I stretch out my hands, but it's always you I find, you only, confronting me, and I've come to hate you. . . . We shall be forever guilty. The night tonight is heavy as the sum of human sorrows.   p. 94

This is the nadir of the pit. Absurdity was recognized, but no leap of faith to a positive assertion followed the recognition. Freedom in isolation has led to nothingness; the isolated individual is swept away and life goes on, with ordinary collective values reasserted in an ordinary human community.

Cross Purpose is one of the few modern plays containing both the
Oedipus and the Jocasta archetypes. Jan, the son, who left his bleak
mountain home as a boy to seek sunnier lands, returns as a married
man, and for reasons obscure to himself visits the inn kept by his
mother and sister without revealing his identity. Unlike Oedipus, the
stranger does not succeed in being adopted where he really belongs;
he makes no contact with his mother, and before morning the two
women, still not knowing who he is, have murdered him for his money
and thrown his body into the river. Thus Jan makes the long return
journey to a home which destroys him, and in his death he is, as his
sister says, 'with the woman he crossed the sea to find' (p. 167). On
his mother, on the contrary, calamity descends, as it descended on
Jocasta, out of a clear sky, while she sits where she has always sat, at
her own hearth. When Jan's previously unopened passport has at
length been read, the mother is herself destroyed by her failure to
recognize the son she loved. Her words could have been used without
alteration by her Greek prototype:

> My heart . . . has learnt again today what grief means, and I am not
> young enough to come to terms with it. In any case, when a mother is no
> longer capable of recognizing her own son, it's clear her rôle on earth is
> ended. p. 153

She knows that the 'absurd' nature of the misunderstanding which
brought about the catastrophe does not lessen its significance:

> It only proves that in a world where everything can be denied, there are
> forces undeniable; and on this earth where nothing's sure we have our
> certainties. And a mother's love for her son is now my certainty. p. 153

When her daughter sneers at the wonderful 'love' that could allow
a son to forget his mother for twenty years, her mother remains
unmoved, her new 'certainties' unshaken:

> Yes, it was a wonderful love that outlasted twenty years of silence and
> brought back to his home a son who seemed forgetful as he was forgotten.
> Say what you will, that love is wonderful enough for me—since I can't
> live without it. pp. 153–4

Such commitment to the irrational certainty of love is paid for with
the equally irrational certainty of guilt. Like Jocasta's the wrong done
was done in ignorance, but ignorance is no palliative. For better or
worse man makes himself and his destiny by his own deeds:

116

... I know that this pain, too, doesn't make sense. But then this world we live in doesn't make sense, and I have a right to judge it, since I've tested all it has to offer, from creation to destruction.   pp. 154–5

The play is, like all Camus' work, a plea for commitment, and the author himself categorically asserts this:

All men's misfortunes come from their failure to speak simply. If the hero of Cross Purpose had said: Here I am. It is me and I am your son, a dialogue would have been possible. . . . There would have been no more tragedy since all tragedies reach their climax through the deafness of the heroes. . . . If we choose to serve the community we choose to serve the cause of dialogue. . . . This is how we can be free together with other people.*

Unlike Sartre, Camus refuses to equate the triumph of the self with death. However mediocre Caligula's victims and opponents may have been, and although there is no image in the play of the natural world and its sensuous delights, which might make life worth enduring, yet the hero's own strident self-assertion in the moment of death is a cry of failure. In *Cross Purpose* the world of love and individual happiness is mirrored in the land which Jan reached and to which Martha longed to escape. Its values are voiced by Maria, Jan's young wife. It is 'a land of endless sunshine beside the sea' (p. 108) where men and women may love passionately, though not for long. Jan himself says to his sister:

Spring over there grips by the throat and flowers burst into bloom by thousands, above the white walls. If you roamed the hills that overlook my town for only an hour or so, you'd bring back in your clothes a sweet honeyed smell of yellow roses.   p. 133

Jan is to be pitied that his sense of guilt for the desertion of his mother led him to renounce this world, and Martha is right to long for it. Her mistake is one of means, for we cannot win love by hate, joy by murder, communion by the attempt at self-sufficiency.

In *The Plague*,† the doctor, Bernard Rieux, voices explicitly his refusal of death as, under any circumstances, a viable goal for man, even though it mean—as it did for Sartre's Mathieu—the momentary achievement of true existence and a free personality, and though, since

* *Carnets 1942–1951*. Tr. P. Thody (London: Hamish Hamilton, 1966, p. 82; New York: Alfred A. Knopf).

† Tr. Stuart Gilbert, Penguin (1960).

'the order of the world is shaped by death' (p. 107), no lasting victory is possible for man.

His justification of the individual's irrational delight and of the demand for social commitment sets up the peculiar tension which is a characteristic of all Camus' best work. In *The Plague* this ambivalence is shown in the refusal of Rieux to condemn Rambert's desire to escape from the city in order to rejoin his mistress, although he himself remains resolutely within it. His own choice of commitment is irrevocable, whatever the cost, for the battle is unending and the man who has found himself must wage it until he is prevented by his own death:

> And, indeed, as he listened to the cries of joy rising from the town, Rieux remembered that such joy is always imperilled. He knew what those jubilant crowds did not know but could have learned from books: that the plague bacillus never dies or disappears for good; that it can be dormant for years and years in furniture and linen chests, that it bides its time in bedrooms, cellars, trunks and bookshelves; and that perhaps the day would come when, for the bane and the enlightening of men, it raised up its rats again and sent them forth to die in a happy city.   p. 252

In *The Fall** the narrator, Clamence, has abused his position in human society by exploiting others for his personal gratification, and he has finally contracted out of all responsibility towards it. He has become an 'ancient mariner' who, fully aware of his own baseness, gloats over a gradual revelation of it to an almost silent listener. Their peregrinations along the misty waterways and subfuse streets of Amsterdam mirror his own journey through the circles which he knows are those of hell. The central incident of the novel fulfils a dual purpose: psychologically it is the catalyst which at last precipitates self-knowledge, formally it is the symbol of the refusal of commitment which is, for Camus, the fatal flaw or sin. One night as Clamence was returning home across the Pont Royal he saw, through the light rain that was falling, the dark figure of a girl leaning over the balustrade. Just after he had passed her, he was halted by the sound of a body striking the water and by a repeated cry which drifted downstream before it stopped abruptly.

> I was still listening as I stood motionless. Then, slowly, in the rain, I went away. I told no one.   p. 53

The memory was successfully repressed for a time; and only later

* Tr. J. O'Brien, Penguin (1957).

became obsessive. At last Clamence thought he had mastered it, but one day, as he stood on the deck of an ocean liner his heart beat wildly at the sight of a floating lump of debris which sank before it reached the ship.

> Then I realized, calmly, just as you resign yourself to an idea the truth of which you have long known, that that cry which had sounded over the Seine behind me years before had never ceased. . . . I realized likewise that it would continue to await me on seas and rivers, everywhere, in short, where lies the bitter water of my baptism.   pp. 79–81

The city of *The Plague* was a kind of *Inferno* in which it was possible that a few men and women could gain knowledge of themselves and afterwards attempt the upward climb to salvation: in *The Fall* the only fully realized character is content to accept the damnation to which he destines himself; as he says 'God is not needed to create guilt or to punish. Our fellowmen suffice, aided by ourselves' (p. 81). The comparison of the city with Dante's Inferno, at first only suggested, is later made explicit:

> We are at the heart of things here. Have you noticed that Amsterdam's concentric circles resemble the circles of hell?   p. 13

Clamence has knowledge of good and evil, or, perhaps it would be more accurate to say, of life and death, but he makes no valid use of it for in any case, he concludes:

> It's too late now. It'll always be too late. Fortunately.   p. 108

This maudlin 'judge-penitent' is at first blind to the truth about himself; then he sees but will not admit it; then he both sees and admits it but still refuses to take up the challenge and attempt to change himself. He and Dr Rieux in *The Plague* are the exact opposite of each other, for Rieux, who also gradually discovers himself and his values, recommits himself to the service of humanity. The totality of Camus' life and work leaves no doubt as to which of the two characters embodies his own purpose and practice.

CHAPTER 5

Franz Kafka: The Journey in the Labyrinth

The bitten apple and the bite in the apple.
T. S. ELIOT. The Dry Salvages

God is the only being who in order to reign does not even
need to exist.   BAUDELAIRE: Fusées

Conscience is a Jewish invention.   ADOLF HITLER

And at that the priest shrieked from the pulpit: 'Can't you see anything
at all?' It was an angry cry, but at the same time sounded like the involun-
tary shriek of one who sees another fall and is startled out of himself.*

THOSE words were not written about Oedipus and the warning
brought to him by Tiresias, but about Joseph K. and the priest
whom he met in the cathedral of his home city. Although he was care-
lessly walking round the building with a tourist's guide book yet K.
was already on the path which was to lead irrevocably to his destruction, just as was Oedipus when Tiresias warned him of the blindness
which, unknown to him, had sealed his eyes. Joseph K. wakened one
spring morning to a calamity as unexpected as the plague which descended on Thebes out of a clear sky. *The Trial* begins with the words:

> Someone must have been telling lies about Joseph K., for without
> having done anything wrong he was arrested one fine morning.   p. 7

In *The Castle*† the first warning of danger comes as suddenly,
though here we know that, as in *Oedipus*, the hero has already made
a long journey from the place of his birth. On his first night in the
territory of 'the Castle' K. is woken suddenly to find a young man
gazing down on him and protests.

At this the young man flew into a passion. 'None of your guttersnipe

---

* *The Trial*, Penguin (1953). First published 1925. Translated E. and W. Muir,
1935, p. 233
† First published 1926. Translated E. and W. Muir, 1930, Penguin Books (1957).

manners!' he cried. 'I insist on respect for the Count's authority. I woke
you up to inform you that you must quit the Count's territory at once.'

p. 12

The structure of the fable thus combines in each case the dynamism
of a sudden shock with the drawn-out tension of the suspense which
follows. From the moment of the warning Oedipus treads a path
ironically direct, deceptively simple. Both Joseph K. and K. lead
themselves, or are led, a labyrinthine dance, but for all three the
direction is equally pre-determined. At the start each protagonist is
perfectly convinced of his own innocence; at the end he is over-
whelmed by his guilt and failure. Oedipus is blind; he is in a darkness
like that of death, but he still has, and uses, his senses of hearing and
touch when he listens to Creon and fondles his daughters. He is still
in the world; his journey is not ended, and he is led by love on a
further pilgrimage. Kafka's heroes end not self-blinded only but self-
destroyed and without hope. Joseph K. has surrendered to his despair
before the actual moment of his execution, which indeed, at one level
of interpretation, is certainly his suicide:

> Without having been informed of their (i.e. the executioners') visit, K.
> was sitting also dressed in black in an arm-chair near the door, slowly
> pulling on a pair of new gloves that fitted tightly over the fingers, looking
> as if he were expecting guests. He stood up at once and scrutinized the
> gentlemen with curiosity. 'So you are appointed for me?' he asked.

p. 245

He makes no resistance to his executioners; in fact he is identified
with them:

> They kept their shoulders close behind his and instead of crooking their
> elbows, wound their arms round his at full length, holding his hands in a
> methodical, practised, irresistible grip. K. walked rigidly between them,
> the three of them were interlocked in a unity which would have brought
> all three down together had one of them been knocked over. It was a unity
> such as can be formed almost by lifeless elements alone.   p. 246

Kafka left *The Castle* unfinished, and his close friend and literary
executor, Max Brod, believes that on his deathbed K. was to have
received from 'the Castle' permission to reside in the village. Even if
this is correct, such permission would have arrived too late to be of
service to K. His search for 'salvation' had destroyed him as surely as
Joseph K.'s search for 'justice' had destroyed him.

No more than Oedipus do Kafka's two heroes suffer for an immoral act, for neither Joseph K. nor K. does wrong by a deliberate choice. Remembering Kierkegaard we may say that the fault of each was not the ethical one of murdering Isaac but the religious one of refusing to do so. They both appeared to be respectable men following the code of the society in which they lived, but they were as ignorant of their own nature as of the nature of the universe of which they were a part and of its demands on them. Oedipus is the image of a man who sees the truth of himself in the propensity to violence and lust which finds fulfilment in the destruction and violation of the most dearly loved object, and he admits his guilt. If such an admission is not made, so Kafka appears to believe, no man can take the 'leap' from contingent to genuine being; no man can receive his acquittal from the high court of justice; no man can gain entrance to the precincts of the Castle.

Sin has no connection with the ethical systems by which man has endeavoured to impose some coherence on the nihilistic horror of a universe whose principle of order—if one exists—is inapprehensible by his intelligence. If this order is to be apprehended it must be by an act of faith, and the relationship between religion and morality which has become axiomatic in Western thought must be broken. This relationship has not always existed, nor does it exist everywhere today. Much religious practice makes or has made holy the ritual murder and the ritual orgy, which are the 'sins' of violence and lust, for which Oedipus, under the compulsion of human society, put out his eyes.

We have been taught, and Kierkegaard has reminded us, that Abraham's sin would not have been the killing of Isaac but the refusal to enter the world where that killing was demanded of him. To Kafka, as to Kierkegaard, the primordial sin was neither lust nor violence, neither the eating of the apple nor the killing of Cain, but the refusal to recognize the reality of the world where the limits of our human reason are transcended, so that good and evil, truth and falsehood, equally with all the modes of human behaviour, must be assessed by faith and imagination before they can be interpreted by reason. Writing in this sense Kafka shows Amalia and her whole family outcast from the Castle's favour not because she accepted but because she refused the lewd advances of Sortini, a castle official. Notwithstanding our ignorance of what is expected of us, freedom for every existentialist or near-existentialist writer is something which can only be achieved by self-committal to a deed, and to Kafka as to Kierkegaard this deed, this first committal, must be to the admission of sin, and the anguish which inevitably accompanies this is identifiable with a sense of sin. It is also a sense of reality.

It is only slowly that the possibility of his condemnation dawns on Joseph K., and although he reaches despair he never admits guilt:

'How do you think it [*i.e. his case*] will end?' asked the priest. 'At first I thought it must turn out well,' said K., 'but now I frequently have my doubts. I don't know how it will end. Do you?' 'No,' said the priest . . . 'Your guilt is supposed, for the present, at least, to have been proved.' 'But I am not guilty,' said K., 'it's a misunderstanding. And if it comes to that, how can any man be called guilty? We are all simply men here, one as much as the other.' 'That is true,' said the priest, 'but that's how all guilty men talk.'   p. 232

'It's a misunderstanding . . . we are all simply men.' In the world of Kafka's creation the second statement is true, but the first is false. There is no misunderstanding except in Joseph K.'s mind. When Oedipus found himself, he had found mankind. Kafka knew as well as another and greater Jew that 'we have all sinned and come short of the glory of God' (Romans III, 23), but this K. does not accept. His year-long wanderings in the purlieus of the court, those 'labyrinthine ways' of his own mind, bring him at last only to the point at which he abandons hope and relaxes into death, 'like a dog' for whom there can be no resurrection. All his efforts were in vain; indeed they were misapplied, for they were directed towards the proof of his innocence, rather than the acceptance of his guilt:

Etre soi c'est se choisir coupable.*   p. 199

Thus Joseph K.'s 'journey' is a flight from self-knowledge rather than a progress towards it. He knows guilt but without admitting it, and therefore he never transcends it. A new bitterness and despair have flooded the old myth. K. is not passive like Jocasta; he strives like Oedipus, but the fate of Jocasta, not that of Oedipus, is his. He dies rather than face the full knowledge of himself.

Louis MacNeice writes that Kafka is reported to have said:

What is sin? . . , We know the word and the practice, but the sense and

* Maja Goth, *Franz Kafka et les lettres françaises* (José Corti).

the knowledge of sin have been lost. Perhaps that is itself damnation, Godforsakenness, meaninglessness.*

René Dauvin† believes that Joseph K. is guilty because he had not taken his total 'I' into account so that he is a thing rather than a person—an example in fact of Heidegger's 'unauthentic man', who fails to enter the world of genuine existence.

This may be so since, although Kafka shows none of his heroes reaching the earthly paradise of Colonus nor the mysterious world to which its cavern gave access, yet he forces us to accept that that world does nevertheless exist. The man in the priest's parable *saw* the light burning behind the gate through which he never passed. Not only that but the entrance to that world existed and had in fact been made expressly that that particular man might pass through it. As he lies dying, after a lifetime spent waiting outside the precincts, the doorkeeper bends over him:

> 'What do you want to know now?' asks the doorkeeper, 'you are insatiable.' 'Everyone strives to attain the Law,' answers the man, 'how does it come about, then, that in all these years no-one has ever come seeking admittance but me?' The doorkeeper perceives the man is at the end of his strength and his hearing is failing, so he bellows in his ear: 'No-one but you could gain admittance through this door, since the door was intended only for you. I am now going to shut it.' p. 237

The door was intended for the man, intended for a specific individual, and after a lifetime's waiting it was shut even as the man gained the knowledge to use it: 'So the doorkeeper deluded the man', said K. immediately, but the priest denied this. By telling the man at the start of his vigil that he could not let him in *at that time*, he had in point of fact shown that ingress was actually possible and by that door, but nevertheless the man never took the necessary step across the threshold. The priest emphasizes that he was a free man, but he never puts his freedom to the test of the final 'leap', although in this case it would have been only a single step.

Although for Kafka failure to take the step, to make the leap, is what involves men in the devastation of guilt, he sees nothing in man's make-up which can aid him in his dilemma. His reason is not fitted to bring him knowledge of reality, and Kafka tells nothing of the

* *Varieties of Parable*, Cambridge University Press (1965), p. 140.
† *Franz Kafka Today*, ed. Flores & Swander, University of Wisconsin Press (1958).

prevenient grace of Christian theology. Yet in his interpretation of the anguish of which he has a knowledge as profound as Heidegger's, more exacerbated than that of Sartre, Kafka is at odds with both these philosophers in that he shares the Christian Kierkegaard's identification of the anguish with guilt:

> Sin is this: before God . . . to be in despair at not willing to be oneself, or in despair at willing to be oneself . . . Sin is despair . . . and the opposite of sin is faith.*

Without the leap of faith guilt is therefore as inescapable and as impersonal as the destiny spun by the fates in the imagination of the Greeks, and man's chance of defying it by an act of free choice is as slender, although probably in a final analysis as real.

Guilt for Kafka, as for the Christian existentialist, is inexpugnable, is unatonable so long as it is unknown and unadmitted. The most primitive reaction to the anguish of self-knowledge is self-punishment, and in its simplest form self-mutilation, but this is ineffective since any punishment short of death requires of the victim continual repetition, as Shakespeare knew:

> *Lady Macbeth:* Will these hands ne'er be clean?
> *The doctor:* See how she rubs her hands.
> *The gentlewoman:* I have known her continue in this a quarter of an hour.

For both the K.s therefore, as for Lady Macbeth, suicide remains the only viable reaction in a world which knows guilt without knowing God.

When Joseph K. looks at the grotesque figures of his 'executioners' it is himself he is seeing and loathing, and his death marks his final despair. The men enter his room unannounced:

> In frock coats, pallid and plump, with top-hats that were apparently uncollapsible . . . 'Tenth-rate old actors they send for me,' said K. to himself. . . . 'Perhaps they are tenors,' he thought, as he studied their fat double chins. pp. 245–6

Thus even the dignity of tragedy is denied to the modern Oedipus, and when the butcher's knife has twice been turned in his heart these repulsive figures are his final vision of himself:

> With failing eyes K. could still see the two of them, cheek leaning against

* S. Kierkegaard, *The Sickness Unto Death*, pp. 208 and 213.

cheek, immediately before his face, watching the final act. 'Like a dog!'
he said: it was as if he meant the shame of it to outlive him.   p. 251

While this poem in fictional form can be set beside the drama of
Oedipus Tyrannus, it also invites comparison with the first part of
The Divine Comedy, for it may well be considered as Kafka's *Inferno*,
and like Dante's it is a dual image, mirroring both a universal, metaphysical guilt and also the exploration of an individual psyche. The
careful analysis made by Hermann Uytersprot* shows that the train of
events in *The Trial* represents with clinical accuracy the story of the
growth of a neurosis ending in suicide. This interpretation depends on,
or is at least strongly re-enforced by, a re-ordering of the chapters, the
order of which was left unspecified by Kafka at his death. Mr Uytersprot bases his arrangement on a meticulous examination of the events
of the plot and also on the indications of the progress of the seasons during the last fateful year of Joseph K.'s life—that from his 30th to his
31st birthday—which is the time-span of the novel. Noting that
Kafka writes in his diary (May 2nd 1913) that he is striving to cure
his own neurasthenia by work, this critic goes on to demonstrate the
stealthy but unremitted development of a neurosis in Joseph K. until
he is portrayed as a man completely alienated from others and concerned only with his own subjective reactions—a state of ego-
obsession to which Dante's pilgrim never succumbed. We see this
disease:

> approach and its ever more penetrating effects: . . . (K.'s) tendency to
> refer everything to himself . . . the discrepancy of which he grows pro-
> gressively more strongly and painfully aware between his will to be normal
> and . . . his torturous wavering between deed and dreams . . .   p. 143

That *The Trial* does indeed, at one level of interpretation, represent
in symbols the struggle in one mind, divided against itself, is suggested
from the beginning of the novel. In the first chapter the men who
enter the hero's bedroom when he is lying between sleep and wake
and whom he never remembers to have seen before, choose exactly
a moment when elements up to then firmly repressed may be likely to
float into consciousness. In the diary for 1st February, 1922, Kafka
specifically refers to his own experience of this:

> The period before falling wearily asleep is really the time when no
> ghosts haunt one; they are all dispersed; only as the night advances do

* *The Trial: its structure*. In *Franz Kafka Today*.

they return, in the morning they have all assembled again . . . and now in
a healthy person, the daily dispersal of them begins anew.   p. 410

The implication is clear: for Kafka himself as for Joseph K. these
ghosts too often remained.

As Joseph K. gets out of bed to face the ordinary demands of an
ordinary day, he realizes, with something of a shock, that he has
already admitted 'the stranger's right to an interest in his actions', and
when he decides to cross the room it means 'wrenching himself away
from the two men (though they were standing at quite a distance from
him)'. They 'had dared to seize him in his own dwelling'. But he
believed he was still free, should he choose to exert his freedom
(pp. 7–11). The warders go on to devour K.'s breakfast and one of
them claims that:

we . . . probably mean better by you and stand closer to you than any
other people in the world.   p. 12

In fact when he wants to show his identification papers the chief
warder cries: 'What are your papers to us?' which if they are indeed
a part of himself is obviously true.

Only after this intimate relationship has been established is the Law
explicitly named. The cold finger of fear touches us when the senior
warder claims that his employers 'as the Law decrees, are drawn
towards the guilty'. If the warders are projections of K.'s own mind,
he here implies his knowledge of his guilt even while he immediately
goes on to deny it:

'I don't know this Law,' said K. 'All the worse for you,' replied the
warder. 'And it probably exists nowhere but in your own head,' said K.
          p. 13

Is it a coincidence that after this the only breakfast K. allows himself
is 'a fine apple which he had laid out the night before' (p. 14) and of
which 'the first few bites' assure him that it is better than any food
the warders might have brought him. Although it is acceptable at a
completely naturalistic level, it cannot fail to suggest also the external
tribunal of the One who walked in the Garden in the cool of the day.

It is the inter-relationship of the two separate 'worlds' in which
Joseph K.'s life comes to be lived that most vividly reproduces the
landscape of a mental break-down. At first the familiar surroundings
and demands of a life where he is admired and successful banish all
thoughts of his trial from K.'s mind. Then for several months the

two worlds are as it were conflated. He carries the obsession with his trial to his place of work, the bank, but while actually there he can still *faire front* to his fellows, disguise his pre-occupation and draw on the resources of his habitual skills to carry him through. As René Dauvin has perceptively remarked,* experiences concerning K.'s private world tend, at the beginning of the story, to occur only at night and on Sundays, that is to say at times when the defences of routine reactions are absent. Increasingly however this dual living so exhausts him, and his obsession becomes so demanding, that thoughts of his trial obtrude continuously in his consciousness, and the conflict induces a lassitude that prevents his carrying on his routine duties effectively. He has moreover continually to defend himself against the prying observation which he senses or imagines from superiors and inferiors alike:

> At last K. was alone. He had not the slightest intention of interviewing any more clients and vaguely realized how pleasant it was that the people waiting outside believed him to be still occupied with the manufacturer, so that nobody, not even the attendant, would disturb him. He went over to the window, perched on the sill, holding onto the latch with one hand, and looked down on the square below. The snow was still falling, the sky had not yet cleared.
>
> For a long time he sat like this, without knowing what really troubled him. p. 147

Very shortly before the thirty-first birthday which was to be his body's death-day, Joseph K. was seized by an irrational impulse to visit his mother whom he had not seen for three years and who was now in extreme old age.† Possibly the fulfilment of the impulse to return to the source of his being might have been significant for him, but the visit was apparently never made since the ability for action was leaving K.:

> he had lately noticed a certain plaintiveness in himself, a tendency to give way without a struggle to all his desires. p. 260

This flaccidity of purpose could lead to death but prevented all search for a source of renewed life. Kafka, however, chose not to develop the symbol, and the chapter was abandoned. Maybe it was completed in another language by another poet in *Molloy*.

---

* *Franz Kafka Today*, p. 146.
† v. Uncompleted Chapters in *The Trial*, Secker & Warburg (1956).

It has already been suggested that it is his own destructive impulses which lead Joseph K. to the quarry where his throat is cut. There is an incident on the walk there which suggests that he had still the power to change his direction had any stimulus to life elicited a response. The only object of possible desire, however, was fleeting and but dimly perceived; it gave no sufficient motive for resistance to the death-wish which held him in its grip:

> He (K.) halted, and in consequence the others halted too; they stood on the verge of an open, deserted square adorned with flower-beds. . . . And then before them Fraülein Bürstner appeared, mounting a small flight of steps leading into the square from a low-lying side-street. It was not quite certain that it was she, but the resemblance was close enough. . . . They suffered him now to lead the way, and he followed the direction taken by the Fraülein ahead of him. . . . (She) meanwhile had bent into a side-street, but by this time K. could do without her land submitted himself to the guidance of his escort.   pp. 247–8

Through a neurosis the introspective man discovers many aspects of his self before unknown to him. In so far as he can come to terms with these and incorporate them into the organization of his conscious self, he can live with them, knowing the truth of himself better than before. In so far as he fails in this task the newly discovered elements of his self will tear his personality apart and destroy him. The story of such an experience is therefore a modern version of the journey into the depths which may or may not be followed by a climb upwards to salvation. Whether the search is for a reconciliation with the self or for a reconciliation with God, man's reason alone is inadequate to bring it to success. Knowledge of the previously unconscious elements of the self is not, in the beginning at least, made available by rational analysis; it comes by way of dreams and images, is apprehended by intuition and its truth proved only by experience. The same is true of the neophyte's search for a divine power external to himself, and the one may therefore be an image of the other. Just as his passage through the Inferno revealed to Dante's pilgrim both his own essence and the evil which was an intrinsic part of the universe outside his self, so Joseph K.'s exploration of his own awareness of guilt and innocence reflects mankind's unending search for the knowledge of an ultimate good—in this case perhaps Justice—which he hopes is a part of universal reality. But the reality which he discovers is flawed by forces of evil and destruction. Unlike Dante's, Joseph K.'s search is unavailing. It leaves him with the belief that if such an ultimate justice exists—and he sees the light burning in the tabernacle of the Law—yet he can never hope to reach it. He must yet he cannot. Unless he is mistaken the dichotomy is absolute:

> Le combat spirituel est aussi brutal que la bataille d'hommes; mais la vision de la justice est le plaisir de Dieu seul.*

Here we may return for a moment to the thought of the seasons. Joseph K. dies in the Spring, and as he says, he dies 'like a dog'—that is like an animal, for whom, in the Western mythos, there can be no resurrection. But Spring, in that same mythos, is the season for both death and re-birth. After the three days in the tomb came Easter morning. Joseph K. dies without hope, but he walks to his death through trees in full blossom, and he sees Fräulein Bürstner moving down a turning off his route. He is still aware of a world which he has not entered. But is the reader justified in assuming that Kafka intends the unfamiliar world into which the heroes of *The Trial* and *The Castle* strive to batter their way as being truly a better or a more important world than the world they leave? Is a precarious mental balance, however much more knowledge it integrates, of more value than a stable organization of less? Is a right relationship with 'Justice', or even with 'God', more important than a right relationship with one's employer or one's employees? Kafka's personal life suggests his positive answer. While writing *The Trial* he deliberately gave up the world imaged by Joseph K.'s bank so that he might devote himself to the different values of the world of his writing. Joseph K. therefore cannot have been condemned by his creator for leaving the sterile though balanced world of his earlier existence. His fault was his failure first to realize the nature of the world of the Law and then to attempt to take it by force, and he receives acquittal neither from himself nor from Another. The tension which informs *The Trial* is exerted between the poles of a rational and sensory apprehension of daily life, and an intuitive apprehension of a hidden righteousness. This latter is the light in the priest's parable, which streams from the sanctuary; that the man concerned has failed to discover a means of entering the door is tragic, not meaningless. The hardness of the journey is the measure of its importance. The necessity moreover of the guidance, which is missing for all Kafka's heroes, suggests something which he

---

* A. Rimbaud. *Une Saison en Enfer.*

must have himself experienced but not something which he believed inevitable. In his diary for 12th May, 1922, he copied the following from the Vedas:

O beloved, even as a man brought blindfold from the land of the Gandharians and then set free in the desert will wander east or north or south, for in blindness was he brought there and in blindness was set free; yet after someone has struck the blindfold from his eyes and said to him: 'Thither dwell the Gandharians, go ye thither', after having asked his way from village to village, enlightened and made wise he comes home to the Gandharians—so too a man who has found a teacher here below knows: I shall belong to this earthly evil until I am redeemed, and then I shall return home. p. 420

With *The Castle* we turn from Kafka's Inferno to his Purgatorio. Its opening is truly Dantesque in quality; K. stands at the foot of Mount Purgatory but the top of the mountain is out of sight.

It was late in the evening when K. arrived. The village was deep in snow. The Castle hill was hidden, veiled in mist and darkness, nor was there even a glimmer of light to show that a castle was there. On the wooden bridge leading from the main road to the village K. stood for a long time gazing into the illusory emptiness above him. p. 11

The mystery is conveyed in the last phrase. Is it the emptiness which is the illusion as mankind gazes in the upper air, or is the castle an imagined one, peopled only with the phantasmagoria of the onlooker's unconscious mind? Only the 'leap' into the Absurd can give man a positive answer to his perpetual and anguished questioning.

The relationship between Dante's universe and Kafka's is only partial, however, for in *The Castle* as in *The Trial*, no helper is at hand; neither Virgil nor Cato finds a representative in Kafka's work, and the attendant angels are represented only by the enigmatic assistants, Arthur and Jeremiah, the illusive Barnabas and the other equivocal officials who descend in their carriages to carry on their master's incomprehensible affairs. Edwin Honig* considers the loneliness of Kafka's seekers after truth to be one of the main causes of their failure to find it:

That Kafka's heroes persistently refuse the didactic aid of helpers or choose the wrong ones is the reason why they fail; . . . It is as though the

* *Dark Conceit: the making of Allegory*, Oxford University Press (1960).

typical formula for the Christian hero, which Dante set up and Bunyan renewed, had been adopted (sic) by Kafka's with all the old terms intact save the consolation of a supernatural grace. Kafka's incomplete adaptation of the formula suggests those picture-puzzles appearing in the old Sunday supplements under the caption, 'What's Wrong with this Picture?' Thus challenged the guileless reader would soon discover the unlikely three-legged table, the one-eyed girl, or the boy without a nose. The lack of real helpers, with the implication of some disorientation of the guiding intelligence, has a determining effect on the allegorical narrative. p. 76

Dante does not only accept the existence of divine guidance; believing in a divinely rational universe, he accepts also the relevance of human reason to the task of exploring it. It is only when the pilgrim has surmounted the last cornice of the mountain and is cleansed from all the sins whose reality was revealed in the Inferno, that human wisdom becomes incapable of guiding him further and resigns in favour of 'Beatrice'. Kafka also allows a meeting between K. and his potential Beatrice, whom he first sees drawing beer in the inn, but the results are different. K. is dimly aware of her as in touch with the world he is so intent to seek and therefore as a messenger of 'grace'; his mistake is to attempt to manipulate her as a means to his own ends. He does not submit to her, reverence her nor in any sense 'love' her; instead he desires to make use of her and finds too late that she has eluded him beyond recapture.

The Trial and *The Castle* are obviously companion pieces. Louis MacNeice has described them as 'Everyman persecuted and Everyman shut out'.* More important is Max Brod's interpretation, given in his *Additional Note to The Castle*:

> In The Trial and The Castle then, are represented the two manifested forms of the Godhead (in the sense of the *Cabbala*), justice and grace.
>
> p. 313

These are the same forms of Godhead as are made manifest even more authoritatively in *The Divine Comedy*.

Camus also distinguishes between the heroes of the two greatest novels; he admits the guilt of Joseph K. in *The Trial* but claims that the guilt of K. in *The Castle* is difficult to establish.† However Maja Goth draws nearer to the heart of Kafka's creation:

---

* *Varieties of Parable*, p. 137.
† v. *Mythe de Sisyphe*, p. 18.

FRANZ KAFKA

Le tort des deux héros consiste dans le fait qu'ils fuient leur être-coupable. La culpabilité est essentielle à leur condition humaine. Ils en sont conscients, mais ils essaient d'en détourner les yeux.*

Here we shall consider the novels as imaging two consecutive phases of the same pilgrimage. Avoiding the destruction which overcame Joseph K. in the first phase, K. succeeds in leaving the world of the daily human round, not, like his predecessor, to sink to his destruction but, after a long journey, to see before him the goal he seeks. When he sees it, however, it is incomprehensible and even unattractive. He uses inappropriate or grossly mistaken means in his efforts to reach it and is destroyed by his efforts as completely as was his namesake in *The Trial*. In contrast to Dante's steady ascent up the spiral of the mountain, travelling by daylight and resting at each recurring dusk, Kafka allots to K. a confused and hectic exploration of lanes which lead nowhere or wind back upon themselves and where the pressure to continue comes not from assured confidence but from near despair of ever gaining the world of the upper air so desperately sought. There is an entry in the diaries† for 16th January, 1922, which conveys something of this dilemma:

> The clocks are not in unison; the inner one runs crazily on at a devilish or demoniac or in any case inhuman pace, the outer one limps along at its usual speed. What else can happen but that the two worlds split apart. . . .

He speaks of 'the wild tempo of the inner process' and continues:

> I can—can I?—manage to keep my feet somewhat and be carried along in the wild pursuit. Where, then, shall I be brought? 'Pursuit' indeed, is only a metaphor. I can also say, 'assault on the last earthly frontier', an assault, moreover, launched from below, from mankind, and since this too is a metaphor, I can replace it by the metaphor of an assault from above, aimed at one from above.   pp. 398–9

The 'assault from above' was a metaphor also to Sartre, when he wrote of Orestes that his freedom crashed down on him like a thunder-bolt, but it was a reality to Sophocles, when he makes the demon strike at Oedipus from without, as it was to Eliot when, in *Family Reunion* Harry submits to 'the love and terror' which pursued him but would not let him fall. Kafka seems at times to hover uneasily

---

* *Kafka et les lettres françaises*, p. 131.
† *The Diaries of Franz Kafka, 1910–1923*. Ed. Max Brod, Penguin (1964).

between the statements of metaphor and those of fact—as Beckett also does by implication, as when, in a world where Godot never comes, 'They' at last convey Molloy to his desired haven. The nature of Kafka's world 'above'—the world of the Castle—is deducible only indirectly even at the end of the novel. An extended metaphor, exactly parallel to that in the diary is the story of the assault launched by K. from the village, upward at the castle from whose threshold descend the officials and servants who forever repulse his efforts. The diary continues pertinently:

> All such writing is an assault on the frontier.   p. 399

Kafka can write with passion of his longing for the straight road. The diary entry for 10th February, 1922, runs:

> Attacked right and left as I am by overwhelming forces, it is plain as can be that I cannot escape either to the right or to the left—straight on only, starved beast, lies the road to food that will sustain you, air that you can breathe, a free life, even if it should take you beyond life.

The route followed by Kafka must have resembled that trodden by K. and Joseph K. It could certainly be claimed for K. that he looks neither to right nor left; his gaze is obsessively fixed on his single aim —to enter the Castle, but the road he follows is a labyrinthine path on which he becomes exhausted while no further than a stone's throw from his starting point.

Before K. realizes the full difficulty of access to the Castle he makes the simplest of his attempts to reach it; he sets out to walk to it, first alone and then with help. The first journey, by the snow-covered road out of the village, leads him in circles until he is thankful to be driven back to the inn on a peasant's sledge. The second begins under better auspices. K. is at the inn:

> A man came cleaving his way with rapid steps through the group, bowed before K. and handed him a letter. K. took it, but looked at the man, who for the moment seemed to him the more important. . . . He was clothed nearly all in white, not in silk of course; he was in winter clothes like all the others, but the material he was wearing had the softness and dignity of silk. His face was clear and frank, his eyes larger than ordinary. His smile was unusually joyous; . . . 'Who are you?' asked K. 'My name is Barnabas,' said he, 'I am a messenger.'   p. 27

A strange angel indeed to one who remembers the great winged figures who guard and lead the souls on Dante's mountain; nevertheless when he believes that Barnabas is returning to the Castle, K. entrusts himself to his protection and guidance:

> K. took his arm. . . . and they moved away from the inn. K. realized indeed that his utmost efforts could not enable him to keep pace with Barnabas, that he was a drag on him, . . . The effort which it cost him merely to keep going made him lose control of this thoughts.   pp. 33–4

Nevertheless K. refuses to let go his hold:

> He took a firmer hold, Barnabas was almost dragging him along, the silence was unbroken. . . . He vowed to himself that however difficult the way and however doubtful even the prospect of his being able to get back, he would not cease from going on. He would surely have enough strength to let himself be dragged. And the road must come to an end sometime. By day the Castle looked within easy reach, and, of course, the messengers would take the shortest cut.   p. 44

The road does come to an end, but K. has been deceived or has deceived himself:

> 'Where are we?' asked K. in a low voice . . . 'At home,' said Barnabas . . . 'Be careful now, sir, or you'll slip. We go down here'. 'Down?' 'Only a step or two,' added Barnabas, and was already knocking at a door.
>
> p. 35

The door is of a cottage on the outskirts of the village; K. is no nearer the Castle. After this he no longer attempts a direct ascent of the mountain.

Any interpretation of K.'s efforts to gain the Castle involves an understanding of the relationship between the village and the Castle and also of that between the village and the land beyond the bridge from which K. came and to which, if he chose, he could return. For there are three regions represented in *The Castle*, not two, as some critics appear to think. Though it may seem rash to put aside the interpretation of Max Brod, the intimate friend who had listened to Kafka talking of the novel as it was being written, yet an alternative to Brod's two world reading does appear to be necessary. In *The Castle* there is first the world from which K. has come and to which Frieda urges him to return, because she is sure that only there can the marriage with K., which she so longs for, be consummated with some hope of peace and joy. In that land is the church with the beautiful tower which, in a moment of nostalgia, K. contrasts so favourably with that of the Castle. It is the land, however, which K. has deliberately left in his search for something 'other', and he absolutely refuses to return. Next there is the village, which K. calls 'this desolate country' with its church, a barnlike structure with no tower, no power to give either courage or hope. Finally there is the Castle, inefficient, unethical and entirely incomprehensible, looking, now that K. is near enough to see it with his own eyes, like a mere huddle of village houses, its tower:

> mantled with ivy . . . and topped by what looked like an attic, with battlements that were irregular, broken, fumbling, as if designed by the trembling or careless hand of a child, clearly outlined against the blue. It was as if a melancholy-mad tenant who ought to have been locked up in the topmost chamber of his house had burst through the roof and lifted himself up to the gaze of the world.   p. 20

Sometimes indeed Kafka's diaries do show him thinking in terms of a simple duality, and then the contrast is between a world of straight-forward sensuous living, which he longs to inhabit, and another of arduous endeavour and existential anguish. Only in the latter can he fulfil the compulsion to write and the equally urgent compulsion to find himself, in freedom from the domination of a loved and hated father and of the family life which at other times he longed to share. Writing of his father on 28th January, 1922, the diary continues:

> He would not let me live in it, in his world . . . I am now a citizen of this other world whose relationship to the ordinary one is the relationship of the wilderness to the cultivated land . . . I am the wretchedest of creatures in the desert too, and Canaan is perforce my only Promised Land, for no third place exists for mankind.

This is not the whole truth as Kafka knows it, however, for later in the famous Letter to his father he speaks of a world divided into three parts, a part for the slaves, a part for the masters and a part where men can live free and happy, and where orders are neither given nor obeyed. Here at last is an image of three spheres of experience, and we can hope that it gives us the clue to the three worlds of *The Castle*. A further quotation suggests that it was his pathological relationship with his father which prevented Kafka from enjoying either the world of family commitments or the world of leadership and power both of which his father's arbitrary authoritarianism made repellent and yet desirable:

> Sometimes I imagine a map of the world spread out flat and you stretched out diagonally across it. And what I feel then is that only those territories come into question for my life that either are not covered by you or are not within your reach.*

From this we may deduce that the 'not very comforting territory' is the village, and K.'s early impression of its inhabitants bears out this interpretation:

> the peasants . . . stood gaping at him with their open mouths, coarse lips, and literally tortured faces—their heads looked as if they had been beaten flat on top and their features as if the pain of the beating had twisted them to the present shape. p. 36

The following diary entry for October 19th, 1921 is also relevant to any interpretation of the novels:

> The essence of the Wandering in the Wilderness. A man . . . is on the track of Canaan all his life; it is incredible he should see the land only when he is on the verge of death. This dying vision of it can only be intended to illustrate how incomplete a moment is human life . . . Moses fails to enter Canaan not because his life is too short but because it is a human life.
>
> pp. 393–4

This reveals the meaning both of the light which the dying man could see within the sanctuary only when he was too weak to reach it and of the message that K. could remain within the Castle's territory, which reached him only on his death bed.

We have now found parallels in Kafka's personal life for the land beyond the bridge and for the village of *The Castle*. The first region K. abandons and to it he refuses to return, although Frieda desires it, and when K. will not take her to it, she leaves him and returns to her ambiguous relationship with the personnel of the Castle. The village is a wilderness where Kafka lived alone and unhappy as he struggled to write, and which K. refused to leave for the sake of marriage with Frieda, although he longed for marriage and believed he loved her. K.'s quest and K.'s frustration are Kafka's own.

And the Castle? It is the region that Kafka believed he had never

---

* Quoted in *Franz Kafka Today*, p. 189.

reached but to which his books surely belong. It is Dante's Paradise, the world of integrated being, the world of artistic achievement, of justice and mercy, the world of God, forever beyond the grasp of man, but for ever sending him messages or intuitions which he cannot interpret but which he neglects at his peril.

> And my ending is despair
> Unless I be relieved by prayer.*

And not by prayer only. Kafka himself used another sword of the spirit, one with which he endowed also his namesake of *The Castle* —persistence. In the last entry of the diary written less than a year before his death, following the words: 'incapable of anything but pain' there comes this concluding paragraph—not a paragraph of despair certainly, although carrying no note of any easy optimism.

> More and more fearful as I write. It is understandable. Every word . . . becomes a spear turned against the speaker . . . The only consolation would be: it happens whether you like it or no. And what you like is of infinitesimally little help. More consolation is: You too have weapons.   p. 423

Kafka can claim to stand with those:

> Who are only undefeated
> Because we have gone on trying;
> We, content at the last
> If our temporal reversion nourish
> (Not too far from the yew-tree)
> The life of significant soil.†

* *The Tempest*, Epilogue.
† T. S. Eliot. *Four Quartets: The Dry Salvages*, p. 33.

CHAPTER 6

Samuel Beckett: The Ambiguous Journey

I thought it was necessary for me... to reject as absolutely false everything as to which I could imagine the least grounds of doubt... thus because our senses deceive us I wished to suppose that nothing is just as they cause us to imagine it to be; and because there are men to deceive themselves in their reasoning .... I rejected as false all the reasons formerly accepted by me as demonstrations. . . . But immediately afterwards I noticed that while I thus wished to think all things false, it was absolutely essential that the 'I' who thought this should be somewhat... 'I think, therefore I am' was so certain... that I could accept it without scruple.

DESCARTES. *Philosophical Works* I

All I know is . . . life without tears, as it is wept.   *Molloy*

i JOURNEYINGS AND WAITINGS

I trundle along rapidly now on my ruined feet.   *Eneug.* 1

Our Father who art no more in heaven than on earth or in hell, I neither want nor desire that thy name be hallowed, thou knowest best what suits thee. . . .*

THIS, the opening of Moran's *Pater*, at first sight blasphemous, proves on closer inspection entirely orthodox, yet although his query, 'Was Youdi's (i.e. Jehovah's) business address still 8, Arcadia Square?'† is no more than pleasantly flippant, a later remark is both heretical and sceptical:

I would never do to my bees the wrong I had done my God, to whom I had been taught to ascribe my angers, fears, desires, and even my body.‡

* *Molloy*, p. 179 (London: Calder, 1959; New York: Grove Press, 1959). First published London 1938.
† Ibid., p. 180.   ‡ Ibid., p. 82.

Here the refusal of Christian dogma is shot through with the nostalgia of 'the wrong I had done my God', and the three quotations, taken together, show up with some fairness the ambiguities of Beckett's mythology, and of the emotional attitudes which underlie it. Perhaps the ambiguities are finally unresolvable, but analysis of the elements of the myths may, it is hoped, elucidate them to some degree.

The Father who is no more in heaven than on earth appears nevertheless with fair regularity in Beckett's works. Mr Knott,* who is perhaps the primordial Nought, walks in the garden in the cool of the day and finds it difficult to see where he is going; Youdi,† whose name, if spelled Yehudi, would recall the Jewish Yahveh, who has his messenger Gaber, a bowler-hatted Gabriel, to carry his enigmatic instructions to men; the suggestively named Mr Godot,‡ for whom the tramps wait, together with Molloy's unnamed They, may all be figments of the minds that project them, but their imperatives are categorical. Moreover there are here no Daughters of God to bear man grace or reconcile truth with mercy.§ The pressure which imposes the pilgrimage appears merely cruel, and together with the predestined culmination in apparent failure it is the hub from which all Beckett's tragedies radiate.

Movement figures in all Beckett's myths. Their characters travel by bicycle, by autocycle, in dung cart, motor or train; helped often by sticks or umbrellas, they walk, hobble, drive each other, swing between crutches or grovel forward flat on belly or back; they may even consider rolling rather than stay inert. Perhaps they first started out with the enthusiasm of the Old Woman in *The Chairs*, who knows that:

> there are some happy people. In the morning they breakfast in an aeroplane, they have their mid-day meal on a train and in the evening they dine at sea. They spend the night in lorries that go rumbling, rumbling, rumbling. . . . ||

The happiness soon fades.

The commands which enforce this frenzied mobility, whether they are believed to come from within or from without the self, are apparently irresistible, although those who obey them retain for the most

---

* *Watt*, Olympia Press (1958), (first published 1953).
† *Molloy*.
‡ *Waiting for Godot* (London: Faber, 1956; New York: Grove Press).
§ v. Psalm 85 v. 10 and 11.
|| Ionesco. *Plays I* (London: Calder; New York: Grove Press).

part a belief in their own freedom or at least in the possibility of attaining it. Their movement leads them nowhere, unless it is circular, so that they return to their point of departure, and this may indeed fulfil their heart's desire.

Molloy believes that he has learnt to travel in a straight line. Since the man without guidance who thinks he is moving in a straight line usually moves in a circle, Molloy decides that by trying to move in a circle he is likely to achieve a straight line. In the matter of escaping from the forest this technique proves valid, which amounts to saying that it works among the nonsensical trivia of everyday life. In the matter of his concern with his mother, however, it is inapplicable, and it is by the completion of the circle that he returns at last to the bed on which he was born.

It is in *Murphy* that Beckett uses most brilliantly the image of the reflection of the self which evokes horror and remorse and is thus a climactic moment, or even a turning point in the Journey. Murphy seeks to escape from the material macrocosm in the belief that his true self can function only when detached from what he calls the 'big world' and concerned solely with the microcosm, or mental 'little world', as apprehended by one single self. In the Magdalen Mental Mercyseat, a mental hospital, he finds in the patients:

> that self-immersed indifference to the contingencies of the contingent world which he had chosen for himself as the only felicity and achieved so seldom.   p. 168

Murphy therefore resolves to leave his Celia and any other small things, such as ginger, which could make the external world attractive to him and emulate the 'absolute impassivity of the higher schizoids', who, 'in the face of the most pitiless therapeutic bombardments', remained secure within the microcosm of their own minds. He fetches from the room he had been sharing with Celia the rocking chair, whose rhythmic movement had proved so far to be the most effective means of obliterating his awareness of external reality, and installs himself at the Magdalen Mental Mercyseat as a male nurse. He has one moment of triumph:

> 'Do you know what it is?' said Ticklepenny, 'no offence meant, you had a great look of Clarke there a minute ago.'
>
> Clarke had been for three weeks in a catatonic stupor. . . .
>
> The gratified look that Murphy disdained to hide so alarmed Ticklepenny that he . . . rose to go.

Murphy is delighted to find:

> that the self whom he loved had the aspect, even to Ticklepenny's inexpert eye, of a real alienation. Or to put it perhaps more nicely: conferred that aspect on the self whom he hated.   pp. 193–4

But Murphy discovered his satisfaction to be an illusion, and he discovered it in this way. Being on night duty he visited an inmate whom he particularly admired for his remoteness, and took the opportunity of seizing the patient's head and gazing intently into his unseeing eyes. This experience Murphy accepts as a revelation of ultimate truth and he formally enunciates it aloud:

> 'The last Mr Murphy saw of Mr Endon was Mr Murphy unseen by Mr Endon. This was also the last Murphy saw of Murphy'. . . .
> A long rest.
> 'Mr Murphy is a speck in Mr Endon's unseen.'   p. 250

After this unnerving revelation Murphy decides to return to the macrocosm and to Celia, and to start again. But during one last taste of oblivion on his rocking chair, he dies in a gas explosion. He had started the second phase of the journey too late.

The most elaborately conceived journeys are those of the pair presented in *Molloy*, and these we reserve for more detailed consideration later. In *How It Is*,* Beckett's last novel, the quality of the nightmare has changed. The humour of *Murphy*, the richly poetic language of *Watt*, together with their varied scenery, have disappeared, and in their place are a sparse laconic speech and bleak vistas of an unending sea of grey mud. After a close-up of one of the 'pseudo couples',† the eternally shifting pairs of victim and executioner, who wallow across it, our vision is extended to include the endless procession of human pairs moving 'abandoned so on infinitely' (p. 149). Dante's descent and re-ascent are here reduced to:

> imagination on the decline having attained the bottom what one calls sinking one is tempted
> or ascending heaven at last no place like it in the end.
> or not stirring that too that's defendable half in the mud half out   p. 112

Since reason can discover no possibility of discharge from this appalling

---

* (London: Calder, 1964; New York: Grove Press, 1964).
† Beckett's own description of Mercier and Commier in *The Unnamable* (London: Calder; New York: Grove Press).

pilgrimage, Beckett, in this work, allows no hope of one to shine even on the distant horizon which Molloy glimpses from the edge of the dark forest.* The only future divined as perhaps endurable is a world where the single slender comfort of our present existence is denied us, along with its corresponding and inevitable anguish:

> one perhaps there is one perhaps somewhere merciful enough to shelter such frolics where no one ever abandons any one and no one ever waits for any one and never two bodies touch.   p. 156

For Beckett time, the destroyer, is continually at work on the erosion of man's feeble constructs, material and mental, and this of course includes both their personal qualities and anything they have achieved of a self.

> Time hath, my lord, a wallet at his back,
> Wherein he puts alms for oblivion.†

In *Waiting for Godot* men stay still, but time moves, and we watch men disintegrate under its flow. People soon cease to recognize one another, and Lucky's famous tirade‡ is the unorganized material of a being completely broken down.

The stripping of the self to its bare bones is a recurrent theme. In *Endgame*, Hamm is even more helpless in his invalid chair than Molloy and Malone in their beds, since unlike them he is blind. Hamm has perhaps made the first half of the journey and lost his sight at the vision of his own failure, which was a failure in love, but although he has not made a single step on the upward path, he yet keeps some dignity in decay. As his memory fades and the dust-bin lids are mercifully closed at last, he retains the power to suffer stoically. Krapp,§ on the other hand, reliving his own past by means of his tape-recorder, is as disorganized and pathetic in his mental masturbation as Lucky.

Winnie,‖ immobilized in her sand-heap, shows that the powers of motion, thought, judgment and feeling steadily recede with the passage of time. The play's pattern in this respect is that of *The Summoning of Everyman*, but for Winnie her lost faculties are replaced not by the words of Knowledge but by the escapist patter of her society's current fashions. The three characters of *Play* have attempted to live more intensely, but their attempts have destroyed them; in the urns which

---

* v. inf. p. 160.   † *Troilus and Cressida*. III. 3.
‡ *Waiting for Godot*, pp. 42–4.   § *Krapp's Last Tape*, Faber (1959).
‖ *Happy Days*, Faber (1962).

confine them after death they are not more ineffective than they were in life and are quite as unimportant.

In describing Murphy's retreat from the Magdalen Mental Mercy-seat Beckett introduces the clothes imagery which figures in other novels and in the plays.

> He raised his face to the starless sky, abandoned, patient, the sky, not the face, which was abandoned only. He took off his shoes and socks and threw them away. . . . He took off his clothes one by one as he went, quite forgetting they did not belong to him, and threw them away. When he was naked he lay down in a tuft of soaking tuffets and tried to get a picture of Celia.   p. 251

'Off, off you lendings'. The process is described in more detail as Moran discards his clothes on the last lap of his journey home:

> But I kept my tie, I even wore it knotted round my bare neck, out of sheer bravado I suppose. It was a spotted tie, but I forget the colour.*

This discarding of the clothes may, as in Shakespeare's plays, betoken an approach to death, for:

> Ah! when the ghost begins to quicken,
> Confusion of the death-bed over, is it sent
> Out naked on the road, as the books say,
> And stricken by the injustice of the skies for punishment?†

It is also a symbolic suicide, though none of Beckett's heroes do in actuality take this way of escape. More important perhaps is the suggestion that time, or the individual himself, is breaking down the machine through which alone the mind can think and know. The mind is thus forced in on itself as the body weakens, and perhaps this is, for some, a way to truth. Molloy is almost helpless physically before he is ordered to write his record of the experience he has amassed. But Malone,‡ equally deprived of all bodily functions, knows that with their surcease the mind dies also.

> It is there I die unbeknown to my stupid flesh. That which is seen, that which cries and writhes, my witless remains. Somewhere in this turmoil thought struggles on, it too wide of the mark. It too seeks me, as it always has, where I am not to be found.   p. 9

---

* *Molloy*, p. 183.
† W. B. Yeats, *The Cold Heaven*. C.P., p. 140.
‡ *Malone Dies* (London: Calder, 1958; New York: Grove Press).

So even the mind is not equated with the self.

Beckett forces us to recognize that no evidence can be found on which to base a belief in the existence either of man or of a deity worthy of his worship, yet at the same time his agnosticism will not permit him to assert the contrary. The machines by which we strive to extend our bodily powers, are like the clothes by which we attempt to disguise our nakedness and are as frail as they; indeed Molloy's bicycle, thrown into a hedge by Lousse, is broken long before his fragile legs lose their power to support him. All this is commonplace, yet it has been suggested that it proves Beckett's pessimism concerning the unreality of any individual identity. Actually it is irrelevant to the possibilities that a conscious and integrated self may or may not be developed to use the body while it exists and functions as a unit in the material universe.

Man's head and feet are there to be made use of while they last; they are scarcely more a part of himself than the hats and boots which sometimes cover them, and which can be lost or exchanged without much importance attaching to the fact. It is not his body man is concerned to find on his hard journey, yet he is never completely successful in discovering any other self, although he gains glimpses which are sufficient to set him up in hope or thrust him into despair. The search for the self is as ambiguous and inconclusive as the search for God. Naturally Beckett shows men's bodies as subject to decay. Whatever we achieve, unless we die before, we shall at last become senile like Krapp, living only on the ever fainter memories of our intellectual attainments and emotional satisfactions.

Occasionally the traveller reaches some kind of an oasis on his journey, in which he escapes for a while from the flux of time. Murphy is seeking such an escape in his rocking chair and in the Magdalen Mental Mercyseat. Watt* inhabits temporarily a region of incomprehensible commandments and events which cannot be verbalized in human speech, and where he discovers a strange peace and even perhaps a purpose, valid though incomprehensible.

For Watt now found himself in the midst of things which, if they consented to be named, did so as it were with reluctance. And the state in which Watt found himself resisted formulation in a way no state had ever done, in which Watt had ever found himself, and Watt had found himself in a great many states, in his day.   p. 88

* *Watt.*

Watt is now in contact with ineffable things:

> Looking at a pot, for example, or thinking of a pot, at one of Mr Knott's
> pots, of one of Mr Knott's pots, it was in vain that Watt said, Pot, pot.
> . . . it was not a pot of which one could say, pot, pot, and be comforted.
>
> pp. 88–9

The place, the journey to it and the anti-climax which ensues is described to Watt by an earlier pilgrim. The peace of the first morning
in Purgatory appears to have been reached, but when the tear-smirched
face looks up, there is no Virgil there to wipe it clean,* and hopes fade
into the macabre grotesqueness of the human condition:

> Then at night rest in the quiet house, there are no roads, no streets any
> more . . . How I feel it all again . . . like a face raised, a face offered, all
> trust and innocence and candour, all the old soil and fear and weakness
> offered, to be sponged away and forgiven! . . . All the old ways led to this,
> all the old windings, the stairs with never a landing that you screw yourself
> up, clutching the rail, counting the steps, the fever of shortest ways under
> the long lids of sky, the wild country roads where your dead walk beside
> you, on the dark shingle the turning for the last time again to the lights of
> the little town, . . . All led to this, to the gloaming where a middle-aged man
> sits masturbating his snout, waiting for the first dawn to break. pp. 42–3

This is reminiscent of Kafka's world; Watt does succeed in reaching
Mr Knott's house, to which he has been summoned, and unlike 'K.'†
is able to enter the mysterious precincts, he does not know how. But
once inside the house its ways are incomprehensible to him, and soon
he is obliged to leave it and tread again his *via dolorosa*, on which he
suffers the mockery of the soldiers and tastes the bitterness of the
sponge, which for him, was dipped not in vinegar but in the filthy
bucket of a jakes. As a recent critic‡ of Beckett has written of *Watt*
and *The Castle:*

> Both novels are however similar in that they are myths, the interpreta-
> tion of which must be a subtle and complex affair, for they have the power
> of haunting the mind on many levels without being explicit: they fulfil the
> function of a symbol of *unassigned* value: it is we who lend the symbol
> meaning from our own hopes and fears.

* v. sup., p. 57.
† In *The Castle*. v. pp. 134–5.
‡ John Fletcher: *The Novels of Samuel Beckett* (London: Chatto & Windus,
1964; New York: Barnes & Noble), p. 89.

To endure under the shadow of an unnamable and unknowable purpose becomes a form of the 'hard journey' of particular significance in Beckett's writings:

> Is there a coming that is not a coming to, a going that is not a going from, a shadow that is not the shadow of purpose, or not? For what is this shadow of the going in which we come, this shadow of the coming in which we go, this shadow of the coming and the going in which we wait, if not the shadow of purpose, of the purpose that budding withers, that withering buds, whose blooming is a budding withering?*

Since so little is achieved by movement it is not surprising that other characters achieve as much by simply refusing to budge. They wait, and in this they fulfil the mystic demands of most religions whether of East or West. Many of Beckett's characters and their activities are described in the words of a great Christian poet:

> Descend lower, descend only
> Into the world of perpetual solitude,
> World not world, but that which is not world,
> Internal darkness, deprivation
> And destitution of all property,
> Desiccation of the world of sense,
> Evacuation of the world of fancy,
> Inoperancy of the world of spirit;
> This is the one way, and the other
> Is the same, not in movement
> But abstention from movement; while the world moves
> In appetency, on its metalled ways
> Of time past and time future.†

Waiting may be as much the symbol of faith as of despair:

> I said to my soul, be still, and wait without hope
> For hope would be hope for the wrong thing; wait without love
> For love would be love of the wrong thing; there is yet faith
> But the faith and the love and the hope are all in the waiting.‡

Images of waiting are frequent in the plays, and the chances of movement are gradually diminished. In *Waiting for Godot* the tramps,

* *Watt*, p. 64.
† T. S. Eliot: *Four Quartets. Burnt Norton.*
‡ *Four Quartets. East Coker.*

hampered by bodily weakness and ill-fitting boots, wait at a cross-roads in open country. Hamm,* confined to his invalid chair, is apparently in a room, but the characters' containing envelopes grow progressively smaller as they mirror more clearly the head to which all our consciousness is confined; where as Moran says: 'all I need is to be found', and which Molloy calls:

> all that inner space one never sees, the brain and heart and other caverns where thought and feeling dance their sabbath.†

The containers—symbols of the body which sustains the thinking entity—include dustbins, beds, a glass jar, a sand-heap and finally urns fitted exactly to the bodies which occupy them. If reality is a mental phenomenon only, place becomes irrelevant and confinement of the body may be freedom. But such a divorce between the two modes of being which man experiences in his sense of identity, is inevitably a source of existential anguish. The total split in Cartesian dualism between a *res cogitans* i.e. a thinking something without spatial extension and a *res extensa* which is spatial, but lacks all mental or conscious being, is accepted as the necessary pre-requisite for scientific thought, a kind of thought which was impossible for medieval man, who 'conceived of himself as embedded in nature and intrinsically united with what he beheld'.‡ On the results of this change in men's psychological attitude to their environment, Dr Karl Stern comments:

> It implies a fearful estrangement. Just think of nature as nothing but a huge, vastly extended soul-less machine which . . . you can run but with which you have lost all contact.

The experience of birth and separation from the mother is of just such a loss of contact, and in Molloy Beckett has created a character whose anguish of alienation can be assuaged only by re-union with the mother whom he haltingly but persistently seeks throughout his adult life.

As Dr Stern insists, the new 'system' made the world a harder place to live in:

> No Pythagorean harmonies were enough to maintain the experience of the world as a shelter.   p. 124

This *Molloy* is concerned to show.

* *Endgame.*   † *Molloy*, p. 10.
‡ Karl Stern: *The Flight from Woman.* Allen & Unwin (1966), pp. 76 ff.

Another poet is equally aware of this dangerous dichotomy and writes of it in connection with a great precursor of Descartes:

> And God-appointed Berkeley that proved all things a dream,
> That this pragmatical preposterous pig of a world,
> its farrow that so solid seem,
> Must vanish on the instant if the mind but change its theme;*

Yeats voices Beckett's central ambiguity. Is the reality of God, like everything else, that of a thought in the mind? Are the 'messengers' His or man's? Has the journey a goal, men's suffering an ultimate solace, his self the possibility of ultimate integration and redemption? Or is the hard journey pains wasted? no more than 'The uncontrollable mystery on the bestial floor?'†

A popular exposition of solipsism finishes with a metaphor which is relevant here:

> Since all our knowledge is of our own mental states, nothing that is other than our own mental states can be known to exist . . . Whether anything in addition to them exists I cannot tell, since, being completely enclosed within the circle of my own ideas, eternally incarcerated in the prison house of my own experience, I cannot penetrate beyond its wall.‡

One last mythical image remains to be considered here — that of the child. The two tramps, Vladimir and Estragon, wait and suffer but not without some measure of hope. Vladimir sees Godot's boy; whether or not he is the bearer of any relevant message is less significant than the fact of his visible presence. C. G. Jung's studies of the child archetype give many examples of the different values projected on to the child, who does not merely function as a retreat from 'the burdens of modern facts and fantasies'. He may also stand for the future and so indicate the possibility of a new personality; he may be the heroic child, 'smaller than small and bigger than big', who can overcome serpents in his cradle. Most clearly he is birth and rebirth, the end and the beginning of the circle. This seems particularly relevant to Beckett's myths of the circular journey.

But the *Puer Eternus*, who is sought but eludes the seeker, is also something other than this, and again therefore Beckett's symbol is ambiguous, for the goal of the search can be an objective one, which

---

* W. B. Yeats: *Blood and the Moon*, C.P., p. 268.
† *The Magi*. Ibid., p. 141
‡ C. E. M. Joad: *A Guide to Philosophy*, Gollancz (1936), p. 56.

appears to recede as it is approached, or it can be the awareness or creation of the self which is struggling towards its birth.

> A child is a frequent symbol of the self, sometimes a divine or magical child, sometimes an ordinary figure or even a ragamuffin.*

On both counts a denial of the child is of fundamental importance:

> The eternal child in man is an indescribable experience, an incongruity and a divine prerogative, an imponderable that determines the ultimate worth or worthlessness of a personality.†

If all touch with the child image is lost despair triumphs. When Clov‡ tells him that a boy is outside but not approaching them, Hamm, who has already once refused to succour a child, faces annihilation:

> It's the end, Clov, we've come to the end.   p. 50

Clov is 'dressed for the road', but one never sees him leave the stage. Like Vladimir and Estragon§ he waits, but unlike his famous predecessors, he waits without companionship, without the awareness of even a name to remember or of anything which could be either an illusion or a hope.

All that Fall is a play of motion in which the journey is made by a number of people in a fantastic assortment of vehicles. Finally they all reach the railway to await the incoming slow train. They have indeed gathered unknowingly at Bethlehem, but the child who is approaching never arrives to be born. He has fallen or been pushed from the train. Perhaps after all he was one of Rachel's children, sacrificed that the true prince might be saved. But here there is promise of no theophany.

> *Mrs Rooney:* Did you hear what kept the train so late? . . . What was it, Jerry?
>
> *Jerry:* It was a—
>
> *Mr Rooney:* Leave the boy alone, he knows nothing! Come on!
>
> *Mrs Rooney:* What was it, Jerry?
>
> *Jerry:* It was a little child, ma'am.
>
> *Mrs Rooney:* What do you mean, it was a little child?
>
> *Jerry:* It was a little child fell out of the carriage, ma'am. . . . . . On to the line, ma'am. Under the wheels, ma'am.   p. 37

* F. Fordham: *Introduction to Jung's Psychology*, Penguin (1953), p. 64.

† 'The Psychology of the Child Archetype' in *Archetypes and the Collective Unconscious*. Collected Works of C. G. Jung, IX. I., p. 179.

‡ *Endgame.*   § *Waiting for Godot.*

At best one human being may discover, or partially discover, another, as Miss Fitt finds her mother, and Maddy and Dan Rooney meet for the return journey and hold each other up in the mud and the rain.

The dramatic works, after *Waiting for Godot*, become progressively shorter, sparer in form and more compressed in content. In the process they lose much of the ambiguity of *Godot* and the greatest novels and with it the resonance of the clash between the worlds of time and of eternity, between mind and body, between hope and despair. This loss is observable also in the last great prose poem, *How It Is*. An explanation of the change is possibly of great importance to a correct interpretation of Beckett's work, but it may well be too early to attempt it. Beckett's *Tempest* is perhaps not written as yet. In the meantime *The Unnamable** still gives us the clearest statement of its author's stoic philosophy. Man may seek deliverance from himself, but more properly his concern is with the fulfilment of a purpose which may exist although it is unknowable and unnamable. Only after this unknown task is fulfilled should he dare to seek the oblivion he craves:

> Yes, I have a pensum to discharge, before I can be free, free to dribble, free to speak no more, to listen no more, and I've forgotten what it is. There at last is a fair picture of my situation I was given a pensum, at birth perhaps, as a punishment for having been born perhaps . . . and I've forgotten what it was.   p. 312

> I've journeyed without knowing it . . . you must go on that's all I know.
>   p. 418

ii *Molloy*

> I cannot help feeling that despite the abyss of nonsense in which we are stuck, we shall all be saved.
> SÖREN KIERKEGAARD. *Journal 1854*

> One of the thieves was saved. It's a reasonable proportion.
> SAMUEL BECKETT. *Waiting for Godot*

Molloy is certainly a myth of the Hard Journey. Although it is a new construct, self-consistent and self-sufficient, its relationships to earlier myths, the Odyssey for example, re-inforce such an interpretation of its admittedly elusive material. Like Odysseus Molloy follows the pathway of the sun, though with a characteristic reservation:

* *The Unnamable* (London: Calder, 1957; New York: Grove Press).

> I was able to continue on my way, saying, I am going towards the Sun, that is to say in theory towards the East, or perhaps the south-east. p. 66

A more direct reference has already been made, when Molloy says he is 'free, on the black boat of Ulysses, to crawl towards the East, along the deck' (p. 54). Hugh Kenner* relates the policeman who arrests Molloy to the Cyclops, and Lousse, by whom he is kept too long in dalliance, to Calypso. The last parallel is close, and its irony is both cutting and amusing; but Lousse is also a contemporary representative of Circe, with her big house, her soft beds and obsequious servants, her 'spells' and delicious, yet—as Molloy believes—drugged, food and drink. The girl who gaily but shyly leaves her friend to approach Molloy as he shelters on the beach is likened by Professor Kenner to Nausicaa, and the hero forces a passage which might suggest the way between Scylla and Charybdis:

> Thus we cleared these difficult straits, my bicycle and I, together.
>
> p. 21

This last comparison is not imaginatively valid, however, for Molloy's straits are not one peril among many; they are the entrance to Bally— or Dublin, the new Jerusalem, Nirvana, what you will—where Molloy's mother lives and where he is later to pass the last stages of his existence as an individual soul. They thus remind us rather of the Clashing Rocks passed by Jason before he could gain the Fleece, or of those straits pictured by Donne as he lay 'a flat map', awaiting death, and saw his way forward through:

> my South-west discovery,
> *Per fretum febris*, by these straits to die,
> I joy, that in these straits, I see my West;
> For, though their currents yield return to none,
> What shall my West hurt me? As West and East
> In all flat maps (and I am one) are one,
> So death doth touch the resurrection.†

The metaphor thus leads to the Christian imagery which is a far more powerful element in Beckett's mythology than that of the Greeks. This, together with the main line of the fable, which is based on Molloy's irrational and passionate need to return to his mother, make it obvious that there is in this novel an unusually close union of the two

---

* *Samuel Beckett: a critical study*, John Calder (1962).
† John Donne: *Hymn to God, my God, in my Sickness*.

themes with the juxtaposition of which this study started: the journeys of Oedipus and of Dante's pilgrim.

The method of threefold interpretation, literal, moral and anagogical, which Dante described in his letter to Can Grande*, is peculiarly appropriate to *Molloy*, which can be enjoyed as a story of events, as a psychological analysis of an individual soul and as an image—anagogical in quality—of the timeless situation of mankind. The interpretation of Beckett's imagery and of his association of ideas is notoriously difficult, and before attempting to think in terms of the second and third references it will be pleasant, even if not absolutely necessary, to comment on the novel when it is considered simply as a narrative. It is then apparent that the setting of the action is described with extraordinary vividness. All the senses are laid under contribution and particularly that of sight. Rarely have the varying qualities of light been more exquisitely conveyed by words:

> Yet I did not despair of seeing the light tremble, some day, through the still boughs, the strange light of the plain, its pale wild eddies through the bronze-still boughs, which no breath ever stirred. p. 91

The fleeting moment which marks the coming in of night is caught in as delicate a noose of words:

> the fields, whitening under the dew, and the animals, ceasing from wandering and settling for the night, and the sea, of which nothing, and the sharpening line of crests, where without seeing them I felt the first stars tremble. p. 11

The sounds of birds and beasts, of forest and seashore, of the very elements themselves are given a similarly lyrical quality. We hear 'the frail keel grating on the shore' (p. 73) as clearly as 'the crackling of the fire, of the writhing brands rather, for fire triumphant does not crackle, but makes an altogether different noise' (p. 161). A description of the sea appeals also to the less definable sense of touch: 'Much of my life has ebbed away before this shivering expanse, to the sound of the waves in storm and calm, and the claws of the surf' (pp. 72–3). The screaming of men and the lowings, bleatings and howlings of other living creatures supply Beckett with some of his most poignant images of the suffering of all sentient things: 'the bellowing of the cattle, that violent raucous tremulous bellowing not of the pastures, but of the towns, their shambles and cattle-markets' (p. 23). Elsewhere the

* v. sup., p. 35.

anguish is communicated by an assault on the most intimate of all the senses—the kinaesthetic:

> ... The bleating grew faint, because the sheep were less anxious or because they were further away . . . it left me with a persisting doubt, as to the destination of those sheep, among whom there were lambs, and often wondering if they had safely reached some commonage or fallen, their skulls shattered, their legs crumpling, first to their knees, then over on their fleecy sides, under the pole-axe, though that is not the way they slaughter sheep, but with a knife, so that they bleed to death.   pp. 30–1

Lastly the dense reality of the environment may be dependent in part on the use of the sense of smell: 'I turned back to look at my house. . . . I offered my face to the black mass of fragrant vegetation that was mine' (p. 137). More often smell seems to be to Beckett, as perhaps it was to Shakespeare, a source of disgust rather than delight; of his mother's bedroom Molloy writes that it: 'smelt of ammonia, oh not merely of ammonia, but of ammonia, ammonia' (p. 18).

Not even Shakespeare goes further than Beckett with the integration of broad and even brutal farce with correspondingly intense pathos and tragedy, and it is, of course, this close integration which gives its peculiar quality to all Beckett's writing about people. The savage mockery of all sexual relationships must be set against such a reflection of their inevitable conclusion as the following:

> From things about to disappear I turn away in time. To watch them out of sight, no, I can't do it . . . Looking away I thought of him, saying He is dwindling, dwindling. I knew what I meant.*   pp. 12–13

Those who watch and those who dwindle beyond sight may be living gargoyles, the objects that they purchase with their pittances the merest trivia; desire is farcical, yet men's fleeting satisfactions are not the less poignant for their brevity:

> But from time to time. From time to time . . . What tenderness in these little words. What savagery.   p. 88

The second level of interpretation, that of psychological analysis, reveals first the peculiar quality of Molloy's relationship with his mother. This is the drive which sweeps him to seek her 'with the clipped wings of necessity' (p. 28) at regular intervals, in spite of the unsatisfying nature of their contact when this is occasionally achieved.

---

* Cf. the description of the disappearance of Watt quoted on p. 168.

Molloy writes of 'this frenzy of wanting to get to her' (p. 36), but the difficulties of the journey were not all external:

> I needed, before I could resolve to go and see that woman, reasons of an urgent nature, and with such reasons, since I did not know what to do, or where to go, it was child's play for me, the play of an only child, to fill my mind until it was rid of all other preoccupation, and I seized with a trembling at the mere idea of being hindered from going there, I mean to my mother, there and then.   p. 16

The punning references to child's play spring from the mutual entanglement between the two of them, an entanglement in which age has become irrelevant and the biological nexus so twisted that it appears to function in reverse:

> She never called me son, fortunately, I couldn't have borne it, but Dan, I don't know why, my name is not Dan. . . . I called her Mag because for me, without my knowing why, the letter g abolished the syllable Ma, and as it were spat on it, better than any other letter would have done.

But the abolition was only partial and the relationship never completely denied:

> For before you say mag, you say ma, inevitably. And da, in my part of the world, means father.   pp. 17–18

In earlier days they had conversed, though not very rationally:

> Dan, you remember the day I saved the swallow. Dan, you remember the day you buried the ring. I remembered, I remembered, I mean I knew more or less what she was talking about, and if I hadn't always taken part personally in the scenes she evoked, it was just as if I had,   p. 18

Mrs Molloy, if that was her name, carried happier memories of her days of love than did her son, who had no recollection even of swallows or rings save for those he shared vicariously with her.

When he is what he calls 'worming his way' into their more recent encounters, Molloy recounts that all verbal communications had become impossible, and he replies to her senile gabblings by a code of punches and whacks only less brutal than Bam's application of the tin-opener to the body of his fellow-traveller across the mud.* Yet when he is thinking of the only two other women whom he can remember, Molloy muses:

* v. *How It Is.*

> And there are days, like this evening, when my memory confuses them and I am tempted to think of them as one and the same old hag, flattened and crazed by life. And God forgive me to tell you the horrible truth, my mother's image sometimes mingles with theirs, which is literally unendurable, like being crucified, I don't know why and I don't want to.   p. 62

Yet in that bedroom lies his only hope of happiness:

> if ever I'm reduced to looking for a meaning to my life, you never can tell, it's in that old mess I'll stick my nose to begin with, the mess of that poor old uniparous whore and myself the last of my foul brood, neither man nor beast. I should add . . . that with this deaf, blind, impotent, mad old woman, who called me Dan and whom I called Mag, and with her alone I—no, I can't say it. That is to say, I could say it, but I won't say it, yes, I could say it easily, because it wouldn't be true.   pp. 19–20

The ambiguity of this approach to a conclusion followed by an immediate and sceptical retreat from it as unbearable is revealing. Determined to avoid any idealization of a situation of the greatest importance to his Everyman, Beckett continues:

> Once I touched with my lips, vaguely, hastily, that little grey, wizened pear. Pah. Did that please her? I don't know. . . . Perhaps she said to herself, Pah. I smelt a terrible smell. It must have come from the bowels.
>
> p. 20

Yet Molloy writes also that when he is 'beat to the world, all shame drunk' (p. 20), it is in that room that he will take refuge, and so at last indeed he does.

Molloy's final journey begins with a vision. He is seated in the shelter of a great rock high up on the hillside, looking at the bare, white road below him. On this road appear two figures, walking in opposite directions, who inevitably meet each other. Molloy calls them A. and C., since in the translation from French into English C. is a change from B., it is presumably significant, and the men can safely be identified with Cain and Abel, and are another example of the pseudo-couple, the eternal executioner and victim who have their habitation within each single individual. Beckett clarifies the image in *Waiting for Godot* when Lucky and Pozzo are lying helpless on the ground:

> *Vladimir:* I tell you his name is Pozzo.
> *Estragon:* We'll soon see . . . Abel! Abel!

Pozzo: Help!
Estragon: . . . Perhaps the other is called Cain . . . Cain! Cain!
Pozzo: Help.
Estragon: He's all mankind.*

Along this road Molloy himself must travel, if he is to fulfil the command within him. On it he will suffer and inflict suffering; he will be his own executioner and endure crucifixion by others and experience the martyrdom of Abel as well as the exile of Cain.

As he makes his journey Molloy himself becomes increasingly grotesque. At first his body, the machine through which alone his mind functions is extended by a bicycle, an old green bicycle, without brakes but still rideable.

> Crippled though I was, I was no mean cyclist, at that period. This is how I went about it. I fastened my crutches to the cross-bar, one on either side, I propped the foot of my stiff leg . . . on the projecting front axle, and I pedalled with the other. It was a chainless bicycle, with a free wheel, if such a bicycle exists. p. 16

When the bicycle is broken, his crutches allow fairly efficient loco-motion, and Molloy can swing himself through the night, his feet off the ground, like some huge, wounded bird. At last even such progress becomes impossible, and all movement is torture:

> Flat on my belly, using my crutches like grapnels, I plunged them ahead of me into the undergrowth, and when I felt they had a hold, I pulled myself forward by an effort of the wrists. . . . And in this way . . . I covered my fifteen paces, day in, day out, without killing myself. pp. 95–6

In the end he admits that he will have to roll if he is to reach his mother's door, but this final ignominy is spared him.

What was it he sought, at first with frenzy and later with inter-mittent but agonizing effort? Molloy's journey through space on a bicycle and crutches is surely a grotesque symbol of man's search for satisfaction and safety. It is the universal nature of the personal security to be found in the parent-child relationship which makes this in its turn—grotesque as it too appears in Beckett's imagination—a valid reflection of man's ultimate quest, the quest for a self which can be absorbed into the absolute. Such a quest, by such a bare, forked animal as man, may properly be shown as ludicrous. Beckett does

* *Waiting for Godot*, pp. 83–4.

show it thus. He shows it also, however, as tragic, and, just possibly, in the end triumphant. In other words it is the intrinsic importance of the personal psychological quest which makes it a valid symbol of a search for the satisfaction of a need even more profound than its own fulfilment. The search appeared to Molloy to be commanded from outside his own mind by 'imperatives' which he could not resist:

> physically nothing could have been easier, but I was not purely physical, . . . Yes, those imperatives were quite explicit and even detailed until, having set me in motion at last, they began to falter, then went silent.

> p. 92

When he is approaching the end of his narrative and death is very close to him, Molloy writes:

> And of myself, all my life, I think I had been going to my mother, with the purpose of establishing our relations on a less precarious footing. And when I was with her, and I often succeeded, I left her without having done anything. And when I was no longer with her I was again on my way to her, hoping to do better the next time. And when I appeared to give up and to busy myself with something else, or with nothing at all any more, in reality I was hatching my plans and seeking the way to her house.

> p. 93

The ineluctable purpose, uncomprehended and incomprehensible, again recalls *The Castle*, and many a religious man could use no stronger language of his own spiritual search; Molloy himself adds the words: 'this is taking a queer turn'.

In the terms then of the third level of interpretation where does the journey take place, and what is its goal? At first one is tempted to answer 'in hell', for the sufferings are so intense, the sin and shame surrounding the traveller so violent. But there is no movement for the damned; damnation is a stasis in a place from which there is no exit. Dante travels through hell just because it is not his proper sphere and he does not suffer its pains. Molloy suffers as he journeys, but his journey is not through either hell or purgatory. From hell there is no exit and from purgatory there is one exit only—the entrance to paradise, and although Molloy does reach a kind of equipoise, it is in no permanent resting place and therefore not a possible image for paradise. In fact it is only when he leaves the dark wood, in which Dante had also wandered, that Molloy moves on from this earthly world, and without the friendly aid of a Virgil, propelling himself forward on back or belly, reaches the open country of the 'other world' at last.

That Molloy's journey until the point where he falls into the ditch and is 'succoured' by the unseen 'them' is through this world, is made plainer by an explicit reference to the Via Dolorosa. Describing the agony which movement became to him, Molloy writes that his journey was to:

> a veritable calvary, with no limit to its stations and no hope of crucifixion, though I say it myself, and no Simon,   p. 83

He describes his experience as 'those brief moments of the immemorial expiation'. The journey is commanded:

> it is forbidden to give up and even to stop an instant. So I wait, jogging along, for the bell to say, Molloy, one last effort, it's the end. That's how I reason, with the help of images little suited to my situation.   p. 87

When Molloy is at last approaching the edge of the forest there comes the first premonition of 'otherness':

> a word about the forest murmurs. It was in vain I listened, I could hear nothing of the kind. But rather, with much good will and a little imagination, at long intervals a distant gong.   p. 95

To this sound, Molloy, the most decrepit of all imaginable Childe Rolands, replies by a hoot on the little horn, last relic of his bicycle, which he still carries in his pocket. It sounds:

> through the cloth of my pocket. Its hoot was fainter every time.   p. 95

Nevertheless he blows it and continues his desperate 'fifteen paces day in, day out'.

> And I even crawled on my back, plunging my crutches blindly behind me into the thickets, and with the black boughs for sky to my closing eyes. I was on my way to mother. And from time to time I said, Mother, to encourage me I suppose.   p. 96

He emerges from the forest by falling into a ditch on its perimeter, and the scene is suddenly flooded with a numinous light.

> I looked at the plain rolling away as far as the eye could see. No, not quite so far as that. For my eyes having got used to the light I fancied I saw,

faintly outlined against the horizon, the towers and steeples of a town.

pp. 96-7*

The city, like other Celestial Cities, is reached only in death. Molloy is carried there by unseen arms, and once arrived he has completed his circle and discovers the nature of his goal. 'In my end is my beginning . . .' just as 'In my beginning is my end'.†

> And the end of all our exploring
> Will be to arrive where we started
> And know the place for the first time.‡

No effort is too great to be demanded of the flesh before it is abandoned or transcended, but at the moment of dissolution help is available.

> For how could I drag myself over that vast moor, where my crutches would fumble in vain? Rolling perhaps. And then? Would they let me roll to my mother's door? Fortunately for me at this painful juncture, which I had vaguely foreseen, but not in all its bitterness, I heard a voice telling me not to fret, that help was coming. Literally. . . . Don't fret, Molloy, we're coming.   p. 97

We are now at the heart of Beckett's mystery. We have been spared not an iota of the horror of existence; we have been allowed not a shred of hope, for there are no grounds for hope; until the end no help has been vouchsafed us. In *Molloy* even the inadequate comfort that friends can occasionally offer each other—such as the carrot which love only can substitute for the undesired turnip,§ are in this novel only memories of the far past, distorted by later sufferings into grotesque parodies of what they may once have been. If Murphy had not been gassed in his rocking-chair he might well have remembered Celia as painfully as Molloy remembered Ruth. And yet . . . and yet . . . and yet . . . We remember: 'Don't fret Molloy, we're coming'. Here there appears the possibility that we have returned, however obscurely, to Dante's world. If so Beckett is less ruthless than Kafka; not a finger or a whisper of help was allowed to reach K.

It is when he is at last carried by unseen hands or in an unseen

---

* Professor Fletcher declares, although without explicit evidence, that Beckett has been influenced by Bunyan. Considering his non-conformist up-bringing it is more than likely, and this passage seems to confirm it.

†T. S. Eliot: *Four Quartets. East Coker*, pp. 15 and 23 (the first and last lines).

‡ Ibid., *Little Gidding*, p. 43.

§ v. *Waiting for Godot*, pp. 19-20 and 68.

vehicle to his mother's empty bed that Molloy leaves 'this earthly world' behind him and is in purgatory at last. There he does penance for his personal inadequacies and for that ultimate and all but unpardonable sin, the sin of being born. To reach this point is a gift, a true charisma. Molloy admits:

> I was helped, I'd never have got there alone. p. 7

For him the refining fire is the writing of his own story. The 'powers' insist that this is done, and thereby they assist the doing in spite of the recalcitrance of the individual soul. Before it is accepted 'anagogically' as an image of purgatory, the writing of the life history may properly be compared to the process of an analysis, so that Molloy's bed becomes the analyst's couch and the writing that painful but curative recollection of the past at the end of which the true self is recognized and accepted. To this the patient is inevitably resistant:

> What I'd like now is to speak of the things that are left, say my goodbyes, finish dying. They don't want that. p. 7

Salvation must depend on the completed confession, the fulfilled penance, and mercy itself must ensure that the task is accomplished so that understanding may follow and bring release.

The mystery is still dense, the ambiguity acute:

> It's my fault. Fault? That was the word. But what fault? p. 8

Nevertheless in the new circumstances renewed movement and a new goal are conceivable:

> It is in the tranquillity of decomposition that I remember the long confused emotion which was my life, and that I judge it, as it is said that God will judge me, and with no less impertinence. p. 26

So far we have drawn our image of Molloy from his own narrative, the narrative which fills Part I of the novel which bears his name. Now we must supplement this picture from the material in Part II which contains the narrative of Jacques Moran. Molloy obeyed an imperative—to seek his mother; Moran's imperative is to seek Molloy, but whereas the source of Molloy's 'frenzied determination' is obscure and can legitimately but not necessarily be interpreted as subjective, Moran's orders come from an external source in whose omnipotence Moran himself unquestionably believes. He is an agent of Youdi who sends his messenger, Gaber, with orders which their recipient, although he grumbles about them, never disputes. Moran, an utterly unimaginative and meticulously accurate civil servant, is strangely reluctant to undertake the quest of Molloy. He procrastinates and only leaves home struggling against obscure but powerful emotion. It is soon suggested that Moran and Molloy are facets of the same individual, and in some sense Moran himself is aware of this. When his vision of Molloy is set beside the portrait of himself which his own words create, the reader realizes that Moran is embarking on the exploration of his own unconscious mind. The pattern is thus that Moran, the rationalist intellectual, is impelled to the search of his irrational self, while Molloy, his unconscious self, is concerned to settle the matter of his relations with his mother and to find redemption or Nirvana outside of time and space. In support of this interpretation of the novel we may notice first the fastidious reluctance of the organized, rational personality to contemplate the possibility of the chaos below the mask he has successfully created:

> If anyone else had spoken to me of Molloy I would have requested him to stop and I myself would not have confided his existence to a living soul for anything in the world.   p. 121

His image of Molloy amply justifies his distrust.

> He panted. *He had only to rise up within me for me to be filled with panting.*
>
> Even in open country he seemed to be crashing through jungle. He did not so much walk as charge. In spite of this he advanced but slowly. He swayed, to and fro, like a bear. . . .
>
> *This was how he came to me, at long intervals. Then I was nothing but uproar,* bulk, rage, suffocation, effort unceasing, frenzied and vain. *Just the opposite of myself, in fact:* it was a change. And when I saw him disappear, his whole body a vociferation, I was almost sorry.
>
> What it was all about I had not the slightest idea.
>
> pp. 121–2 (italics the present writer's)

The resentment and fascination felt at the intruding elements are brilliantly suggested, but for Beckett no self is neatly divided into two halves, and having established a specific relationship between Molloy and Moran he hastens to subtilize and confuse it:

> Between the Molloy I stalked within me thus and the true Molloy, after whom I was soon to be in full cry, over hill and dale, the resemblance

cannot have been great. . . . The fact was there were three, no, four Molloys. He that inhabited me, my caricature of same, Gaber's and the man of flesh and blood somewhere awaiting me. To these I would add Youdi's. . . . There were others too, of course. But let us leave it at that, if you don't mind, the party is big enough.   pp. 123–4

Moran is drawn as sufficiently intelligent to realize the dangers of the quest on which he set out and the improbability of his returning from it unchanged. All the security he had painfully built up by limiting his desires to those which he might reasonably hope to fulfil —'These fragments I have shored against my ruins'*—was threatened. Leaning on the post of the little wicket-gate he looked back at home and garden, hesitating before he started on his quest. In the stillness he could hear only the tiny quivering sounds that came from the hen-houses:

> And so I turned again a last time towards my little all, before I left it, in the hope of keeping it.   p. 137

As Moran moves slowly forward to self-knowledge he loses much of his obsessive perfectionism and his assertive self-confidence. He becomes more like Molloy and in so far as he does so becomes progressively less efficient as a human mechanism. He is crippled by a sudden and incomprehensible injury to his knee and broods alone in his little shelter of boughs until he drags himself down to a nearby stream:

> I lay down and looked at my reflection, then I washed my face and hands. I waited for my image to come back, I watched it as it trembled towards an ever increasing likeness.   p. 156

He is horrified by the image he evokes:

> what I saw was more like a crumbling, a frenzied collapsing of all that had always protected me from all I was condemned to be. Or it was like a kind of clawing towards a light and countenance I could not name, that I had once known and long denied.   p. 159

It is a literal description of what happens when the elaborately created persona collapses, but here also another dimension is suggested. He whom we beg to lift up the light of his countenance upon us and give us peace, cannot be apprehended by the skills of reason.

This experience is followed by a recognition of a dawning new self,

---

* T. S. Eliot: *The Waste Land*, 1. 430.

inchoate, bi-sexual and immature; the image is of quite extraordinary subtlety:

> What words can describe this sensation at first all darkness and bulk, with a noise like the grinding of stones, then suddenly as soft as water flowing. And then I saw a little globe swaying up slowly from the depths, through the quiet water, smooth at first, and scarcely paler than its escorting ripples, then little by little a face, with holes for the eyes and mouth and other wounds, and nothing to show if it was a man's face or a woman's face, a young face or an old face, or if its calm too was not an effect of the water trembling between it and the light. pp. 159–60

Immediately after this nascent intuition of a previously unknown self, Moran is faced with a *doppelgänger*, a sinister and threatening replica of the self he was attempting to discard:

> There I was face to face with a dim man, dim of face and dim of body, because of the dark. . . . the face . . . vaguely resembled my own, less the refinement of course, same little abortive moustache, same little ferrety eyes, same paraphimosis of the nose, and a thin red mouth that looked as if it was raw from trying to shit its tongue. . . . I do not know what happened then, But a little later, perhaps a long time later, I found him stretched on the ground, his head in a pulp. pp. 161–2

This close connection between the mirror image of truth and the false persona has been described by Jung:

> Whoever looks into the mirror of the water will see first of all his own face. Whoever goes to himself risks a confrontation with himself. The mirror does not flatter, it faithfully shows whatever looks into it, namely the face we never show to the world because we cover it with the *persona*, the mask of the actor. But the mirror lies behind the mask and shows the true face. This confrontation is the first test of courage on the inner way. . . .*

Events move quickly now, and it is not long after the slaying of the discarded *alter ego* that the messenger again seeks and finds Moran. Gaber reads from his notebook of instructions: 'Moran, Jacques, home, instanter' (p. 175). Moran believes he is now physically incapable of reaching home, but presuming Youdi is not mistaken as to the possibilities, he sets out. He stumbles through a whole winter of intense cold, but he does at last reach what was his home. It is a derelict shell

* *The Archetypes and the Collective Unconscious*, C.W. IX. i, p. 20.

now. His bees are dead, his hens have disappeared, the housekeeper he bullied has gone, while the son he tormented had escaped long before. Moran begins his new life alone except for his birds.

> They were the longest, loveliest days of all the year. I lived in the garden. I have spoken of a voice telling me things. I was getting to know it better now, to understand what it wanted, . . . I understand it all wrong perhaps. That is not what matters. It told me to write the report. Does this mean that I am freer than I was? I do not know. I shall learn. pp. 188–9

Jung again sheds light on Beckett's imagery when he writes of the self as an image gradually built up in consciousness, as essential as it is unreal. In his 'Two Essays on Analytical Psychology'* he relates the making and discovery of the self to a journey:

> the self has somewhat the character of a result, of a goal attained, something that has come to pass very gradually and is experienced with much travail. pp. 237–8

At the end of his journey Moran is approaching that goal, and the fruits of his travail have also been described by Jung:

> the more we become conscious of our selves through self-knowledge, and act accordingly, the more . . . there arises a consciousness which is no longer imprisoned in the petty, over-sensitive, personal world of the ego. . . . This widened consciousness is no longer that touchy, egotistical bundle of personal wishes, fears, hope and ambitions which always had to be compensated or corrected by unconscious counter-tendencies. p. 176

Beckett never shows his characters undertaking the next stage of the journey as Jung describes it: 'Instead it (i.e. consciousness) is a function of relationship to the world of objects, bringing the individual into absolute binding and indissoluble communion with the world at large'. This is a course which Molloy, Moran, Malone and all the other named and unnamable heroes are set at all costs to avoid. The communion they seek is with another world than this.

In spite of, or perhaps it is rather because of, his experiences, Moran is sure that he is still the man who set out to find Molloy and who is now, in part, integrated with the object of his search:

> Physically speaking it seemed to me I was now becoming rapidly unrecognizable. . . . but I had a sharper and clearer sense of my identity than ever before, in spite of its deep lesions and the wounds with which it

* C.W. VII.

was covered. And from this point of view I was less fortunate than my other acquaintances. p. 182

The juxtaposition of the double journey — Molloy's and Moran's — suggests that a recognition of the self is as necessary as the transcending of the self, that in fact the former is an essential prerequisite of the latter, and 'from this point of view' Moran may well have been more, not less fortunate than his acquaintances.

iii Conclusion

Only the poet has re-integrated
the world that in each self disintegrates.
The strangest beauty he's authenticated,
even what tortured him he's celebrated,
and ruin so infinitely expurgated
that norm appears in what annihilates.
Baudelaire. R. M. Rilke. *Poems 1906–26*
tr. J. B. Leishman

It is precisely the task of human apprehension to understand that there is something it cannot understand and also what that something is . . . The paradox is not a concession but a category . . . which expresses the relation between an existing apprehending mind and eternal truth.

These words are from the Journals of Kierkegaard in 1847. A year later we can read there of 'the inner sufferings involved in becoming a Christian, the fact of giving up reason and being crucified to a paradox'.

The dilemma is Beckett's also, and he refuses the 'leap of faith' by which, for Kierkegaard, it was resolved, so that in his creative work the nature and goal of the hard journey remain for ever ambiguous. It is becoming fashionable to call Beckett a humanist, and the word may well be valid. Yet his humanism abounds in the paradoxes, the ambivalences, the overtones and undertones, which are associated more easily with a religious than with a sceptical mind. Moran learns more truth about himself; Molloy awaits redemption or oblivion in the shelter he sought; the self is not finally integrated; salvation is not visibly achieved, but the validity of the conception of such possibilities is not denied. All man's dreams, fantasies and idealisms — virtue, religion, love, justice, friendship even—have been derided and dragged through the mire, but above the harrowed, blasted surface of 'an Egypt without bounds, without infant, without mother' the stars tremble though unseen in the sky, and below them men continue to journey for no certain reason to no certain goal. *The Unnamable* is a more terrifyingly pessimistic book than *Molloy*, but its last words are a bang not a whimper:

> You must go on, I can't go on, you must go on, I'll go on . . . where I am, I don't know, I'll never know, in the silence you don't know, you must go on, I can't go on, I'll go on.　　　　　　　p. 418

The Hard Journey has never been presented to our contemplation as harder than this, and from such stoical endurance Beckett allows only one 'lightening', the fleeting human contact that is, of its nature, ephemeral and the fore-runner of renewed anguish.

One last illustration of the paradoxical juxtaposition of ruthlessness and tenderness at the heart of all Beckett's work must end this slender study of the man who may well be the greatest living writer in the English language. It is ironic that one who is so violent in the dis-membering of the individual personality, should also be the man to achieve the most sensitive of all contemporary writing on personal relationships. The last of his journey images to be quoted here shall be of the approach of two friends to each other and of one's retreat from their friendship. Watt and Sam take the air in two adjacent gardens and occasionally they meet by crossing a fragile bridge which spans a little brook, never dry, and flowing now slow, now with torrential rapidity, in the ditch which divides them. One day the bridge is broken, and with infinite pains the two men repair it, each beginning at his own end. They could not stand upright on it so they lay on their stomachs in order to work. At last the breach was mended, the ludicrous passage was accomplished and they met, forehead touching forehead, in a grotesque intimacy.

> And then we did a thing we seldom did, we embraced. Watt laid his hands on my shoulders, and I laid mine on his (I could hardly do other-wise), and then I touched Watt's left cheek with my lips and then Watt touched my left cheek with his (he could scarcely do less), the whole coolly, and above us tossed the over-arching boughs.　　　　p. 169

So was the immeasurable distance conquered but not for long. Soon the movement was reversed, and Watt moved backward through his garden, stumbling among the undergrowth, knocking against the trees, falling to the ground, until he disappeared:

> And from the hidden pavilions, his and mine, where by this time dinner was preparing, the issuing smokes by the wind were blown, now far apart, but now together, mingled to vanish.   pp. 234–5

CHAPTER 7

Bertolt Brecht : The Communist Journey

According to Marxist precepts . . . the steps of the dance, or
at least its precise limits, are traced on the floor of the stage.
G. STEINER. *Tolstoi and Dostoievsky*

I make friends with people. And I wear
A derby on my head as others do.
I say: they're strangely stinking animals.
And I say: no matter, I am too.
B. BRECHT, *Concerning Poor B.B.* Selected Poems

i BRECHT AND DANTE

Little mother, . . .
The bereaved one, whose sons are in the war.
Who is beaten with fists, but full of hope.
Who weeps when she is given a cow
And is surprised when she is not beaten.
Little mother, pass merciful sentence on us, the damned!
Caucasian Chalk Circle, p. 79

IT is not contended here that the imaginative reach of Brecht's
writing, in either its scope or its depth, can be equated with that of
Dante, yet there are common factors in the works of the two men
which make comparisons between them of value. In the first place,
Brecht stands with Dante as a creative artist who accepts an inclusive
social and philosophical system and is content to write within it,
clarifying it, and both giving and receiving support in the process.
Moreover they both wrote their greatest works while in exile for the
political cause which they supported. Dante, looking back at this,
writes lines true of both writers and of their enemies:

For with a savage fury shall they play
The ingrate, and defame thee; yet anon
Not thou shalt feel thy forehead burn, but they—
Fools all, and proved so by their goings-on;
Paradise. xvii. 64–7

The reactions of the two men to this situation are however diametrically opposed, for Dante continues:

> Well shall it be for thee to have preferred
> Making a party of thyself alone.   ll. 68–9

This last course Brecht refused to contemplate, whatever the temptations to do so may have been.

In *The Inferno*, Dorothy Sayers lists among 'the greater images' of *The Divine Comedy*, the Empire and the City, and these invite a political interpretation and concern social as well as individual redemption. A good deal of the *Paradiso* is concerned with the social justice* which reflects 'that living Justice' which is the will of God (XIX. 68), and for the men of the Middle Ages this was prefigured in the Roman Empire which Dante was so eager to see re-established in a new form.

Dante castigates the failure of the human community in the sins of Florence and the Papacy. His beloved birth-place is actually described as the off-spring of Lucifer himself, and the attack on the church which immediately follows this reference is as violent as Milton's own.

Like the priests in *Lycidas* these shepherds neglect their sheep, or themselves play the part of the wolf:

> Dust gathers on the Gospels, gathers low
> On the great Doctors, while they thumb and scrawl
> O'er the Decretals, as the margins show.
> That's the whole lore of pope and cardinal
> Alike; to Nazareth that felt the beat
> Of Gabriel's wings they give no thought at all.
> *Paradise*. IX. 127–37

This is a hatred with which Brecht could have sympathized though he never would have willingly accepted Dante's solution, which is that of an autocracy:

> Justice, as Dante conceived it philosophically, is an absolute standard of righteousness. . . . The antithesis of justice, which provokes injustice, is greed or covetousness. . . . How can this (a just society) be brought about? Only by a universal Monarch, a single world Emperor, who alone,

---

* E.g., Justinian Canto VI, and the imagery of the eagle in Cantos XVIII and XIX.

of all temporal rulers, would be free from covetousness and disposed, therefore, to act in accordance with the maximum justice possible on earth.*

The diagnosis is indeed close to Brecht's; only the remedy is distinct. Brecht realized, of course, that he was trail-breaking. Because his philosophy was alien to western culture he knew his style also must embody a new convention. Of the methods of the *avante-garde* writer of the twentieth century he himself says:

> No longer did the artist feel himself bound to create 'his own world', and, taking the actual world as known and unalterable, feel bound to enrich the catalogue of images which are really images of the image-makers; rather did he feel himself bound to take the world as alterable and unknown and to deliver images which give information more about the world than about himself.†

One of the most important sources of the imagery in both drama and narrative poetry is characterization, and here also comparison with Dante is illuminating, for Dante also is a great creator of individual character—not extended in time and space as are the characters of a dramatist but portrayed in vignettes of extraordinary vigour and power. One has only to recall Francesca, Ulysses, Ugolino; there in embryo are three characters each able with little further development to be the central figure in a full length play. Yet Dante puts at the climax of his poem a vision, not of men but of mankind, in perfect, irrefutable order. Gazing at the thrones and their occupants which make up the petals of the Celestial Rose, S. Bernard says:

> In this wide kingdom no contingency
> Can find a place in the minutest fact,
> No more than sadness, hunger, thirst can be.
> For here eternal law doth so enact
> All thou beholdest, that the measurements
> Between the ring and finger are exact.
>
> *Paradise:* xxxii. 52–7

Professor Auerbach sees a similar order in the souls peopling irrevocably the circles of hell, and his comment on the effect of the individual seen as an individual in a setting which transcends individuality is as relevant to the Communist's ordered society as to the Christian's, since

---

* Barbara Reynolds, *Introduction to Paradiso*, Penguin (1962), p. 51.

† From 'Prospectus of the Diderot Society', quoted by E. Bentley in *Life of the Drama*, Methuen, (1965).

171

both claim that only within a comprehensive organism can individuality be given its true significance. Of the inhabitants of the *Inferno* Auerbach writes:

> Their eternal position in the divine order is something of which we are only conscious as a setting whose irrevocability can but serve to heighten the effect of their . . . humanity. . . . The result is a direct experience of life which overwhelms everything else.

Paradise also has its social significance:

> The community of the blessed in the white rose of the Empyrean is at the same time also the goal of the historical process of salvation.*

In the imagined final order there is no room for the eccentricities which make up 'character'; there man is revealed in his essence, and every person is a representative and known by the place he fills in the whole. Although individuals had inevitably an importance for Dante that they could not have for Brecht, since to the Christian their fate was of such moment to their Creator that he permitted the crucifixion of his son that a way of salvation might be found for them, yet in his greatest work Brecht reveals that he shares to some extent such a belief in their value. To all believers in an ordered universe, however, individuals must, in the last resort, be subservient to the collective, whether they be the workers in a valley of Azerbaijan† or the unnumbered saints in the white rose of Eternal Love.

There is no such direct reflection of the writer's own spiritual journey to be found in Brecht's work as there is in Dante's, though such a journey—from the position of the young, romantic-nihilist of *Baal* to that of the committed Marxist of the later plays—must certainly have taken place. The journeys dramatized by Brecht are those of his characters, and in *St Joan of the Stockyards*‡ he challenges us to remember the *Inferno*. Three times his captions tell us we are about to see Joan's descent into the abyss. The circles of Brecht's hell reveal the horrors of the Chicago meat-markets, previously used by Upton Sinclair to stigmatize capitalist society.§ Joan's journey, however, is a means of salvation neither to herself nor to others. For Brecht mankind's upward journey has still to be made, and he nowhere

---

* *Mimesis*, p. 201.   † v. *Caucasian Chalk Circle*.

‡ All quotations from Brecht's plays except *Galileo* are from the collected edition published by Methuen.

§ v. *The Jungle*, Heinemann (1906), Penguin (1937)

makes any attempt to represent it—unless perhaps in his last original play, *The Caucasian Chalk Circle*. Nevertheless the knowledge which only the downward journey and its agony can make available to men, is essential to human progress, and as such it is dramatized here.

Joan, a Brechtian incarnation of Shaw's Major Barbara, works for the Black Straw Hats, who deal out soup and consolation to the starving proletariat. Scene II is headed: *Joan's first descent into the depths*. In this episode she enters a kind of Limbo, a threshold from which the lower circles will be later approached and raises there the banner of her hopes:

> We wish to re-introduce
> God. . . .
> Therefore we have decided
> To beat the drum for Him
> That He may gain a foothold in the regions of misery
> And His voice may ring out clearly among the slaughterhouses.
>
> pp. 95–6

On her 'second descent into the depths' (Scene IV) she has a guide; her Virgil is Slift, the meat king's broker. He has already warned her without effect of what she will find and opens the next scene with the words:

> Now Joan, I will show you
> The wickedness of those
> For whom you feel pity, and
> How out of place the feeling is.   p. 112

The people are indeed wicked; a man has fallen into a boiling vat, and his body has been carried into the bacon-maker. A sycophantic apprentice is rewarded with his job, and his wife's passionate complaints and enquiries are stifled by the promise of free dinners for three weeks. A worker who has lost his arm in the slicing machine foregoes his vengeance on the foreman when the management promotes him to the man's job, and he tempts Joan also to accept work in which he knows she will certainly be maimed or killed. When the wife recognizes her husband's cap in the canteen and hears the man who wears it say laconically:

> I got it off a man that fell into a boiling vat,

she feels sick and goes out, but she calls to the waiter:

> Leave the plate where it is. I'm coming back.   p. 117

173

Brecht does not deny the wickedness, but unlike Dante he puts the responsibility for the fall not on the tempted but on the tempter. Joan answers Slift:

> Certainly she would have liked
> To be true to her husband, as others are . . .
> But the price was too high: it amounted to twenty
>   meals . . .
> Not the wickedness of the poor
> Have you shown me, but
> *The poverty of the poor*. . . .
> O thoughtless rumour, that the poor are base:
> You shall be silenced by their stricken face!   p. 118

Joan's 'third descent into the depths' (Scene IX) is in a dream. In it she sees the crowd of the faceless that haunted also the vision of Dante and of T. S. Eliot. She watches a procession move across a little field.

> I saw a bunch
> Of people: I could not make out how many, but . . .
> There were far more of them than all the sparrows
> That could find room in such a tiny place . . .
> So the procession moved, and I along with it
> Veiled by snow.   pp. 152–3

Joan has refused to make a moral judgment of wickedness, but because she still believes in a morality of goodness, she leads the faceless crowd of workers to defeat. Dying, she realises her mistake:

> Like an answer to their prayers I came to the oppressors!
> Oh, goodness without consequences! Intentions in the dark!
> I have changed nothing.

This is the fate of Brecht's pilgrim, the 'moral' of his *Inferno*; Joan dies without hope, having lived without guidance, and her fate is irrelevant to the order she challenged and which she understood too late; she has indeed 'changed nothing'.

In contrast to the 'commitment' which gives to both writers their strongly masculine quality, there is an opposite element which again, though less obviously, they share. Both reveal that 'androgynous mind' which Coleridge has declared to be the hall-mark of the great artist, and they reveal it through their use of a feminine image representing the intuitions which can be shown to be the inspiration of their own work.

Brecht, as has been said already, has made no image of his personal life central to any of his plays, but he is incapable of entirely eliminating from them all reflection of the self which created them, and this in spite of an apparent fear of his own emotion which is betrayed by the very barriers he erects to suppress it. Yet 'Beatrice' appears to Brecht, and she elicits from him the fury of compassion which was the driving force of all he came to be and do. Thus both poets are men who—to use Dante's vocabulary—receive the feminine bearer of 'grace', just as both seek also the City of God as the final over-riding Good. Dante is the more fortunate. For him the Beatrice who brings his personal salvation, is concerned also with the building of the future City, and his vision of this, as of absolute Truth and Goodness is subsumed in the Rose of Paradise. For Brecht it is far otherwise. For him there are no absolutes, and the foundations of the City are the selves of those who—as they could—served it and were destroyed in their task:

> Alas we
> Who wished to lay the foundations of kindness
> Could not ourselves be kind.
> But you, when at last it comes to pass
> That man can help his fellow man,
> Do not judge us
> Too harshly.*

Of the other self, the *anima*, which is hidden below the conscious level of the mind Jung writes:

> The first bearer of the soul image is always the mother; later it is borne by those women who arouse the man's feelings, whether in a positive or a negative sense.†

Because of the ubiquity of the 'paired opposites' in the psyche's experience of living, the image of the *anima* is projected with equal strength on to figures of light and of darkness, on to the virgin and the harlot, the saint and *la belle dame sans merci*, unless or until these figures are synthesized in one mysterious and immaculate Mother of God. Brecht nearly always uses the harlot, and he gives her a touch of the numenous beauty which distinguishes the figures which rise from a myth-making stratum of the mind.

* *To Posterity:* Selected Poems (London: Calder; New York: Grove Press), 1959, pp. 175–6.
† *Two Essays on Analytical Psychology*, C.W. VII, p. 195.

Dante's poem presents among many other things the process by which a man accepts and integrates the feminine into his conscious self; he is estranged from Beatrice, rediscovers her and is again at one with her before he receives the beatific vision. Brecht never presents us with an image of such an achievement, but as we should expect, he has not kept the representation of his *anima* out of his work, and in it she is continually betrayed and destroyed by the male with whom she is associated. Perhaps the most tender of Brecht's earlier poems is *In Memory of Marie A.*, in which the betrayer is apparently the poet himself, who is writing seven years after the kiss described in the first verse:

> One day in the blue month of September
> Silently I held her under the young plum tree,
> I held her there, my pale and silent loved one,
> And like a gentle dream within my arms was she.
> And over us in the fair summer heavens
> Was a cloud that fleetingly I saw,
> Very white and terribly far above us,
> And as I looked up it was there no more.
>
> . . . .
>
> Even the kiss I should have quite forgotten
> If there had been no cloud there, long ago.
> I see it still and I shall always see it
> For it was white and drifted down like snow.
> Perhaps the plum trees bear their yearly blossoms,
> Perhaps the woman has her seventh child,
> And yet that cloud bloomed only for a minute
> And as I looked up vanished in the wind.*

Beatrice, it has been said, is 'for Dante the embodiment of his experience of love',† and since this love included the love of God its embodiment is always held in awe:

> Of all that I have looked on with these eyes
> Thy goodness and thy power have fitted me
> The holiness and grace to recognize.
>
> *Paradise:* xxxi. 82–4

The tenderness with which Brecht regards the women he remembers or imagines is suffused not with awe but with pity. The charisma

* *Selected Poems*, p. 45. † B. Reynolds, op. cit., p. 51.

brought by their slender figures may be accepted for a moment, but it can be retained no longer than the innocence and youth that brought it, for it is as fleeting as they. The girl Nanna sings her own song; she remembers the grace she once brought her lover and shared with him, but she knows it has slipped away:

> Good Sirs, at seventeen summers
> I went to Lechery Fair
> And plenty of things it's taught me.
> Many a heart-ache,
> That's the chance you take.
> But I've wept many times in despair.
> (After all I'm a human being, too.)
> Thank God it's all over with quickly,
> All the love and the grief we must bear.
> Where are the tears of yesterevening?
> Where are the snows of yesteryear?*

In these poems there has appeared the snow image which is re-iterative in Brecht's writing and which is always associated with the poet's pity for the women destroyed by the society which exploits them. Marie Farrar gives birth in the snow to her illegitimate child which she afterwards kills.

> With her last strength, she says, because
> Her room had now grown icy cold, she then
> Dragged herself to the latrine and there
> Gave birth as best she could (not knowing when)
> But toward morning. She says she was already
> Quite distracted and could hardly hold
> The child for snow came into the latrine.
> And her fingers were half numb with cold.
> *You too, I beg you, check your wrath and scorn*
> *For man needs help from every creature born.*†

The Threepenny Novel closes with the apocalypse granted to the soldier-tramp Fewcombey shortly before he was hanged for a murder he did not commit. In his vision the figure of a woman comes towards him. She is Mary, worn down to despair by her unavailing struggle to keep herself and her children alive by sweatshop trade and casual

---

* *Nanna's Song. Selected Poems*, p. 87.
† *Concerning the Infanticide of Marie Farrar. Selected Poems*, p. 25.

whoring. Fewcombey knows her preciousness and welcomes her to all he can give her—his pity, pure and cold as snow, but necessarily as fleeting:

> 'I wanted to ask you whether it is cold where you come from, Mary,' he said loudly, 'but I can see that the question is unnecessary. I see that it *is* cold where you come from.'
>
> Then he saw that she was tired, so he said to her:
>
> 'Sit down, Mary. You have walked too far.'
>
> She looked round for a chair, but there was none there.
>
> The judge rang again. And it snowed out of the air, but only in a thin column, no thicker than the trunk of a medium-sized tree, until a bank of snow was there on which she could sit down. The judge waited until the snow stopped, and then he said:
>
> 'It will be a little cold; and when it becomes warm, it will melt, and you will have to stand up again. But there is nothing else I can do!'*

In other poems Brecht's images may be those more familiarly associated with love and grief. The fragile beauty of the fruit blossom appeared in the poem to Marie A., and the drowned Ophelia is recalled in the water imagery of *Concerning a Drowned Girl*.†

> Weeds and algae clung about the corpse
> Until they slowly weighted down the maiden.
> Cool fish swam about her legs till she
> On her last trip, with plant and beast was laden.
>
> . . . .
>
> As her pale body rotted in the river,
> It happened (very slowly) that God forgot her,
> First her face, her hands, at last her hair,
> Then she was carrion with the carrion in the water.

Sometimes the poet's pity is expressed not through tenderness but through anger. Jenny, the dockside tart and barmaid, is utterly destroyed. Her song is a scream of hatred, a fantasy of death for all the men who have patronized her and abused her, but the significance of the poem lies not in her madness but in the anger of the poet at the desecration wrought on innocence by lust and greed:

> Good Sirs, today you see me rinsing out the glasses
> And I make up the beds for all of you.

---

* *Dreigroschenroman* (1934). *Threepenny Novel*, tr., D. I. Vesey, Penguin (1961).
† *Selected Poems*, p. 49.

And I get penny tips and I thank the clientele
And you see me in rags in this filthy hotel
And you don't know who you're talking to.
But one fine evening there'll be screams in the harbour
And they'll ask: what can it be that we hear?
And they'll see me laughing as I wash out the glasses
And they'll say: her laughter's very queer.

     And a ship with eight sails
     And with fifty cannons
     Will tie up at the pier.

. . . .

And a hundred men toward midday will all come ashore
And march by the shadowy water
And quickly haul every one into the street
And put them in irons and lay them at my feet
And they'll ask me: which ones shall we slaughter?
And the harbour will be silent on this midday
When they ask: now who shall it be?
And then you'll hear me cry aloud: all of them!
And with each head that falls I'll shout: hurray!

     And the ship with eight sails
     And with fifty cannons
     Will vanish with me.*

Joan, in *St Joan of the Stockyards*, is perhaps Brecht's last picture of these lost girls. Like Mauler, the meat-king, whom she challenges to unequal combat, Joan is an emblem rather than an individual, but in her death she captures the tragedy which distinguished her prototypes in the poems. She dies, significantly enough, in a snow-storm and is covered by the falling flakes of Brecht's pity as well as by the flags with which her enemies celebrate the apotheosis in which they intend to smother all memory of her crusade. In the disillusionment of her death, when she cries: 'I have changed nothing', Joan touches a grandeur which Brecht rarely allows his characters to reach. In order to destroy the society which itself destroyed the conflated figure of the Jennys, the Maries, the Joans and the Nannas who proffered it the tenderness it scorned, Brecht became the Marxist who demanded not the finding but the sacrifice of the self.

Such searing tenderness is not called out only by the youthful

* *Jenny the Pirate. Selected Poems*, p. 67–8.

victims who first lit it; one of its fiercest flames is kindled by the vision of the two old Tuscan peasants, the parents of the 'little monk' who so faithfully served Galileo. Here is his loving description of them:

> I see my parents. I see them sitting by the fire with my sister, eating their curded cheese. I see the beams of the ceiling above them, which the smoke of centuries has blackened, and I see the veins stand out on their toil-worn hands, and the little spoons in their hands. They scrape a living, and underlying their poverty there is a sort of order. . . .
>
> They draw the strength they need to sweat with their loaded baskets up the stony paths, to bear children, even to eat, from the sight of the trees greening each year anew, from the reproachful face of the soil, which is never satisfied, and from the little church and the bible texts they hear there on Sunday.*

The dignity and suffering of a peasant community have never been more respectfully and lovingly reported. It is a vision which one might have hoped to find in the *Divine Comedy*, for it is essentially Christian and medieval, but there it is missing. Emile Mäle in *The Gothic Image*,† writing of the medieval representations of the labours of the seasons to be found inside and often on the doorways of so many French churches,‡ comments:

> The Christian of the thirteenth century, who stopped on the threshold to contemplate found, according to his outlook in life, different subjects for meditation. The labourer recognized the unceasing round of work to which all his life he was destined, but the statues of the Saviour or of the Virgin looking down on those things of earth reminded him that he did not work without hope. p. 66

Brecht could not have found a clearer image of the contrast between the immediate past and the new world to which Galileo's labours served as midwife.

In 1938, after he had written *Mother Courage* and *The Life of Galileo*, Brecht returned to use his earlier image and made the archetype of the innocent harlot the heroine of one of his major plays. It

---

* *Galileo*, tr. Charles Laughton, in *From the Modern Repertoire II*, ed. Eric Bentley, Indiana University Press, (1952).

† Fontana Library (1961). First published by Dent as *Religious Art in France: XIII Century* (1913).

‡ Also of course in other countries, e.g. the stone figures in the baptistry of Padua and the wooden poppyheads of the pews at Blytheborough, Suffolk.

will be convenient therefore to consider *The Good Person of Szechwan**
here rather than among the later plays. Shen Teh, its heroine, is the
most developed of Brecht's *anima* figures, but she is not helpless
although she is betrayed. The pity, always implicit when Brecht is
concerned with one of these women, is expressed first by Shen Teh
herself. In the scene with the unemployed airman under the willow
tree on which he had attempted to hang himself, she says:

> *Shen Teh:* When we were children we had a crane with a broken wing . . .
> in the autumn and the spring, when the great flocks of birds flew over
> our village, he became very restless, and I could understand why.
> *Sun:* Stop crying.   p. 236

But like Brecht's own, Shen Teh's compassion is not called out only
by the person she loves; it flows to all the oppressed, the hungry, the
homeless, the maimed, the old, and above all to the helpless child. In
succouring them, as she believes it is the will of the gods she should do,
she soon finds that she will lose not only her own livelihood but the
very means by which she is striving to do good to others. To avoid this
she changes the face of her personality. Instead of 'yang', or light, she
offers the world 'yin', or darkness. In Jung's language the *anima* is
replaced by the *animus*, and the animus is male. Shen Teh imperson-
ates her own 'cousin' Shui Ta, and in her male clothing she makes use
of all those supposedly masculine characteristics in herself which make
living in a cut-throat society possible. At last, however, she is brought
to 'justice', and the magistrates turn out to be the gods themselves.
She appeals to them:

> *Shen Teh:* Your original order
> To be good while yet surviving
> Split me like lightning into two people. . . .
> The hand which is held out to the starving
> Is quickly wrenched off! He who gives help to the lost
> Is lost for his own part! . . .
> O gods, for your vast projects
> I, poor human, was too small.   pp. 307–8

The earlier request of the old waterer is surely not extravagant:

> A slight reduction of the precepts, Illustrious Ones.
> A slight alleviation of the bundle of precepts, O
> gracious ones, in view of the difficulty of the times.   p. 284

* *Plays II.*

Brecht is not wholly consistent in the use of the male and female avatars. Shen Teh is able, as her feminine self, to refuse her lover the money he needs because it is owed to her old neighbours, although she loses him through her action. To safeguard the welfare of her unborn son, however, she assumes her masculine 'shape' and runs a tobacco factory where she exploits her own erstwhile protégés and uses her ex-lover as overseer. The dramatist is concerned with showing neither Shen Teh's guilt nor a final integration of her personality. Since she is a woman her dominant but not her sole part must remain that of the *anima*, although the price will be hard:

> *Shen Teh:* Oh no, Illustrious Ones! Do not go away!
> Don't leave me! . . .
> *First God:* You can manage . . .
> *Shen Teh:* But I must have my cousin!
> *First God:* Not too often!
> *Shen Teh:* Once a week anyway!
> *First God:* Once a month: that will be enough!
> . . . *As Shen Teh stretches desperately towards them they disappear upwards, waving and smiling.*   pp. 309–10

But no path upward is opened for the humans left behind them; the dichotomies of *yang* and *yin*, body and spirit, altruism and egoism, remain distinct and continue to split like lightning the personalities who strive to integrate them and so find their essential and unified selves

ii BRECHT THE DRAMATIST

> Praise ye the tree which grows exultant from carrion unto
>   heaven!
> Praise ye carrion,
> Praise ye the tree that ate of it
> But praise ye the heavens likewise.
>
> *Grand Chorale of Thanksgiving*

> You actors of our time,
> The time of change
> And the time of the great taking over
> Of all nature to master it
> Not forgetting human nature,

BERTOLT BRECHT

This is now our reason
For insisting that you alter.
Give us the world of men as it is,
Made by men and changeable.
An Address to Danish Worker Actors.
Poems on the Theatre.

The individual, now in a state of complete dissolution, still goes on being developed within his own limits, but only as parts for actors—whereas the late bourgeois novel at least considers that it has a science of psychology which has been worked out to help it analyse the individual—as though the individual had not simply collapsed long ago.

So Brecht—writing on characterization and the place of the individual character in drama, in his notes to *The Threepenny Opera* (1928). As a young man Brecht had not believed this doctrine, and as a mature dramatist he created 'individuals' of an unsurpassed liveliness and charm, but the belief that 'the human being must be regarded as the totality of all social relationships'* was a dominating influence on all but his very earliest work.

His first play, *Baal* (1918), has been described as the 'search for a self in a world of faceless beings.' When for example the girl who loves him says: 'My name is Sophie Bargel', Baal answers: 'You must forget it'. 'In insisting that his partners be faceless, however, he too disappears'.† Baal, alone among Brecht's heroes, makes his personal journey through the sins of the *Inferno*: he allows the girl he has seduced to drown herself; he murders his friend in a fit of jealousy; he repudiates God, and having denied all love, human and divine, he dies alone in the mud of the forest floor.

The play depicts an anarchistic attempt to create personality in a depersonalizing world, and death becomes the metaphor for Baal's failure.‡

Brecht did not pursue what he soon held to be the exploded theory of the importance of personality. Man, he came to believe, is what he is made to be by society. It is not the self but the forces that make the self that demand attention, and these forces are indifferent to the

* *Plays I.* Methuen (1964), p. 187.
† G. Weales: 'Brecht and the Drama of Ideas', in *Ideas in the Drama*, ed. J. Gassner, Columbia University Press (1964).
‡ Ibid.

development of any admirable or complete personality and therefore in actuality are inimical to it.

> *Peachum:* But there's a little problem of subsistence:
> Supplies are scarce and human beings base.
> Who would not like a peaceable existence?
> But this old world is not that kind of place.
>
> *Polly and*
> *Mrs Peachum:* I fear he's right my dear old Dad:
> The world is poor and men are bad.*

Macheath's son is also sadly relevant, and so is its chorus:

> *Chorus:* So, gentlemen, do not be taken in:
> Men live exclusively by mortal sin.†

The individual is not only unimportant, he is in fact completely expendable. In a conversation with Brecht reported in *Brecht on Theatre*‡ concerning the play *Man is Man*, we read that the play 'is about a man being taken to pieces and rebuilt as someone else for a particular purpose . . .

> *Question:* Is the experiment a success?
> *Answer:* Yes. . . .
> *Question:* Does it produce the perfect human being?
> *Answer:* Not especially.

On this laconic dialogue Brecht's comment is equally laconic:

> No doubt you will go on to say that it's a pity that a man should be tricked like this and simply forced to surrender his precious ego, all he possesses (as it were); but it isn't. It's a jolly business.§

The forces which destroy the individual are social, for society does not require 'individuals' in order to function efficiently. The *Ballad of the Dead Soldier*‖ tells the story of the man who 'died a hero's death'. His body, dug up and reclothed, is quite adequate to carry out a soldier's function and is taken on a triumphal march held up by two nurses:

> Around him so many danced and howled
> That none could him espy.

---

* *The Threepenny Opera: Plays I*, p. 130.   † Ibid., p. 153.
  ‡ *Conversation with Bertolt Brecht* in *Brecht on Theatre*, tr. John Willett (London: Methuen; New York: Hill & Wang).
  § Ibid., p. 16.   ‖ *Selected Poems*, pp. 57 ff.

BERTOLT BRECHT

You could only see him from above
Where stars looked down from the sky.

The image of the stars, which can watch from above the wretchedness unnoticed by the madly milling crowd of fellow-mortals, is unusual in Brecht; in the 'city' of which we are members even the vision of the deepest compassion is unable to save the victims it can observe.

Jimmie, the lumberjack hero of *The City of Mahagonny*, attempts the most elaborate of the bids for individual freedom to be dramatized by Brecht. He succeeds in making 'You may do it' the operative words in the city of pleasure, but finds that living by them cannot be long sustained. One of his friends uses his freedom literally to eat himself to death, and Jimmie at last is judged for what inevitably remains the cardinal sin under a capitalist system—inability to pay his bills. He finds neither defence nor defender and is hanged.

Jimmie is not found again in Brecht's theatre for his creator became more and more concerned with the group. In *Man is Man* (1924) occurs the *credo* of the dramatist's middle years:

Why all this fuss about people? One's as good as none at all. It's impossible to speak of less than 200 at a time.

From *Drums in the Night* (1922) to the end of the decade Brecht is concerned to preach the voluntary sacrifice of personality for the sake of the collective good. One of the *Badener Lehrstücke* tells the story of a fallen plane. Three of the airmen face their personal inadequacy, but the fourth refuses to do so. They are all instructed that men cannot help men by kindnesses, such as the gift of a pillow or a cup of soup; men must understand their condition. Since the play is not yet published in book form in English a long quotation from the translation in the Tulane Drama Review* may be useful.

The dialogue between the Learned Chorus and the Fallen Mechanics leads to the hub of the argument:

Learned Chorus:
  Who are you?
Fallen Mechanics:
  We are the ones who flew over the ocean.
Learned Chorus:
  Who are you?

* Tr. Lee Baxandall, Vol. IV, May 1960.

185

Fallen Mechanics:
  We are some of you.
Learned Chorus:
  Who are you?
Fallen Mechanics:
  We are nobody.
Leader of Learned Chorus to the Crowd:
  They are nobody.
Fallen Flyer:
  I am Charles Nungesser.
Learned Chorus:
  And he is Charles Nungesser.

Later the Learned Chorus demands that the 'plane be handed over:

> So give us now the motor
> Wings and undercarriage, all
> That enabled you to fly and
> Was made by some of us.
> Give it up!

Fallen Flyer:
  I'll not give it up.
  What is
  The airplane without the flyer?

The wrecked 'plane is, however, carried off by the fallen mechanics.

Four of Learned Chorus:
  1. If he existed . . .
  2. He existed.
  1. What was he?
  2. He was nobody.
  3. If he was someone . . .
  4. He was nobody.
  3. How did he become recognized?
  4. By being employed.

The Flyer refuses to submit: 'I cannot die'. But the answer is:

Learned Chorus:
  Now you must depart. Leave quickly.
  Do not look about, go
  Away from us.

  The singer of the Fallen Flier leaves the podium.

In *He Who Says Yes* (1929–30) the young idealist, who at first insists on relieving individual suffering instead of following the party policy that his group shall only work for a mass revolt, submits to the judgment of his comrades and to their sentence of death. It is said to have been the protests of the boys who acted this morality play that led Brecht to write an alternative ending in which the idealist was re-prieved.

In *The Measures Taken* (1930) the man who tears off the mask of anonymity under which like all the rest he has been taught to hide his face, later agrees that his body shall be thrown into the lime pit where all traces of individuality will again be obliterated. The dramatist thus returned to what he held to be the path of Marxist orthodoxy:

> Everything or nothing. All of us or none.
> One alone his lot can't better.
> Either gun or fetter.
> Everything or nothing. All of us or none.*

This self-imposed limitation on characterization persists into the next decade. Although the plot of *St Joan of the Stockyards* (1931) is fully, even over-elaborately, developed, the characters, in spite of the sympathy demanded for Joan, do not show development; they remain puppets, carrying only the doctrine of the play. In *The Mother* (1930–2) Brecht did perhaps achieve a more dramatically satisfying balance between character and propaganda, and in 1933 came his exile from Germany. With the loss of all opportunity directly to influence political affairs a change came over his work. The quality of emotional involvement in this fresh situation is made clear in the poems written at this time—the poems on exile and return, on Germany, on war and on Fascism.

The first play in which the new attitude is strongly marked is *Fear and Misery in the Third Reich* (1935). The structure remains non-naturalistic; the characters are 'distanced' in various ways, and the whole is a 'morality' of complete orthodoxy. But the author's personal feelings sweep through the whole with a passion which inevitably modifies all theory. The characters become individuals and are seen and felt for as individuals caught in a trap too strong for them to open.

In spite of the terrible pressures exercised by the Nazi regime, the Fascist state is only a particularly vicious example of collective power

---

* *All of Us or None. Selected Poems*, p. 103.

over all fragile human beings who can be terrorized into self-destruction. In presenting a universal image of the misuse of power Brecht's passion informs even the minor characters with authentic personality. To begin with they cling desperately to their personal loves and their personal lives. Too easily, however, they give way, each with his own peculiar treachery, to the forces which are moulding them into the white-faced dummies manning the panzer truck which at intervals hurtles across the stage. The doctor lets the Jewish wife he loves go over the frontier 'for a short rest'; the teacher placates the son he fears will betray him, the mother cannot protect her daughter's innocence. Even the priest falters in his witness, and the parlour-maid who, recognizing the metamorphosis of the boy she loved into the man who has betrayed his workmates murmurs: 'How they've changed him', can only weep for him.

It is in the years 1939–1945 that occurs the period of extraordinary productivity which gives us *Mother Courage and her Three Children*, *The Trial of Lucullus*, *The Life of Galileo*, *The Good Person of Sechzwan*, *Puntila and his man Matti*, *Arturo Ui*, and, as a crowning glory, *The Caucasian Chalk Circle*.

In this the last group of original plays, the great characters of Brecht's maturity are all to be found. In several the journey which leads to the meeting with the self is discernible, and it is here that the English reader may become aware of the possible comparison with Shakespeare. 'Courage',* Galileo,† and Azdak‡ all challenge comparison with Falstaff, while Grusha§ and Katrin‖ are peasant reflections of Rosalind and Cordelia. The Shakespearean quality is emphasized by the fact that Shakespeare's plays also are set within an ordered society, and that his greatest characters are inclined to break through its boundaries as do Brecht's. Falstaff makes nonsense of Hal as the hero-prince, and Shylock would do the same to Antonio and Bassanio as Christian merchants and gentry, if Shakespeare had allowed us time to notice the fact. Cordelia is the centre of a play that has little to do with the Tudor hierarchy, and even in the comedies the heroines bring with them the breath of a vitality which, had the dramatist given it rein, would have made them difficult partners in the ordered dances of their married lives. Brecht's characters are now no more 'faceless' than Shakespeare's, and their geographical wanderings are parallel

---

* *Mother Courage and her Children. Plays II.*　† *The Life of Galileo.*
‡ *The Caucasian Chalk Circle. Plays I.*　§ *The Caucasian Chalk Circle. Plays I.*
‖ *Mother Courage and her Children. Plays II.*

with a gradual revelation of the self, although this may or may not be recognized by the character concerned.

Brecht writes in his Notes to *The Life of Galileo** that Galileo has 'the urge to research, a social phenomenon no less delightful or compulsive than the urge to reproduce'. He is no simple cut-out of the conventional scientist; his creator represents him as a truly divided character. Moreover Galileo recognizes conflict in himself between the devoted thinker and the greedy hedonist—and when, under the duress of society, he chooses the second part, he is broken in his own eyes. Before the Inquisition he had his moment of vision, made his choice, recognized and finally loathed himself. When he returns to his waiting followers 'he is changed, almost unrecognizable', and his only comment on their disillusionment and despair at his recantation is the single line:

> Unhappy is the land that needs a hero. p. 468

In reward for his conformism he receives shelter, warmth and ample food, and secretly he continues to write and preserve the banned Discorsi. Galileo in confinement, eating his goose cooked with apples and onions, is like Falstaff enjoying his sherris sack and consigning 'honour' to the devil. Both men are rich, engaging personalities, for Galileo shares all Falstaff's gaiety and ebullience; both therefore have value in the world of individuals, but neither makes his rightful contribution to the 'collective'. Falstaff never faces this truth; his rejection by Hal appears to him not merely wrong but completely incomprehensible. He cannot assimilate or master it, and so it kills him. Galileo, on the other hand, knows perfectly well what he is doing. He is outspoken about it:

> I have no patience, Sagredo, with the man who doesn't use his brains to fill his belly. p. 438

The discontinuity of Galileo's acts is as clear as that between the acts of Shen Teh and Shui Ta, but Brecht appears to have denied to the scientist the built-in mechanism of self-judgment which makes Shen Teh's masculine *persona* such a continual torment to her. Only occasionally does he look at himself with clear eyes. Close reading does however make it plain that Brecht imagined his hero as both seeing and condemning himself at the climactic moment of his recantation. In this he is therefore comparable to two figures with whom this study was

* *Plays I*, p. 340.

first concerned. Like Oedipus and Dante's pilgrim, Brecht's Galileo sees his own baseness. After this he differs from them, for he makes no use of his self-knowledge, attempts no upward climb. Brecht explicitly states, what is indeed clear in the text, that the secret writing of the *Discorsi* was no deliberately planned course of action, no dangerous heroism, but the continued indulgence of a lifetime's enthusiasm. When Andrea, one of his former disciples, visits him, their dialogue contains lines central to the interpretation of the play and its hero. Andrea has just learned of the existence of the Discorsi manuscript and believes that his adored master had submitted in order to complete and preserve his work. But Galileo denies this:

> *Galileo:* I recanted because I was afraid of physical pain.
> *Andrea:* No!
> *Galileo:* They showed me the instruments.
> *Andrea:* It was not a plan?
> *Galileo:* It was not. pp. 471–2

And there follows the self-judgment.

> I have come to believe that I was never in real danger; for some years I was as strong as the authorities, and I surrendered my knowledge to the powers that be, to use it, no, not *use* it, *abuse* it, as it suits their ends. I have betrayed my profession. Any man who does what I have done must not be tolerated in the ranks of science. p. 473

When Andrea leaves, Galileo refuses his proffered hand and goes over to his meal. He knew where he was—among the traitors in the ice of Cocytus—and he made himself as comfortable there as he could:

> Somebody who knows me sent me a goose.
> I still enjoy eating. p. 473

Mother Courage and her Children, the play set amid the destructive campaigns of the Thirty Years' War, presents an even stranger ambiguity in the central character. The audience who did not mourn for Anna Fierling tugging her tattered wagon towards the darkening future, would need to have resisted the dramatist's most skilful use of his theatrical technique. The single lonely figure on the empty stage, silhouetted against a wide grey sky could only be designed to elicit sympathy. Equally strong, however, should be the realization that Courage is herself her own destroyer and has herself sent to their deaths the three children whom she had set out to cherish.

Eric Bentley places Galileo and Anna Fierling side by side when he writes:

> The plays take their life from the author's ambivalence. Mother Courage and Galileo are fascinating characters because of this ambivalence. The author disapproves of both of them as cowardly old reprobates. What he does not seem to have realized is that his love for them peeps through all the cracks.*

But it is misleading to write as though such an ambivalence is unique or even rare; plenty of authors have loved the most disreputable of the characters they created. In Brecht's case it is more important to identify the 'empathy', which Bentley rightly detects, with the furious partisanship for all whom society forces into bad ways which, as we have seen, is the driving force of Brecht's Marxism.

Unlike the leading characters of the three other major plays, Anna Fierling achieves little or no self-knowledge, and she faces no facts about herself for long. As she introduces herself so she remains:

> They call me Mother Courage 'cause I was afraid I'd be ruined. So I drove through the bombardment of Riga like a madwoman, with fifty loaves of bread in my cart. They were going mouldy, I couldn't please myself.

She is concerned with the virtues of courage, wisdom and loyalty but evaluates them in her own way:

> In a good country virtues wouldn't be necessary. Everybody could be quite ordinary, middling, and, for all I care, cowards.   p. 17

Mother Courage follows the armies up and down Europe for twelve years, but she remains oblivious of the significance of the journeys she makes through time and space, and the lessons they bring her she cannot learn. When her son, 'Swiss Cheese', is captured and faces summary execution she could buy him off by selling her wagon, since she knows all men are—thank God!—corruptible, but she keeps back part of her purchase price; the drums of the court martial roll, and her ceaseless busy activity is stilled for the moment as she mutters: 'I believe—I've haggled too long' (p. 39). She had her moment of choice, but she did not recognize it and soon forgot her mistake. Unlike Galileo she does not know what she has betrayed, and in the next scene she is advising an angry young soldier to pocket up his wrongs and accept what comes to him:

* *Brecht:* Tulane Drama Review, IV, May 1960.

How long won't you stand for injustice? One hour? Or two? You haven't asked yourself that, have you? And yet it's the main thing.   p. 42

Mother Courage had chosen not to 'sit in the stocks', and her choice did in fact reflect her true self. She merely confirmed this when she refused to recognize her son's body and allowed it to be thrown into the carrion pit. At only one point in the play does she admit any knowledge of the nature of the war by which she lives and is at last destroyed, and her creator draws attention to this moment by adding a note on its importance. Katrin had been sent to bring back some articles which her mother had bought in the town at a bargain price, and on her return journey she was attacked by a soldier who, in an attempt to steal the goods, slashed her across the face, permanently disfiguring her. She admits that perhaps she had insisted too much on the safe-keeping of her property and contnues:

> *Mother Courage:* She's all but finished now. . . . I'll not see Swiss Cheese again, and where my Eilert is the Good Lord knows. Curse the War!
>
> p. 55

Brecht's note reads:

> Those who look on at catastrophes wrongly expect those involved to learn something. . . . They learn as little from catastrophe as a scientist's rabbit learns of biology. It is not incumbent on the playwright to give Mother Courage insight at the end—she sees something at about the middle of the play, at the close of the sixth scene,* then loses again what she has seen—his concern is that the spectator should see.   p. 86

Near the end of the play Courage indeed refuses the shelter of the cook's bar when he will not allow her to bring Katrin with her. She seems to have been changed by her experiences for she risks economic security—though not economic independence—for her child's sake. But the change does not go deep. She leaves Katrin alone in charge of the wagon while she hunts for some new bargains, and when she returns she finds her shot by the enemy soldiers. 'If you hadn't gone off to the town to get your cut, may be it wouldn't have happened', says a peasant, but Courage admits no liability and prepares to carry on as before, dragging her nearly empty wagon and selling to the last regiment that remains in the field:

> I hope I can pull the wagon by myself. Yes, I'll manage, there's not much in it now. I must start up again in business.   pp. 80-1

* This is the scene referred to above.

All Mother Courage's three children have moments when their true selves are revealed to others, but if they do recognize themselves they are given no time to make use of the knowledge. This happens for Swiss Cheese when he flings the regimental cash-box into the river and is tortured and killed by his enemies. For Eilert the moment occurs when he is executed for practising, in time of so-called peace, the brigandage which brought him glory in time of war:

> *The Chaplain:* What shall we tell your mother?
> *Eilert:* Tell her it was no different. Tell her it was the same. Tell her
> nothing. p. 64

Katrin alone finds self-fulfilment before her death, for she is able to die for the children whom all her life she has longed to bear and to cherish. While the peasant woman prays: 'Be mindful of the children in danger, especially the little ones . . . O Lord', Katrin makes her triumphant climb on to the roof with a drum and sends her warning to the threatened citizens until the soldiers shoot her down (pp. 76–9). As her mother says on her return: 'You shouldn't have told her about the children' (p. 80).

The plot of *The Caucasian Chalk Circle* falls into two parts, each with a leading character who meet only in the last scene. Grusha has much in common with Shen Teh. Both are shown to be concerned with the material necessities of food, shelter, money and hard work. Both know that 'Terrible is the temptation to do good',* and both succumb to the temptation. Both place the care of a child above the demands of sexual love, but Shen Teh expresses the emotions of a lover, which for the most part Grusha is content to imply. Still the old magical tenderness gleams now and then in the later play. Simon courts Grusha because she is 'healthy as a fish in water' and strong to work and bear children, but Grusha, in the flush of their courtship, responds with the seasonal poetry endemic to lovers from the days of the first love songs and strengthens it with images from her immediate experience:

> I will be waiting for you under the green elm
> I will be waiting for you under the dry elm . . .
> When you return from the battle
> No boots will lie before the door
> The pillow beside mine will be empty
> My mouth will be unkissed. p. 19

* *Caucasian Chalk Circle*, Scene 2, p. 19.

Rather than the lover, Grusha is however the virgin mother. The child she rescues and risks her life for is both hers and not hers. From the burning city she travels through forests and meadows, over glaciers, rivers and chasms, and across the mountain chains. The child, the future saviour—he is actually a little prince as in a fairy tale—is taken safely to the land of Egypt until he is able to return to his home. The sacred harlot, mother of the divine godling, is just suggested in one of the folk songs which Grusha sings him.

> Your father's a thief
> Your mother's a whore:
> All the nice people
> Will love you therefore
>
> The son of the tiger
> Brings the foals their feed
> The snake-child milk
> To mothers in need.   p. 43

The first aspect of herself that Grusha discovers is this power of maternal love. She does not want to discover it, for she knows it will take her away from her lover, perhaps for ever. But she also knows that to deny it would equally separate them, for she would be denying the self that could both love and be desired. In her imagination she hears the voice of the abandoned child:

> 'Don't you know, woman, that she who does not listen to a cry
>   for help
> But passes by shutting her ears, will never hear
> The gentle call of a lover
> Nor the blackbird at dawn, nor the happy
> Sigh of the exhausted grapepicker at the sound of the Angelus.
> Hearing this she went back to the child.
> . . . Terrible is the temptation to do good! . . .   pp. 24–5

To preserve the child she is forced to marry a peasant, and when Simon returns she would have lost him for ever were it not for the 'happy ending' contrived by the revolutionary judge Azdak. She continues, however, unashamed of her 'sin', although she finds it impossible to explain or justify it. Unhappy that she is, she cannot heave her heart into her mouth but loves her fosterling according to a bond she cannot analyse but dare not break.

Azdak on the other hand, condemns himself and seeks punishment.

He conceals a starving fugitive and feeds him with some of his scanty hoard of cheese only to find he has unwittingly succoured the chief enemy of the revolution. He runs to the people's court with a rope round his neck but is himself made judge. He dispenses a long course of 'Robin Hood' justice until the tide of revolution turns and he is in danger of retribution. Now he sees his true self and finds he is a coward. He does not like the sight, but he makes no attempt to change:

> The game is up! But I'll give no man the pleasure of seeing human greatness. I'll beg on my knees for mercy. Spittle will slobber down my chin. The fear of death is upon me.   p. 82

Again however the tide swings, and Azdak is back on the bench to decide between Grusha and her baby's true mother, who both claim the child's custody. It is at this point that another folklore motif is introduced, for the people's judge decrees that the two women shall compete as to which can drag the child out of the chalk circle. By this means Azdak, the wise fool, demonstrates to all that it is Grusha who loves the child with a true mother's love and is the best fitted to rear him.

Before this, however, he and Grusha, the two characters who know themselves, find that they can also know each other. He tempts Grusha to give the child back to his rich mother:

> *The Singer:* Listen now to what the angry girl thought,
> > But didn't say:
> > He who wears the shoes of gold
> > Tramples on the weak and old
> > Does evil all day long
> > And mocks at wrong. . . .
>
> > Hunger will he dread
> > Not those who go unfed:
> > Fear the fall of night
> > But not the light.
>
> *Azdak:* I think I understand you, woman.   p. 93

The play is the last of Brecht's important original works; it is his '*Tempest*', and its archetypal images have a positive value which has already outlasted countless changes of social system and philosophical theory. With Grusha's journey the material changes from the fairy-tale lore of the opening—the christening, the images of the wicked stepmother and the evil godmother, the answering of the small creature's voice by the cast-out youngest sister, and so forth—to the elements of true myth. Grusha's search is rather for treasure than for the self, but it is an upward climb as she carries the child through winter to spring. While she is waiting for the new year to dawn, her brother's house is the inn with no room for the sacred child, and its leaky attic the stable of his refuge. With the spring the forces of good and evil return, and the struggle is precipitated once more. All is resolved only by the wisdom of the holy fool. Through Azdak the prince is preserved, and the treasure which Grusha sought and at last finds is revealed as Justice.

> *The Singer:* What there is shall belong to those who are good for it, thus
> The children to the maternal, that they thrive;
> The carriages to the good drivers, that they are driven well;
> And the valley to the waterers, that it shall bear fruit.

p. 96

It is the only play in which Brecht allows a character to succeed both as an individual and as a member of a society, and in which the terrible temptation of personal goodness is yielded to without an ensuing calamity. Yet the framework of the class war and the struggle for justice remain as clear as in the early *Lehrstücke*. The structure of the play is therefore basically paradoxical, and in its ambiguity lies its peculiar power.

Epilogue: Angels and Ministers

What is it, in the end, that induces a man to go his own way
and to rise out of unconscious identity with the mass as out
of a swathing mist? ... It is what is commonly called vocation:
an irrational factor that destines a man to emancipate himself
from the herd ... Any one with a vocation hears the voice of
the inner man: he is *called* . . . The original meaning of 'to
have a vocation' is 'To be addressed by a voice'.
                    C. G. JUNG. *The Development of Personality*

Send Your Word upon the earth by Your Messengers. We
recount their works, but it is You who work in them that they
may bring forth a living soul.
                    ST AUGUSTINE

WHEN Oedipus left Corinth he was seeking divine guidance, and
it was the oracle which turned his steps on to the road to Thebes.
A second oracle set him on the journey dramatized by Sophocles at the
end of which he discovered what he was, and finally divine guidance
assured his arrival at the grove of the dread goddess and the chasm
which was to be the scene of his assumption.

For Dante also, the journey was divinely prompted through
Beatrice. We may interpret this as meaning that Dante's memory of
Beatrice was re-activated and led to a new search for truth on his part,
but he himself would certainly have held that such was at least only
a half-truth. The Christian must always believe that the Good Shepherd set out to find the lost sheep, that God came down to earth and
that His grace, on which mankind is dependent for salvation, is given
from without. T. S. Eliot is of course working in this tradition. Harry
is called by 'the bright angels', and Agatha and Mary minister to him;
the Guardians are active in the *Cocktail Party*.

With the secularization of culture however the mythological format
necessarily changed. For most writers since the Middle Ages man's
fate rests in his own hands; whether he is to start either the downward
or the upward journey will depend on his own decision only. Nevertheless to the most calloused materialist deep contemplation of death
retains the power to give something of the primitive *frisson*, and even

197

today the horrors of war remain horrors partly for this reason. It is as might be expected, therefore, that though the start of man's journey may be marked by no supra-human or mantic occurrence, the last phase, leading to his death, is still, although in disguised form, heralded by the significant message. Shakespeare gives Death, the 'mighty messenger' of *Everyman*, some strange disguises. Perhaps the strangest and most endearing is the figure of the countryman who brings Cleopatra her asps hidden by fig leaves. His bawdy prattle expresses both his own essential kindness and also the wilful ways of women, for which his queen and goddess is to die. It is of every woman he speaks when he tells her of one who made a good report of the worm:

> A very honest woman, but something given to lie as a woman should not do but in the way of honesty.

It is strange that she uses of him almost the same words with which Dante pays his last tribute to Beatrice. 'Thou hast led me, a slave, to liberty' (Paradise. xxxi. 85) he says to her, and Cleopatra says of her clown, 'He brings me liberty' (Antony and Cleopatra V.1.). We may remember the words, undoubtedly familiar to both poets: 'Where the spirit of the Lord is, there is liberty'.*

Osric is a more sinister figure; the feathered hat that he is so loath to put to its proper use could well be designed so as to suggest some baroque 'pompes funèbres', and his chatter about poignards and rapiers, with their assigns and carriages, barely covers the fact that he is summoning Hamlet to his death. The prince himself knows it well enough. Hamlet is the only Shakespearean hero clearly called to the start of his journey by a voice from another world. Whether the ghost calls for punishment or for purification it is his words which set his son's feet upon the path which leads at last to wisdom: 'The readiness is all'. Matching the supernatural opening, comes the hint of the supernatural at the close:

> Goodnight sweet prince
> And flights of angels sing thee to thy rest.   V. 3

But Shakespeare remains ambiguous. In Quarto I Hamlet has the words: 'Heaven receive my soul', and perhaps Shakespeare wrote them. Later however they became 'The rest is silence'.

Ibsen is writing in a world more secular by far than Shakespeare's, but he too desires to mark the mystery of the 'rite of passage', and he

---

* S. Paul. *II Corinthians*, III, 17.

uses Shakespeare's device of the disguised messenger with great skill. Brand's angel of death is a mad girl luring him towards the snow fields as she fires her rifle at a hawk; Peer Gynt is summoned by the Button-moulder, in leather apron, carrying his casting ladle; Ulrik Brendel, grotesque in Rosmer's cast-off clothing, is the catalyst which precipitates John's and Rebecca's leap into the mill-race. Hilde Wangel is more tidily but not more congruously clad in climbing clothes when, alpenstock in hand, she knocks on Solness' door.

Sartre resolutely eschews all supernatural overtones, but even he allows to the men who discover themselves in death an *ambiance* of mystery at the last. The white moonlight of the night when Mathieu chooses a rifle and goes to die with his friend, calls up the funeral lilies with which men of faith have symbolised the beauty of death and men of none have tried momentarily to disguise its terrors. Brunet, who has found his self before he dies, finds it to the music of machine-gun fire on the cold whiteness of the snow-covered hillside. Daniel is not granted the last release, and the angel that leads him to renewed torment is all too human in form. He is the beautiful boy standing silent on the bridge, watching the waters of the Seine slipping by beneath his feet.

With Kafka the numenous light has returned, though its function is mainly to throw strangely distorting shadows over the landscape. Mysterious messengers reach both the K.s in time to start them upon journeys which might, it would seem, lead them on to the upward path to life. It is when such guidance is refused or not comprehended that the messages became those of death. The two men who begin Joseph K.'s story by his arrest one spring morning, open his eyes to the need and to the possibility of redemption, but when he fails to pass through the door that was expressly made for him, they become his executioners. We are not told the form of the message which led K. to offer his services as land-surveyor to 'the Castle', but later Barnabas explicitly though modestly, assumes the rank of angel: 'I am a messenger'. He is entrusted however with no clear message, and the gleam of hope which he brings to K. is quickly extinguished.

In Beckett's world God, whether He has withdrawn from the universe He created or whether He is indeed dead as Nietzsche discovered, has left much of His mystery and many surrogates behind Him: Mr Knott, Gaber, and the strange figures who haunt Molloy in the dark wood, come from an unknown world. So do the children who appear unwelcomed or unrecognized and return whence they came in silence.

Brecht's characters move in a world whose messages reach them for the most part through their stomachs, but they are not the less important for that, and they invite to a journey which demands man's body and soul as inexorably as did the older pilgrimages in search of God. To one character, however, a different 'angel' calls: 'Woman', it said, 'help me'. And Grusha heeds the voice and sets out on her journey carrying the child to safety—his safety and, ultimately, her own.

Again and again we see that the voyagers who have made the Hard Journey have been driven to it by a command which they resented or failed to understand but obeyed because it spoke with authority. If no such voice is heard the effort is not made. It is not pleasant to descend into the abyss, nor is it easy to climb the mountain. Modern man interprets the command as coming from levels of his own self for which his reason cannot account. His guilt, when he fails to respond, is even more mysterious to him, and not less desolating than the guilt felt by his forebears. Thus Grusha obeyed the voice not only of the child but of her own maternal love, while the heroes of Beckett and Kafka too often failed their own unconscious promptings.

In *The Fall* Camus has a fine image of the interior voice projected outside the self but clearly speaking from the individual's own self-knowledge. After the hero has heard, like Grusha, the inarticulate human cry 'Help me!' and has ignored it, it is only after a lapse of several months that he first hears the summons to self-judgment. On the Pont des Arts he thinks he hears a laugh behind him:

> Taken by surprise, I suddenly wheeled round; there was no one there; no barge or boat. I turned back towards the island and again heard the laughter behind me, a little farther off as if it were going down stream. . . . At the same time I was aware of the rapid beating of my heart.

In this case the messenger is resisted; his voice therefore leads only to its hearer's destruction.

The messengers in Ibsen's plays who summon the heroes to their final struggle can also be viewed as projections of a part of the character they visit. Brand had faced absolute defeat before he met Gerda. Before he was challenged by the Button-moulder Peer Gynt had already peeled the onion, and passed judgment on himself. Hilda's temptation was not different from the desperate fear of his old age which Solness was fighting long before he fulfilled her demand that he should climb his tower; Brendel's words did no more than echo Rebecca's own guilt and longing for atonement. Like Borkman and Rubek these all followed their own irrational imperatives into the unknown.

Turning the pages again we see that Cleopatra had herself invoked the death that brought her liberty and that Hamlet had freely elected to return to Denmark in order to quit Claudius, although clear warning of the price came to him from his own unconscious mind:

Thou wouldst not think how ill's all here about my heart. V. 2

Dante, who certainly believed that the God who created him willed and made possible his salvation, yet knew also that Virgil in one 'sense' was his own wisdom, and that his recognition and acceptance of Beatrice was due to his own knowledge of the power of love. More remotely but perhaps even more profoundly, the oracle that set Oedipus in flight from Thebes voiced what Sophocles himself recognized as a universal desire springing in man's own breast:

Jocasta: Nor need this mother-marrying frighten you;
Many a man has dreamt as much.   p. 55

The messenger who brings the command or the challenge is not necessarily the same figure as the minister who helps towards its fulfilment. Oedipus is ministered to by neither god nor priest but by Antigone, who is both the daughter whom he loves and also, in Jung's terms, the *anima* or projection of his own 'feminine' self. But though he can respond to her in love and gentleness Antigone has no divine power by which to influence him. She is unable to soften in any way his arrogance, and harshness to others, as is plain when she attempts to mitigate his wrath against his sons. In this respect Dante is more happily placed than Sophocles. The philosophy within which he worked and which set his imagination free to soar as well as to plumb the nether pit, allowed also a unity unattained by any of the poets writing outside the Christian tradition. The dual figure of Beatrice-Virgil was able both to inspire the journey and to protect and guide the pilgrim during its trials.

Everyman is called by Death, who then leaves him as desolate as Peer Gynt was left by the Button-moulder, to seek the next cross-roads alone, but although earthly friends forsake him he is finally supported by Good Deeds, Knowledge and Confession. The sex of these figures is left indeterminate, but it is tempting to think that in Good Deeds the *anima* persists and in Knowledge the image of the masculine reason. For Harry* the call comes from the Erinnyes and

* *The Family Reunion.*

the succour from the old and young feminine figures of Agatha, the spiritual mother, and Mary, the virgin mistress.

In Shakespearean drama only Cordelia plays a rôle analogous to that of Beatrice. Supported by her masculine counterpart, Kent, she challenges Lear to face the truth about her as she is and therefore about himself also. At first Lear understands neither of them. When he does undertake his journey Cordelia returns to succour him, but she offers him human, not divine, love. She knows no way by which to lead him past the gates of death, and from the Earthly Paradise, in which he meets her again, they are soon expelled.

In many contemporary myths human beings do sometimes succeed in ministering to each other, although without the knowledge and authority of those earlier ministers who were also the messengers of God. One of the most unexpected of the human comforters is the little child of three who led Strindberg to temporary peace along the paths and heaths of a Danubian valley. In *Inferno* Strindberg tells how, during one of his most terrible periods of schizophrenia, he visited his parents-in-law and saw for the first time his youngest daughter, Christine. When he came to make creative use of this material in *The Road to Damascus* he does not mention this experience, but since he himself calls the child his Beatrice, the episode is worth relating here.

'My little Beatrice,' he writes, 'was waiting for me, and for the mistletoe bough I had promised her.'

At this crisis in his life, only his child had the power to reach the unhappy, tormented man who believed the whole world was his enemy. To take her walks he gave up even the time sacred to his writing. She brought him unwonted peace, and when she wept he was desolate:

I felt deprived of the light this child had shed on my gloomy soul. I kissed her, carried her in my arms, collected flowers and pebbles for her, cut a switch and pretended to be a cow that she was driving out to graze.

Then she was happy and pleased and life smiled on me once more. Fancy being allowed to expiate a crime by making oneself loved! In truth the powers are not so cruel as we.

Where the hope of other-worldly and numenous comforts fades, the ministering image is frequently no longer female. It is noticeable that in *Hamlet* the feminine minister fails the hero through her weakness, and that it is on Horatio that he relies for comfort. This is indeed a portent of what is to come, although in Ibsen the feminine images still hold pride of place. The Agnes whom Brand fails and the Solveg whom Peer Gynt deserts could both have saved a man who was willing to accept their aid, and the same is true of the women deserted or destroyed by the heroes of the last plays. Because of their failure to recognize the angel all these men—except John Rosmer and Rubek—go lonely to their end. Increasingly, however, the contemporary heroes seek support in relationships with their own sex. In *Roads to Freedom* it is Pinette not Marcelle who is the instrument of Mathieu's salvation, and Vicarios reveals to Brunet all he is to know of love. In the rigorous rationality of Sartrian existentialism women are capable only of betrayal by their *mauvaise foi*. Kafka and Beckett with their more intuitive and imaginative pattern of living occasionally allow women a more positive rôle, but Fraülein Burstein* disappears, and Frieda† deserts K., although she loved him. Maddy Rooney leads the blind Dan on his way, but more usually women, lost in 'the sensual sty', only hinder the heroes on their way.

The services human beings can render each other are small indeed when set against our desperate needs, yet they may be infinitely precious and are our only hope. The fragile contact between Sam and Watt gave both a fleeting peace, and the carrot that Vladimir produces from the bottom of a dirty pocket and offers to Estragon is truly a sacramental wafer:

> Tomorrow, when I wake, or think I do, what shall I say of today? That with Estragon, my friend, at this place, until the fall of night, I waited for Godot? . . . He'll tell me about the blows he received and I'll give him a carrot. Astride of a grave and a difficult birth. Down in the hole, lingeringly, the grave-digger puts on the forceps. . . . He is sleeping, he knows nothing, let him sleep on.   *Waiting for Godot.* pp. 90–1

    * *The Triai.*   † *The Castle.*

Index

INDEX